THE WRITINGS OF
A SELECTION

Ronald Duncan was born in Zimbabwe in 1914, and educated in Switzerland and at Downing College, Cambridge. From 1939 until his death in 1982 he lived on a farm in Devonshire where he wrote the many books which reflect his varied interests, including architecture, music, husbandry, film, pacifism and, above all, poetry and the theatre. His *Collected Plays* were published in 1971 and his *Collected Poems* in 1981. Among his other works are the screenplay for *The Girl on a Motorcycle* (1969), the libretto for Benjamin Britten's *The Rape of Lucretia* (first performed in 1946) and three volumes of autobiography, *All Men Are Islands* (1954), *How to Make Enemies* (1968) and *Obsessed* (1977). The philosophy of Gandhi, whom he met in 1937, was a lifelong influence.

How can you be my guru
if you dont have your
own bible ?!

merry Christmas ↪1984
Patricia

THE WRITINGS OF
GANDHI

———

A selection edited and
with an introduction by
RONALD DUNCAN

FONTANA / COLLINS

First published by Faber & Faber Ltd 1951
First issued in Fontana Paperbacks 1971
Second impression November 1974
Third impression, in this format, September 1983

Introduction, notes and arrangement of selection
copyright © Ronald Duncan 1971

Printed in Great Britain
at the University Press, Oxford

CONTENTS

ACKNOWLEDGMENTS TO ORIGINAL EDITION

The Editor wishes to acknowledge with gratitude the assistance he has received from Admiral Earl Mountbatten of Burma, the High Commissioner for India, Mr Devedas Gandhi and Shri Pyarelal Nuyar in collecting this material; and also the permission to reprint it, obtained from the Navajivan Trust, the Marquess of Linlithgow and Sir Robert Tottenham.

ACKNOWLEDGMENTS TO FONTANA EDITION

The Editor gratefully acknowledges Shri Pyarelal Nuyar for permission to use additional material from *The Last Phase*, and Mira Behn for the extracts from *Gandhi's Letters to a Disciple*. The extracts from *Nehru, the First Sixty Years* and *Mahatma Gandhi's Ideas* are included by permission of The Bodley Head Ltd, and George Allen and Unwin Ltd respectively. For permission to reprint 'The Call of Truth' from *The Modern Review* grateful acknowledgment is made to the executors of Rabrindranath Tagore.

INTRODUCTION

What are my credentials for making this selection or for writing about Mahatma Gandhi? The reader has a right to ask that question. Before he can assess the accuracy of an account, he must first know something about the historian. There is no such thing as complete objectivity especially in human relationships and we delude ourselves when we pretend that there is. Though detachment must always be the biographer's aim, he can never achieve it; and more often than not he succeeds in revealing nothing but himself. This being so, perhaps he should in the first place admit to those factors which have probably limited his vision and thus give the reader the chance to make adjustments accordingly. With this purpose in mind, the following facts concerning myself may not appear wholly irrelevant.

In 1937 I was only twenty-two, and that is probably not the best age at which one can assess the achievements or the personality of a philosopher of sixty. Furthermore, the nineteen-thirties produced a particularly raw type of young man, to which I was no exception. It was a decade of political arrogance and spiritual apathy: the air was thick with so-called progressive thought which approved of nothing in the past, but for all that claimed to be omniscient with regard to the future; the lessons of history were disregarded, tradition was derided; and though everything was explained, nothing was understood. It was a period of *naïveté*.

As soon as I came down from the University, I busied myself about reforming everything, excluding myself. Many of my friends were equally active in the same conveniently extrovert fashion. On one side it must be said that we were genuinely perplexed by the seeming paradox of poverty amongst plenty which we saw around us, and in various ways we sought to do something about this condition. At this time there were nearly three million unemployed; and this factor accounted for the extreme views to which many

of us then inclined. We made the mistake of assuming that
the cure for this social disease was as obvious as the
symptoms were apparent. It proved otherwise.

For several months I worked in a Yorkshire coal-field as
a miner. My duties were to look after the pit ponies at the
bottom of the shaft. I was not a member of any political
party; I was not an agitator, and if I had been, the work
down the mine was so exhausting that I should not have
had the energy for such activities. I told myself I was living
as a working man in order to understand him. Perhaps it
was merely an adventure. However, this is not the place to
describe it.

Soon after I left the colliery and returned to London,
a stay-in strike occurred in the Rhondda Valley. I immediately went there, for I now had some practical knowledge
of the miners' conditions: they had been my own. The
miners had struck without their Union's support. For four
days and nights thirty of them had remained down, refusing
to come to the surface. I stood with the worried women
at the top of the shaft.

It then occurred to me that if only these strikers could
refrain from all violence and continue their passive resistance they might in time arouse the conscience of the
owners and the nation; and, by these means, achieve for
themselves more than political theories could do for them.
Their wives prepared food to be lowered down the shaft. I
smuggled some chewing tobacco into the basket and a note
to their leader urging him to continue his non-violent
resistance. But to no avail. The Communists exploited the
situation; violence broke out, the police had then sufficient
cause to act; the public lost their sympathy with the strike
and it eventually petered out. I myself was denounced by
the Communists who informed the police that I was an
agent provocateur. I was arrested as a vagrant, but eventually allowed my freedom.

This experience convinced me of the importance of passive resistance. I could see the need of personal discipline
even in industrial disputes. This realization turned me from
all the current political theories with their ridiculous sim-
plifications. Dimly, I perceived that what our age needed
most was saints, not politicians.

True to type, I wrote a pamphlet about the matter and
as nobody would sell it when it was printed, I posted the

copies away to anybody whose name came to my mind. One of these was, of course, Mahatma Gandhi.

To my surprise, he treated my silly essay seriously and wrote a long letter to me on this question of discipline. This raised another dimension. We continued to correspond. There was no air mail then, it took me six weeks to get an answer. With my usual impatience I sent him a post card suggesting we should meet. He took me at my word and cabled his reply: 'Meet me Wardha on the 23rd inst.'

I remember that I was sitting playing chess in Amen Court with the late Dick Sheppard at the time when I received it. The first thing was to find an atlas to discover the whereabouts of Wardha. I then realized that if I was to keep the appointment I had to get to the very centre of India within a month. Sheppard advised me to go. He was at this time running the Peace Pledge Movement and urged me to ask Gandhi's advice on several matters.

So within a couple of days I left London. Benjamin Britten and Henry Boys came as far as Paris with me. There was a feeling I should never return and Britten worried lest I might become a yogi in Tibet.

The journey was uneventful except for the fact that I discovered a detective had been detailed to accompany me. We used to play poker together.

I reached Wardha on the 23rd. At the station I looked for a taxi. There were none. I was persuaded to hire a primitive vehicle called a tonga. It resembled Boadicea's chariot, it had wooden wheels without any kind of rims or tyres, three hand-sawn planks constituted the body and these were nailed direct on to the axle. The emaciated driver sat on the shaft and steered the lean bullock by twisting its bony tail. There were no reins, no springs and no road. It was all ruts and bumps. I do not know how far Gandhi's Ashram was from Wardha station. I shall always believe it was too far. After half an hour of bumping across an arid, infertile scrubland I could do no more than cling on for I now lacked the strength to fling myself off.

Suddenly the sadistic and reckless driver pointed out some figure walking towards us; I was too shaken to be interested. But the driver pulled up and there was Gandhi smiling mischievously above me. He had walked three miles to meet me. I crawled off my tonga quite expecting him to congratulate me on my survival, or at least make some comment on my arrival, for I had travelled several thousand miles to keep this appointment.

'As I was saying in my last letter,' he began before I had time to dust the tonga off my back, 'means must determine ends and indeed it's questionable in human affairs whether there is an end. The best we can do is to make sure of the method and examine our motive. . . .'

Whereupon we began to walk across this desert scrub, continuing our discussion as though neither time nor place had interrupted our correspondence. I noted Gandhi never referred to my arrival—which I suppose was one way of making me feel at home and saved us the time of discussing something of no consequence.

For the rest of our walk he continued to discuss the ethics of action and he explained what he meant by 'selfless action'—'I will give you a Gita as soon as we get in'. He also asked me about the pacifist organizations in England.

I told him that one of their difficulties was the expense of propaganda. He smiled ruefully at this.

'The right action contains its own propaganda and needs no other,' he said. 'It's the same with all these movements, societies, or sects, they waste their time and energies saying what everybody ought to do, but if they themselves were to act up to their own principles that would be sufficient and arresting propaganda. Truth needs no publicity other than itself and like a small stone thrown into a pond, its ripples will in time inevitably reach the circumference. The only thing to consider is the solidity and the weight of the stone. . . .'

Eventually we reached Gandhi's Ashram and he immediately showed me round. He called it 'Segoan' and had settled there some years before when he announced his intention of withdrawing from Congress and devoting his life to the betterment of the Indian villages.

I think he had chosen this site for two reasons—firstly, because the neighbouring village was one of the most backward in the country; and secondly because the natural conditions could not have been more difficult. It looked like a desert; indeed it was one, except where Gandhi's efforts had produced this small oasis of fertility around his Ashram.

This tiny settlement built of adobe had now become the political and spiritual centre of India. It consisted of a simple one-roomed house with verandas on two sides. We ate our meals on one and I kept my belongings on the other. There was no furniture or decorations of any kind. The walls were of mud or adobe: the floor was swept earth, trodden hard. This was Gandhi's workroom. There was a rug and a spinning wheel on the floor and in front of this a soap box which served as his desk. I observed that it was inscribed with the word 'Lifebuoy'. Yet it contained his library; there were five books; I noticed one was by Tolstoy.

Adjoining Gandhi's cell were several others in which Miss Slade and the other members of the Ashram lived. Here, too, they used to teach the village children.

These buildings were enclosed by a bamboo stockade in one corner of which three or four villagers were pressing sugar cane and, in another, a great draught bullock trod an endless journey drawing water from a well to water the extensive kitchen garden.

Outside the stockade, Gandhi showed me his idea of a lavatory. This consisted of a narrow hand-dug trench with a portable shelter.

'You've no idea how difficult it is to persuade the villagers to bury their excreta,' he told me. I little guessed then that I was soon to discover.

The kitchen consisted of a pump and a fire, both in the open. On the veranda opposite sat a middle-aged woman shelling peas with remarkable dexterity. Gandhi introduced me to her. It was his wife, Kasturbai. She seemed very shy and could not speak English. As soon as we had moved away he told me that twenty years ago he had undertaken a vow of chastity. And with the amazing frankness which later I was to take for granted, he said that he had married at an early age. He paused. 'I was only thirteen.' He told me how Hindu parents waste so much time and money over the marriage celebrations of their children, who are themselves often unaware of their betrothal. And how his father and mother had decided to stage one extravagant celebration and marry him and his two brothers off in a grand triple wedding. Only when he was measured for new clothes did he realize that his wife had been chosen. He told me, too, of the shyness and the agony of intimacy he and his wife felt when thrust into this premature wedlock.

I formed the impression that Gandhi, the reformer, was born on his own wedding night.

'The marriage was unhappy at the start owing to my

jealousy and I have never forgiven myself for all the sensualism I indulged in which left me no time to teach my wife. She remains almost illiterate. As you notice, she cannot speak English.'

For my part I had thought no less of her for this lack and indeed her homeliness had attracted me as a relief from Gandhi's own intellectualism. I was unable to understand his sense of guilt in this respect, nor could I appreciate his concern that Kasturbai could only speak Gujarati. After all, I thought, she can shell peas.

But even so, I realized then that Gandhi's child marriage had left him with a deep sense of shame which nobody could remove. There is a tragic passage in his autobiography which reveals this:

'The time of which I am now speaking is my sixteenth year. My father, as we have seen, was bedridden, suffering from a fistula My mother, an old servant of the house and I were his principal attendants. I had the duties of a nurse, which mainly consisted in dressing the wound, giving my father his medicine, and compounding drugs whenever they had to be made up at home. Every night I massaged his legs and retired only when he asked me to do so or after he had fallen asleep. I loved to do this service. I do not remember ever having neglected it. All the time at my disposal, after the performance of the family duties, was divided between schools and attending on my father. I would only go out for an evening walk either when he permitted me or when he was feeling well.

'This was also the time when my wife was expecting a baby—a circumstance which, as I can see to-day, meant a double shame for me. For one thing I did not restrain myself, as I should have done, whilst I was yet a student. And secondly, this carnal lust got the better of what I regarded as my duty to study and of what was even a greater duty, my devotion to my parents, Shraven having been my ideal since childhood. Every night whilst my hands were busy massaging my father's legs, my mind was hovering about the bedroom—and that too at a time when religion, medical science, and common sense alike forbade sexual intercourse. I was always glad to be relieved from my duty and went straight to the bedroom after doing obeisance to my father . .

'The dreadful night came. My uncle was then in Rajkot.

I have a faint recollection that he came to Rajkot having had news that my father was getting worse. The brothers were deeply attached to each other. My uncle would sit near my father's bed the whole day, and would insist on sleeping by his bedside after sending us all to sleep. No one had dreamt that this was to be the fateful night. The danger of course was there.

'It was 10.30 or 11 p.m. I was giving the massage. My uncle offered to relieve me. I was glad and went straight to the bedroom. My wife, poor thing, was fast asleep. But how could she sleep when I was there? I woke her up. In five or six minutes, however, the servant knocked at the door. I started with alarm. "Get up," he said, "Father is very ill." I knew of course that he was very ill, and so I guessed what "very ill" meant at that moment. I sprang out of bed.

' "What is the matter? Do tell me!".

' "Father is no more."

'So all was over! I had but to wring my hands. I felt deeply ashamed and miserable. I ran to my father's room. I saw that, if animal passion had not blinded me, I should have been spared the torture of separation from my father during his last moments. I should have been massaging him and he would have died in my arms. But now it was my uncle who had had this privilege. He was so deeply devoted to his elder brother that he had earned the honour of doing him the last services. My father had forebodings of the coming event. He had made a sign for pen and paper and written: "Prepare for the last rites." He had then snapped the amulet off his arm and also his gold necklace of *tulasi*-beads and flung them aside. A moment after this he was no more.

'The shame, to which I have referred in a foregoing chapter, was this shame of my carnal desire even at the critical hour of my father's death, which demanded wakeful service. It is a blot I have never been able to efface or forget, and I have always thought that, although my devotion to my parents knew no bounds and I would have given up anything for it, yet it was weighed and found unpardonably wanting because my mind was at the same moment in the grip of lust. I have therefore always regarded myself as a lustful, though a faithful, husband. It took me long to get free from the shackles of lust, and I had to pass through many ordeals before I could overcome it.'

Gandhi then went on to speak to me about the necessity of continence and chastity in the pursuit of Brahmacharya. I felt that our respective ages gave him a natural advantage in this discussion.

After he had shown me round the rest of his Ashram, he introduced me to Miss Slade, or Mira Behn, to use the Indian name she adopted when she became a devoted follower of the Mahatma. She wore a plain white Indian costume, not a *sari*, but such as the Untouchable beggars wear. Her grey hair was entirely shaven. This forbidding appearance did nothing to conceal the warm kindness of the woman. Often I used to go to her bare little cell and watch her teaching the village children to spin cotton or attend to their filthy sores, I was always struck by the essentially English thoroughness of her work. No shaven head or loin-cloth of coarse linen could hide those qualities. I formed the impression that she was a character as courageous and as resolute as Florence Nightingale.

I also met Rajkumari Amrit Kaur, an Indian princess who had given her estate away and joined the community. She was a most educated and very beautiful woman who combined the best of the West with all the grace of the East.

Others in the Ashram included Gandhi's two pretty granddaughters who were devoted to him, and a young man called Pyarelal who had abandoned a promising university career for a religious life. He acted as Gandhi's amanuensis.

I was then told the discipline which the Ashram followed. 'We rise at 4 a.m. for communal prayers,' Gandhi said slyly, 'but I shall not expect you to attend. After which we do our toilet, breakfast, and then work.'

He suggested that I should talk with him alone for two hours every morning and then accompany him on his walk. He outlined the rest of the day. Every moment was devoted to service to the neighbouring village—except for those times which were given to regular prayer and meditation.

I had brought a bed-roll with me and the first night I slept on this on the veranda. I was wakened by the sound of a chant; its rhythm was the most complex I have ever heard. The stars were still shining; it was 4 a.m. All the members of the Ashram were sitting in a circle round a log fire in the open, Gandhi was reading the vedas and after each *sloka* the others chanted the responses. I did not understand a single word but the rhythm was articulate by itself.

After this service we used to wash and breakfast on figs and the green loose-skinned nagpuri oranges. Then everybody would go to their tasks just as it became light. The Ashram was veterinary college, dispensary, hospital and school to the village, to which the peasants used to come with their ailing animals and children for free medical service and instruction in husbandry and rural crafts.

'Patient example is the only possible method to effect a reform,' Gandhi told me as we walked through the sugarcane plantations, towards the little village which was a mere collection of fly-blown and squalid shacks, an eyrie for wellfed vultures.

'This is the real India,' said the voice beside me, 'it is one which visitors to the Taj Mahal seldom see.'

The hovels were improvised, not built. Their walls were of mud, their roofs of flattened petrol cans, tattered mats in place of doors; and none of them could boast a window. But it was not the extreme poverty and filth of the place which appalled me most, but the complete inertia of the derelict inhabitants. They were too emaciated for work, too apathetic for hope. There they sat in front of their homes without even the energy to remove the flies settling on their sores. I tried to compare this sight before me with the slums of the Rhondda Valley, but there was no point of comparison. The dour streets of inhabited tombstones in which the colliers lived were gay and neat cottages compared to this.

Gandhi let me absorb the scene. 'Hardly the brightest jewel, is it?' he said. 'There are tens of millions living like this; usury has brought them to it—they are mortgaged three generations ahead and what they sow the moneylender and the tax collector harvest.' He told me of the injustice of a fixed charge, that is to say, taxes which are not computed on the yield of the harvest, but a relentless burden when drought produces insufficient even for next year's seed.

As we stood there I noticed four or five men were squatting in front of us. They were relieving themselves. I glanced around me: what I had taken to be the droppings of dogs was, I realized, all human excreta. It was outside the hovels, it was beside their only well . . . no wonder the people were ridden by disease and the children poxed with sores.

Gandhi stood silent. A look of intense pity and sorrow came into his face. There was no anger. He did not step forward and give them a lecture on hygiene or modern sanitation. He did not plead, cajole or reprimand. But with the same expression of abject humility as though he himself was personally to blame for all this suffering and filth, began to scavenge the excreta and bury it with his own hand. As we did this together, the villagers at first stood by and watched. Then the example of their beloved Mahatmaji worked upon them. He was clearing their filth away without a look or a word of complaint. Within a few minutes the villagers began to follow his example. Gandhi's act of selfless action, of service, had achieved in a moment what coercion or teaching could not have done in a century.

Here was an example of practical politics, of applied religion, an excellent introduction to philosophy. I had come to India to talk to Gandhi—but this incident taught me more than all the discussions we had.

When we had finished cleaning round the well, Gandhi took me into one of the 'houses'. It was dark, entirely unfurnished, a sort of noisy grave with tubercular children in fly-blown corners. The smell made me feel sick. To my surprise I saw that his face was now radiant with pleasure. I looked for the cause. In a corner of the room sat a woman using a *charka*, or home-made spinning wheel. Another example of his had been followed.

As we walked home, he told me something of the economics of rural India and how many of the village crafts had been so discouraged and neglected as to be forgotten.

'For instance, they go without sugar though these palms above them will yield it if only they are tapped in the proper manner. And the Government has, by taxing Indian cloth to encourage Lancashire exports, left us almost naked, though cotton will grow here and used to be spun in the homes.'

He explained his Khadi Movement and how he had made a vow many years ago to spin so many yards of yarn every day. The result was that cheap Indian cloth could now be bought in many villages. And that evening he gave me a portable spinning wheel which was fitted into a little case and a blue rug made from cloth he himself had spun.

'The spinning wheel is not only the very symbol of passive resistance,' he said, 'it is also a means of meditation. And so long as the peasants spin they have their self-respect and a measure of independence.'

I began to understand what he meant by the relation of religion to politics. 'Every act', he would repeat almost daily to me, 'has its spiritual, economic and social implications. The spirit is not separate. It cannot be.' This point of view was, I think, his most important contribution to twentieth-century thought. It was the base of all his activities. Those people who ask whether Gandhi was a saint or a statesman do not begin to understand him or his achievement. He was one because he was the other; in him they were identified, and this was the secret of his success as a politician and his integrity as a religious man.

The midday meal at the Ashram was taken squatting on the veranda. I used to sit next to Gandhi for he was most concerned that I should eat enough. The food was vegetarian and was quite delicious. I was particularly fond of the hand-ground bread with white butter. The only condiment allowed was salt, as Gandhi disapproved of all seasoning and would not permit the Indian curry to be served as he maintained that such seasoning not only ruined the palate but was bad for the health and aggravated the senses. He said curries were aphrodisiacs.

He told me that though he had been born into a religious sect which practised strict vegetarianism, he had once tried meat eating. Apparently when he was at school the doggerel rhyme—

> Behold the mighty Englishman
> He rules the Indian small
> Because he is a meat eater
> And is five cubits tall.

—had persuaded him to change his diet. This step meant breaking with the habits of his parents and the strict rules of his religion and had to be done in secret. But he told me, 'Since I wanted to be strong and daring and free my country from the English, I decided on the experiment.' He and a friend went to a lonely spot by a river and there ate some goat's flesh. That night he had a nightmare and dreamed that a live goat was bleating inside him. He persisted in these surreptitious feasts for a time but eventually returned to the diet of his forefathers.

Such detailed principles of diet and behaviour did not make Gandhi a prig or deprive him of his sense of humour. One day I noticed that whereas I and other members of the Ashram ate off brass plates, Gandhi used an old battered tin bowl. I asked him why he preferred it.

'It was given to me when I first went to prison, and as I'm always ready to go back there it's only right that I should continue to use the bowl.'

He spoke of his prison days with joy and with genuine gratitude to those who had detained him. You cannot punish a man who is grateful for the punishment and insists on regarding his jailer as his host. Every privation only enriched him. His dignity lay in the acceptance of every humiliation.

Yet in counterpoint to these qualities he had a wry and mischievous side to him. I was never sure when he was not teasing me. And when people began to praise him to excess or almost deify him, as some of his followers did, his defence was to turn imp.

I remember once when he asked me to accompany him to Wardha where he had promised to attend a conference of Anglican bishops in India. We did not travel by tonga; an open car called for us. As we drove into the town, the car was pelted with flowers and surrounded. One earnest devotee, a girl of about twenty, jumped on to the running board in order to touch the Mahatma's garment. As she leaned over to do so, Gandhi broke the spell by boyishly pulling her nose.

'I am not a god,' he used to complain to me, 'if the truth were known I am tempted more than most men—but perhaps less than those who are sinners.' In that distinction was all of tolerance.

Another time, I myself had been asking him earnest questions about his 'Fast Unto Death'—for there is no doubt that he would have died voluntarily on that occasion if the Government had not been persuaded by opinion to act at the last moment.

'Do you know what I did on the first day of that fast?' he asked me. 'I got the prison dentist in to measure me up for this set of false teeth.'

Whether he meant by this that he had had no intention of fasting to death, or that he had ordered the teeth as an act of faith that the Government would recognize the righteousness of his cause, he didn't say. But in fact I discovered that the latter was his reason, though Gandhi told me the story in order to suggest the former out of modesty, and to make me believe that his will power was not as great as his reputation.

To say the least, I was most ill-prepared for the religious discipline and austerity of Gandhi's Ashram. I had come merely to talk—there is nothing so comfortable as a discussion on remote ideals, but Gandhi would always take my theory gently by the scruff of its neck and rub my nose in the practical and personal implications. It was a useful but painful lesson. In this connection, one day he interrupted one of my more abstract dissertations with a little story from the life of Buddha, which I suspect I have not remembered correctly, but it is probably well known.

'The Buddha had a young disciple', Gandhi told me, 'whom the Master left in the desert promising to return to him in three years to see how he had progressed. During this time the disciple built a house which he proudly showed the Buddha when he returned. The Master examined it and then told the disciple to take the house to pieces and erect it again a few paces farther away, promising to return in another three years. The disciple did as he was instructed. The Master returned, examined the house again, but told the young man that he must now abandon it altogether and sit by the river and meditate, promising to return again at the end of another three years. The disciple did as he was instructed. When the Master at last returned he asked the disciple what he had done with his time. "I can now walk across on the surface of the river without getting my feet wet," the young man boasted. "Then you have wasted your time," said Buddha, "for there is a ferry just round the corner." '

The implications of this parable were not entirely lost on me. Gandhi was the most practical man I have ever met. He would always drive any thought to its personal implication and practical application.

When I arrived at the Ashram I was a heavy smoker— and of course nobody there indulged in that habit. I used to steal off somewhat furtively into a field of sugar cane where I had first to overcome my horror of snakes before hiding in the crop to light a cigarette. But Gandhi was not to be deceived. He took my addiction to this habit very seriously, and in order to help me break it he told me how he and a friend had once become fond of smoking and used as children to pick up the ends of cigarettes which his uncle threw away. 'The stumps were not very satisfactory and so we began to steal the servants' pocket money in order to buy them. But even so we found it intolerable to have to smoke in secret and eventually we became so disgusted with these parental restrictions that we decided to commit suicide. We stole off into the jungle and tried to poison ourselves with some seeds but were so frightened of dying we only took sufficient to give us stomach-ache. However, it cured me of smoking—but not from thieving. I once stole some gold out of my brother's amulet and was then so overcome with remorse that I wrote out a full confession and gave it to my father. He read it. He said nothing. He only wept. This was for me an important object lesson in *ahimsa*—of love.'

As Gandhi told me this incident, I was again made aware of how most of his convictions sprang from his experiences as a child. His love for his parents and the fact that they were both deeply religious people were factors which could not be underestimated in assessing the growth of his character.

His concern about my smoking became of great importance to him. Urgent matters of political moment, correspondence with the Viceroy, were all put aside to keep me provided with toffee made out of the palm sugar as a substitute for cigarettes.

'If you can't master yourself in this,' Gandhi used to say, 'how can you hope to do anything else?' And he would then quote the Gita and tell me that detachment from the senses was the first step in the ladder, without which nothing.

And even after I left the Ashram, Gandhi continued to worry. When I arrived at Bombay to take a boat home, a large parcel of toffee was already on the boat to help me on the voyage. When I reached Port Sudan, there was a letter already there, in his own hand, begging me not to smoke.

After lunch, it was the custom for the members of the Ashram to retire and meditate. I soon realized that a voyage up the unexplored regions of the Amazon would be an easy expedition compared with a journey into my own mind. It is an extremely embarrassing experience to discover the shallowness of one's own thought and complete inability to concentrate.

'Meditation is not for him who eats too much, nor for him who eats not at all, nor for him who is over-addicted to sleep, nor for him who is always awake.'

After a few days, Gandhi took me for a long walk till we came to a little hut in a clearing. The occupant had put himself under Gandhi's teaching. He is what is termed a Yogi; and had been in this place for over a year. The hut was no more than a summerhouse and contained no furniture except a table and a chair. There were no paper or books. I commented on this. 'The sacrifice of wisdom is superior to any material sacrifice; for, O Arjuna, the climax of action is always Realization,' he murmured. I stayed talking to him for several hours. This man had the physique of a boxer and the poise of a dancer. There was about him a lake of calmness; being with him was a kind of solitude. He emitted peace in the same way as a heater radiates warmth.

When I was taking my leave I noticed there was a chill in the evening air. I glanced round his bare hut—'Don't you ever catch cold?' I asked him.

'No,' he said with a simplicity which was without a trace of pride, 'I do not allow them. . . .'

So, that night, I foolishly abandoned the luxury of my bed-roll on the veranda and followed Gandhi out into the open where he used to sleep on the damp ground. I awoke with a heavy dew on me and a severe chill. However, I persisted in sleeping in the open till the chill got steadily worse. Gandhi was sympathetic but in no way alarmed at my sneezes. I also had a temperature and the discomfort of a stiff neck. Eventually, when leaving the Ashram to visit a colony of Untouchables, he sent me to an osteopath who strapped me into a vertical machine. A lever was pulled and the contraption flung me violently on to my back. I was released—not a single trace of my influenza remained.

As I had daily conversations with Gandhi, I had a unique opportunity to study both the man and his ideas. But I was too young to appreciate much at the time. I can correct some of my youthful impressions, but no more; what was hidden from me then, cannot be recalled now.

There is no need to describe his appearance: his features were frequently photographed. But I shall always remember the anachronism of the large cheap watch which dangled on a safety-pin attached to his loin-cloth: worn this way, time itself appeared to be a toy, an invention of the Western mind.

His face was too animated to give the impression of serenity; his mind too active to suggest repose. Though his dress was almost comical in its simplicity, with his shaven head, steel-rimmed glasses and single tooth, yet one was unaware of his appearance, and only impressed by his extra-ordinary strength of will. His humility was so complete as to be the very essence of dignity. His hands, like all Indians', were extremely beautiful—with thousands of years of craft in his long supple fingers, by comparison with which any Western hand is a clumsy paw.

During these discussions he never raised his voice above a whisper and the spinning wheel was never still.

I told him of my experience of the stay-in strike in the coal-mine at the Rhondda Valley, and asked him what training was required for passive resistance. His answer was, of course, such as to leave English politics far behind. 'There is no short cut,' he told me, 'but the way of the spirit which is one of detachment, of self-abnegation, of being unattached to all desires. If such truth resides in one man, all follows inevitably from him. But without that essence, nothing.'

All conversations, whatever their point of departure, returned to the teachings of the Gita, the gospel of selfless action. And there was always his insistence that there was no life but a spiritual life.

There was no need for me to ask him why he concerned himself with politics, for I had seen him clean round that village well. To him it was all service, selfless action, action that is a prayer.

'I do not believe that the spiritual law works on a plane of its own' he used to say and he had no patience with what he called 'the futility of mere religious knowledge'. To Gandhi the whole of life resided in every part. He did not allow the distinctions—religion, culture, politics or art. His insistence on the necessity of being unattached to the senses reminded me of Jerome's vow not to read poetry. I could not understand him when he used to tell me that all sensual gratification is sin. And I used to disagree. I remember that I argued on the lines that it did not matter what one loved but how; the object being unimportant, the quality, the purity of love, being all-important. To my mind the legend of 'Le Jongleur de Notre Dame' is an example of this.

Gandhi saw sin in every sensual pleasure. It seemed to amount to a nausea with life itself. I was at times reminded of the pettiness of English Puritanism and I suggested that perhaps the most perverse sensual gratification was to be obtained not by satisfying one's senses, but by denying them satisfaction. Gandhi smiled at this : 'That is also a danger,' he said, 'but there is no point in renouncing an object that one still desires.'

With infinite patience and good humour he tried to make me understand the difference between what I called Puritanism and what he referred to as Brahmacharya. 'What you are talking about amounts to a mere negation of this life, but what I am talking about is a means to an everlasting life. There is a difference between renouncing an object and relinquishing it.' As usual he quoted the Gita. 'The sages say that renunciation means forgoing an action which springs from desire, and relinquishing means the surrender of its fruit.'[1]

This last phrase 'the surrender of its fruit' was always on Gandhi's lips. It was the key to the philosophy of selfless action.

But in spite of his endless patience with me in these discussions, I refused to understand—for at that age I was determined not to do so. In retrospect I realize that I did, but would not admit it. And in order to preserve my own tastes and habits I subconsciously began to seek points of disagreement with all the desperation of a goldfish clinging to the little bowl I knew in preference to the lake I did not dare to experience.

One day during a walk, he defined sin to me as 'being acted upon by the senses'. I remember I instantly asked him if he considered listening to Mozart was a sin. The question was all-important to me.

'All attachment to the senses is death', he replied. It may seem strange but I used Gandhi's light dismissal of Mozart as the reason for refusing his invitation, which he made

1. For these quotations I have used the excellent translation of the Gita from the original Sanskrit made by Shri Purhit Swami (published by Faber and Faber, London, 1935).

later to me, to return to India again and live with him for a year.

We were, of course, often talking at different levels, yet I was reminded that most of his early influences had been Western in origin. It was Ruskin's *Unto this Last*, Carlyle's *Heroes and Hero Worship*, Tolstoy, and even Mrs Besant and the literature of the Theosophical Society in Bayswater, which had all influenced Gandhi as a young man. But these writers only awakened a spiritual strength which was already there.

I discovered that most of his ideas concerning self-sufficiency, rural crafts and vegetarianism were derivative from Tolstoy. But the derivation is unimportant. The essential contribution Gandhi made to twentieth-century thought was his insistence on the need for a lower standard of living, in opposition to the Western notion that progress lies in an accumulation of material prosperity. He maintained that the essence of civilization consists not in the multiplication of wants but in their deliberate and voluntary renunciation.

He preached a higher standard of spiritual living and maintained that a lower level of material well-being was a necessary prerequisite. His ideas were the very antithesis of both Marx and Ford. This being so, can his importance to contemporary thought be over-estimated?

I do not think they can, and I have made this selection because I believe that Gandhi's teaching is of permanent value especially to the West, which is so bemused with the experiments of science that it is completely blind to the potentialities of the spirit.

Gandhi's political efforts were entirely without 'concern for the fruit'. And in the tragic *Delhi Diary* one reads of his self-doubts as to the value of realizing his great ambition. He had devoted his life to obtaining the independence of India. In the whole course of history there is probably no other example where such a great political accomplishment depended on the efforts of one man. And then it was not a military victory but a triumph of his own will. Yet, as the *Delhi Diary* reveals, if there is one thing worse than failing in one's ambitions, it is to achieve them. For to do that is often to see their value.

From the moment that Gandhi achieved independence for India, he suffered intense introspection, first appealing to one side to abandon communal strife, then pleading with the other, till he was again forced to fast. Not only did he do this; but as ever, led the nation in a practical example by touring the most dangerous areas, and going into the houses of Moslems in preference to those of Hindus.

Page after page of this tragic *Diary* shows his disillusionment as he witnessed the scramble for power and the way it corrupted many of his own supporters. He alone could find no cause for rejoicing at his achievement and was to the last filled with foreboding for India's future.

At the age of seventy-eight 'with nothing but agony in his heart', on 12th January 1948, he announced his intention of undertaking a great fast in an effort to quell the violent antagonism between India and Pakistan. This final act of self-sacrifice was not in vain, but caused the Government of India to pay over certain assets to Pakistan which they had been withholding pending a settlement of the Kashmir dispute. And only when the two governments pledged themselves to protect the life and property of the minorities, did Gandhi break his fast on 18th January.

But two days later, a bomb was thrown into the garden at Birla House where the Mahatma lived and held his prayer meetings. The explosion caused no loss of life. Gandhi instantly intervened with the police on the would-be assassin's behalf.

On 26th January, when India was celebrating Independence Day, Gandhi at his prayer meeting asked what was the cause of their rejoicing. 'Now that we have independence we seem to be disillusioned. At least I am, if you are not.' He then continued to speak against the violence and corruption growing around him.

He knew that the final sacrifice was inevitable. And two days later he told his secretary to bring him all his important letters. 'I must reply to them to-day, for to-morrow I may not be.' This done he went into the grounds for his prayer meeting. A Hindu youth broke from the crowd and almost knelt before the Mahatma, then fired into his stomach. Gandhi fell chanting 'Ram, Ram' (O God, O God), his hands held in an attitude of prayer.

What would Gandhi have done if he had not been assassinated? There can be little doubt that the self-searching and distress he felt at the events which followed immediately after Independence, and which he expressed in his *Delhi Diary*, would have led him to fast to death. The only question is, which event he would have selected for his sacrifice.

There was the continued rift between Hindu and Moslem which he sought to heal; there was the political degeneracy of Congress from which party he had withdrawn, but faced with the petty bureaucracy and careerism which Congress soon manifested, not to mention the growth of materialism and the gradual overthrow of the spiritual disciplines which he had advocated, there is no doubt that here would have been found many reasons which would have suggested a course of self-purification to him. And if he had not chosen the degeneracy of Congress as an issue, I think he would have taken the failure of India to solve the problem of Untouchability. After twenty years, it is still a sore for the whole world to see. Nor do I think Gandhi would have stood by when Nehru moved against Goa; nor is it likely that he would have approved in 1969 when Mrs Gandhi nationalized the banks and made out-of-date gestures towards the Left, since the Mahatma had made many éxplicit statements that he did not think socialism was an answer. And it is, of course, quite certain, that he could not have survived the war between India and Pakistan. Though had he lived, it is probable that this would not have occurred. None of his followers would have dared face him with the borrowed panoply of Delhi round their shoulders, aping the Imperial gesture.

Gandhi was the one restraining influence on Congress, and after his death Gandhism remains, even now, the only spiritual leavening to a party which is obsessed with the ideals of materialism, but is neither competent nor coherent enough to put them into effect. It is clear that Congress as a political party is disintegrating but probable that Gandhism will survive it.

My interest in editing this book derives from my conviction that Gandhi is a relevant figure to the contemporary scene, and that he has a profound contribution to make to it and to the future.

The Government of India can be criticized for failing to project Gandhi's philosophy to the rest of the world. And the Centenary celebrations of 1969, which might have provided an opportunity for making his ideas explicit, have done little to show the immediate relevance of some of his political ideas and spiritual values.

A few people who knew Gandhi and understood his philosophy, such as Lord Mountbatten, are able to assess the Mahatma's value accurately, but many others, who are often powerful publicists, are less well-informed. Mr Malcolm Muggeridge, for instance, wrote in the *Observer* an article celebrating the Centenary of the Mahatma's birth, that the 'great mistake of Gandhi's life was that he meddled with politics.' It is hard to think of a misunderstanding of the man or his philosophy as complete as this statement indicates. Gandhi's whole philosophy was based on the oneness or the wholeness of life. He maintained again and again to me personally that there was no such thing as a religious act without political implications, or a political act without religious overtones. He did not see any way of separating these two subjects, and in my opinion it was this integration within the man that constitutes his most profound contribution to both philosophy and political action. Have we not had enough of the so-called professional politician driving a sick world further insane? Do we not need the saint who can commit himself to action as well as prayer? Are not the events in, say, Budapest or Prague, evidence that without the leadership of a man with spiritual criteria, violence merely begets violence and one tyranny is merely overthrown to make way for the next? Will we not very probably see racial troubles in America which, without the influence of a Martin Luther King, who was partially derivative from Gandhi, worsen into civil war? And can the growing resistance to Communism behind the Iron Curtain become articulate or translated into effective political action, unless the method and strategy of non-violence is used? What happened in Prague without it surely answers that question.

And clearly, too the anomaly of the growth of nationalism which the twentieth century has witnessed, in a world of easy communications, is another sphere where Gandhi's influence would be useful. Although Gandhi achieved political independence for India, he was not himself a nationalist in the narrow sense of the word. His purpose in obtaining independence was to retrieve dignity and responsibility for the Indians. His plan was to move towards an equal partnership between India and Britain.

His insistence that Mountbatten should become the first Governor-General was an immediate and practical gesture in that direction.

It could be said that in the latter part of the twentieth century there was political fervour and religious indifference. Is it not possible that the political disasters were consequent to there being no spiritual criteria? Albert Einstein remarked that 'now we have all the means it would appear that we have forgotten what our goals are.'

The two people that have had most political or social impact this century are probably Gandhi and Lenin. It is therefore not irrelevant to compare them. And to do this one need only look at Lenin's dictum: 'In politics there is no morality, only expediency,' to assess which of these two figures the world would have done well to be without.

And there is also another parallel between Gandhi and Einstein. They had what the latter called a 'cosmic consciousness', both being devoutly religious men and to each a dogma was irrelevant.

Surely, too, as the social and political complexities of this century increase, all politicians and religious leaders have this to learn from Gandhi: the ability to admit that they are sometimes completely wrong.

As the bibliography shows, Mahatma Gandhi had many books published; yet he was neither a prolific writer nor a deliberate author. Many of his books consist of reports of speeches which he delivered, or collections of articles written for his weekly journal, *Harijan*, or were printed in the magazine, *Young India*.

In making this selection, I have tried to bear three things in mind: firstly, my intention to present material of permanent interest as opposed to comments on day-to-day political matters; also to show the development and to give the essence of his philosophy of *satyagraha*, and its basis in the religious teachings of the Gita; and thirdly, I have tried to emphasize those ideas which, though they may not seem immediately applicable to Western life, should be of considerable relevance to contemporary thought.

We live to-day in a period which has much in common with the Dark Ages—though ours is the darkness of the neon light—in the way that many of us are isolated though we are surrounded by means of communication; and inarticulate in spite of innumerable late-editions. In such a time, Mahatma Gandhi was an oasis of meditation in our vast and garrulous vacuity.

His insistence that spiritual value should be the basis for all action, and his belief that all culture is merely a manifestation of religious beliefs (or the lack of them), stands in complete opposition to the materialistic flood from Asia and America which, if not arrested, will certainly engulf these ruins, the remnants of Christendom. European culture arose from a spiritual impulse; and I suggest that it can ultimately only be defended by precisely the same dynamic which produced it.

Gandhi understood these essentials of philosophical strategy; that is, he could distinguish between ends and means, and was aware that it is impossible to mend a delicate wrist-watch with a sledge-hammer. He knew, too, that freedom consists of discipline; and that a higher standard of living is not to be confused with the acquisition of or attachment to a greater number of mere things. He knew that the spirit can ultimately only be defended by the spirit; and that the means for our survival are not visible nor material.

I have not included his account of his campaign of *satyagraha* in South Africa, nor the great tour which he undertook in his last days amongst the North-west Frontier Pathans, as both of these accounts are reported elsewhere and extracts could not do justice to them. Similarly, I have not attempted to give a full picture of his life since my friend, Shri Pyarelal, has written a comprehensive biography.

But since so much of Gandhi's political action was in opposition to the British Raj in India, I have included some correspondence between him and the Marquis of Linlithgow, who was Viceroy of India during a crucial period in the relationship between the two countries, and also a few letters from Lord Mountbatten, the last Viceroy and the first Governor-General. I believe that this correspondence not only shows the deep respect in which Gandhi was held even by the Government which he sought to overthrow, but that Lord Linlithgow's and Lord Mountbatten's letters reveal the best qualities of English authority. Their letters are not only tolerant but friendly; they are dignified and firm, yet also kind. They show the virtues of a governing class over a mere bureaucracy. They are also fine examples of the epistolary style; and I believe that when history comes to assess the achievements or failings of the British in India, then these qualities of tolerance and impartial judgment which these letters from the Viceregal Lodge contain, must weigh to our advantage.

RONALD DUNCAN

PART I

Anasakti Yoga, or the Gospel of Selfless Action, an Extract from Gandhi's Commentary on the Bhagavad Gita

———————

Now about the message of the Gita.

Even in 1888-9, when I first became acquainted with the Gita, I felt that it was not an historical work, but that, under the guise of physical warfare, it described the duel that perpetually went on in the hearts of mankind, and that physical warfare was brought in merely to make the description of the internal duel more alluring. This preliminary intuition became more confirmed on a closer study of religion and the Gita. A study of the Mahabharata gave it added confirmation. I do not regard the Mahabharata as an historical work in the accepted sense. The Adiparva contains powerful evidence in support of my opinion. By ascribing to the chief actors superhuman or subhuman origins, the great Vyasa made short work of the history of kings and their peoples. The persons therein described may be historical, but the author of the Mahabharata has used them merely to drive home his religious theme.

The author of the Mahabharata has not established the necessity of physical warfare; on the contrary he has proved its futility. He has made the victors shed tears of sorrow and repentance, and has left them nothing but a legacy of miseries.

In this great work the Gita is the crown. Its second chapter, instead of teaching the rules of physical warfare, tells us how a perfected man is to be known. In the characteristics of the perfected man of the Gita I do not see any to correspond to physical warfare. Its whole design is inconsistent with the rules of conduct governing the relations between warring parties.

Krishna of the Gita is perfection and right knowledge personified; but the picture is imaginary. That does not mean that Krishna, the adored of his people, never lived.

But perfection is imagined. The idea of a perfect incarnation is an aftergrowth.

In Hinduism, incarnation is ascribed to one who has performed some extraordinary service of mankind. All embodied life is in reality an incarnation of God, but it is not usual to consider every living being an incarnation. Future generations pay this homage to one who, in his own generation, has been extraordinarily religious in his conduct. I can see nothing wrong in this procedure. It takes nothing from God's greatness, and there is no violence done to Truth. There is an Urdu saying which means, 'Adam is not God but he is a spark of the Divine'. And therefore he who is the most religiously behaved has most of the divine spark in him. It is in accordance with this train of thought, that Krishna enjoys, in Hinduism, the status of the most perfect incarnation.

This belief in incarnation is a testimony of man's lofty spiritual ambition. Man is not at peace with himself till he has become like unto God. The endeavour to reach this state is the supreme, the only ambition worth having. And this is self-realization. This self-realization is the subject of the Gita, as it is of all scriptures. But its author surely did not write it to establish that doctrine. The object of the Gita appears to me to be that of showing the most excellent way to attain self-realization. That which is to be found, more or less clearly, spread out here and there in Hindu religious books, has been brought out in the clearest possible language in the Gita even at the risk of repetition.

That matchless remedy is renunciation of fruits of action.

This is the centre round which the Gita is woven. This renunciation is the central sun, round which devotion, knowledge and the rest revolve like planets. The body has been likened to a prison. There must be action where there is body. Not one embodied being is exempted from labour. And yet all religions proclaim that it is possible for man, by treating the body as the temple of God, to attain freedom. Every action is tainted, be it ever so trivial. How can the body be made the temple of God? In other words how can one be free from action, i.e. from the taint of sin? The Gita has answered the question in decisive language: 'By desireless action; by renouncing fruits of action; by dedicating all activities to God, i.e. by surrendering oneself to Him body and soul.'

But desirelessness of renunciation does not come for the mere talking about it. It is not attained by an intellectual feat. It is attained only by a constant heart-churn. Right knowledge is necessary for attaining renunciation. Learned men possess a knowledge of a kind. They may recite the Vedas from memory, yet they may be steeped in self-indulgence. In order that knowledge may not run riot, the author of the Gita has insisted on devotion accompanying it and has given it the first place. Knowledge without devotion will be like a misfire. Therefore, says the Gita, 'Have devotion, and knowledge will follow.' This devotion is not merely lip worship, it is a wrestling with death. Hence the Gita's assessment of the devotee's qualities is similar to that of the sage's.

Thus the devotion required by the Gita is no soft-hearted effusiveness. It certainly is not blind faith. The devotion of the Gita has the least to do with externals. A devotee may use, if he likes, rosaries, forehead marks, offerings, but these things are no test of his devotion. He is the devotee who is jealous of none, who is a fount of mercy, who is without egotism, who is selfless, who treats alike cold and heat, happiness and misery, who is ever forgiving, who is always contented, whose resolutions are firm, who has dedicated mind and soul to God, who causes no dread, who is not afraid of others, who is free from exultation, sorrow and fear, who is pure, who is versed in action and yet remains unaffected by it, who renounces all fruit, good or bad, who treats friend and foe alike, who is untouched by respect or disrespect, who is not puffed up by praise, who does not go under when people speak ill of him, who loves silence and solitude, who has a disciplined reason. Such devotion is inconsistent with the existence at the same time of strong attachments.

We thus see, that to be a real devotee is to realize oneself. Self-realization is not something apart. One rupee can purchase for us poison or nectar, but knowledge or devotion cannot buy us either salvation or bondage. These are not media of exchange. They are themselves the things we want. In other words, if the means and the end are not identical, they are almost so. The extreme of means is salvation. Salvation of the Gita is perfect peace.

But such knowledge and devotion, to be true, have to stand the test of renunciation of fruits of action. Mere knowledge of right and wrong will not make one fit for salvation. According to common notions, a mere learned man will pass as a *pandit*. He need not perform any service. He will regard it as bondage even to lift a little *lota*. Where one test of knowledge is non-liability for service, there is no room for such mundane work as the lifting of a *lota*.

Or take *bhakti*. The popular motion of *bhakti* is soft-heartedness, telling beads and the like, and disdaining to do even a loving service, lest the telling of beads, etc. might be interrupted. This *bhakti*, therefore, leaves the rosary only for eating, drinking and the like, never for grinding corn or nursing patients.

But the Gita says: 'No one has attained his goal without action. Even men like Janaka attained salvation through action. If even I were lazily to cease working, the world would perish. How much more necessary then for the people at large to engage in action?'

While on the one hand it is beyond dispute that all action binds, on the other hand it is equally true that all living beings have to do some work, whether they will or no. Here all activity, whether mental or physical, is to be included in the term action. Then how is one to be free from the bondage of action, even though he may be acting? The manner in which the Gita has solved the problem is, to my knowledge, unique. The Gita says: 'Do your allotted work but renounce its fruit—be detached and work—have no desire for reward and work.'

This is the unmistakable teaching of the Gita. He who gives up action falls. He who gives up only the reward rises. But renunciation of fruit in no way means indifference to the result. In regard to every action one must know the result that is expected to follow, the means thereto, and the capacity for it. He, who, being thus equipped, is without desire for the result, and is yet wholly engrossed in the due fulfilment of the task before him, is said to have renounced the fruits of his action.

Again, let no one consider renunciation to mean want of fruit for the renouncer. The Gita reading does not warrant such a meaning. Renunciation means absence of hankering after fruit. As a matter of fact, he who renounces reaps a thousandfold. The renunciation of the Gita is the acid test of faith. He who is ever brooding over result often loses nerve in the performance of his duty. He becomes impatient and then gives vent to anger and begins to do unworthy things; he jumps from action to action, never remaining faithful to any. He who broods over results is like a man given to objects of senses; he is ever distracted, he says good-bye to all scruples, everything is right in his estimation and he therefore resorts to means fair and foul to attain his end.

From the bitter experiences of desire for fruit the author of the Gita discovered the path of renunciation of fruit, and put it before the world in a most convincing manner. The common belief is that religion is always opposed to material good. 'One cannot act religiously in mercantile and such other matters. There is no place for religion in such pursuits; religion is only for attainment of salvation,' we hear many worldly-wise people say. In my opinion the author of the Gita has dispelled this delusion. He has drawn no line of demarcation between salvation and worldly pursuits. On the contrary he has shown that religion must rule even our worldly pursuits. I have felt that the Gita teaches us that what cannot be followed out in day-to-day practice cannot be called religion. Thus, according to the Gita, all acts that are incapable of being performed without attachment are taboo. This golden rule saves mankind from many a pitfall. According to this interpretation murder, lying, dissoluteness and the like must be regarded as sinful and therefore taboo. Man's life then becomes simple, and from that simpleness springs peace.

Thinking along these lines, I have felt that in trying to enforce in one's life the central teaching of the Gita, one is bound to follow Truth and *ahimsa*. When there is no desire for fruit, there is no temptation for untruth or *himsa*. Take any instance of untruth or violence, and it will be found that at its back was the desire to attain the cherished end. But it may be freely admitted that the Gita was not written to establish *ahimsa*. It was an accepted and primary duty even before the Gita age. The Gita had to deliver the message of renunciation of fruit. This is clearly brought out as early as the second chapter.

But if the Gita believed in *ahimsa* or it was included in desirelessness, why did the author take a warlike illustration? When the Gita was written, although people believed in *ahimsa*, wars were not only not taboo, but nobody observed the contradiction between them and *ahimsa*.

In assessing the implications of renunciation of fruit, we are not required to probe the mind of the author of the Gita as to his limitations of *ahimsa* and the like. Because a poet puts a particular truth before the world, it does not necessarily follow that he has known or worked out all its great consequences, or that having done so, he is able to express them fully. In this perhaps lies the greatness of the poem and the poet. A poet's meaning is limitless. Like man, the meaning of great writings suffers evolution. On examining the history of languages, we notice that the meaning of important words has changed or expanded. This is true of the Gita. The author has himself extended the meanings of some of the current words. We are able to discover this even on a superficial examination. It is possible that, in the age prior to that of the Gita, offering of animals in sacrifice was permissible. But there is not a trace of it in the sacrifice in the Gita sense. In the Gita continuous concentration on God is the king of sacrifices. The third chapter seems to show that sacrifice chiefly means body-labour for service. The third and the fourth chapters read together will give us other meanings for sacrifice, but never animal-sacrifice. Similarly has the meaning of the word *sannyasa* undergone, in the Gita, a transformation. The *sannyasa* of the Gita will not tolerate complete cessation of all activity. The *sannyasa* of the Gita is all work and yet no work. Thus the author of the Gita, by extending meanings of words, has taught us to imitate him. Let it be granted, that according to the letter of the Gita it is possible to say that warfare is consistent with renunciation of fruit. But after forty years' unremitting endeavour fully to enforce the teaching of the Gita in my own life, I have, in all humility, felt that perfect renunciation is impossible without perfect observance of *ahimsa* in every shape and form.

The Gita is not an aphoristic work; it is a great religious poem. The deeper you dive into it, the richer the meanings you get. It being meant for the people at large, there is pleasing repetition. With every age the important words will carry new and expanding meanings. But its central teaching will never vary. The seeker is at liberty to extract from this treasure any meaning he likes so as to enable him to enforce in his life the central teaching.

Nor is the Gita a collection of do's and don'ts. What is lawful for one may be unlawful for another. What may be

permissible at one time, or in one place, may not be so
at another time, and in another place. Desire for fruit is the
only universal prohibition. Desirelessness is obligatory.

The Gita has sung the praises of Knowledge, but it is
beyond the mere intellect; it is essentially addressed to the
heart and capable of being understood by the heart. Therefore the Gita is not for those who have no faith. The
author makes Krishna say:

'Do not entrust this treasure to him who is without
sacrifice, without devotion, without the desire for this
teaching and who denies Me. On the other hand, those
who will give this precious treasure to My devotees will,
by the fact of this service, assuredly reach Me. And those
who, being free from malice, will with faith absorb this
teaching, shall, having attained freedom, live where people
of true merit go after death.'[1]

1. Extract from *The Gospel of Selfless Action* or *The Gita
according to Gandhi*, by Mahadev Desai, Ahmedabad, Navajivan
Publishing House, 1946, pp. 123-31.

PART II

The Gita and Satyagraha: the Philosophy of Non-violence and the Doctrine of the Sword; a Letter from Tolstoy to Gandhi

---

THE GITA AND SATYAGRAHA

I have admitted in my introduction to the Gita known as *Anasakti Yoga* that it is not a treatise on non-violence, nor was it written to condemn war. Hinduism, as it is practised to-day or has even been known to have ever been practised, has certainly not condemned war as I do. What, however, I have done is to put a new but natural and logical interpretation upon the whole teaching of the Gita and the spirit of Hinduism. Hinduism, not to speak of other religions, is ever evolving. It has no one scripture like the Koran or the Bible. Its scriptures are also evolving and suffering addition. The Gita itself is an instance in point. It has given a new meaning to *karma, sannyasa, yajna,* etc. It has breathed new life into Hinduism. It has given an original rule of conduct. Not that what the Gita has given was not implied in the previous writings, but the Gita put these implications in a concrete shape. I have endeavoured, in the light of a prayerful study of the other faiths of the world, and what is more, in the light of my own experiences in trying to live the teaching of Hinduism as interpreted in the Gita, to give an extended but in no way strained meaning to Hinduism, not as buried in its ample scriptures, but as a living faith speaking like a mother to her aching child. What I have done is perfectly historical. I have followed in the footsteps of our forefathers. At one time they sacrificed animals to propitiate angry gods. Their descendants, but our less remote ancestors, read a different meaning into the word 'sacrifice', and they taught that sacrifice was meant to be of our baser self, to please not angry gods but the one living God within. I hold that the logical outcome of the teaching of the Gita is decidedly for peace at the price of life itself. It is the highest aspiration of the human species.

The Mahabharata and Ramayana, the two books that millions of Hindus know and regard as their guides, are undoubtedly allegories as the internal evidence shows. That they most probably deal with historical figures does not affect my proposition. Each epic describes the eternal duel that goes on between the forces of darkness and of light. Anyway, I must disclaim any intention of straining the meaning of Hinduism or the Gita to suit any preconceived notions of mine. My notions were an outcome of a study of the Gita, Ramayana, Mahabharata, Upanishads, etc.

(Harijan, 3rd October 1936)

TRUTH[1]

The word 'Satya' (Truth) is derived from 'Sat' which means being. And nothing is or exists in reality except Truth. That is why 'Sat' or Truth is perhaps the most important name of God. In fact it is more correct to say that Truth is God, than to say that God is Truth. But as we cannot do without a ruler or a general, names of God such as King of Kings or the Almighty are and will remain more usually current. On deeper thinking, however, it will be realized that 'Sat' or 'Satya' is the only correct and fully significant name of God.

And where there is Truth, there also is knowledge, pure knowledge. Where there is no Truth, there can be no true knowledge. That is why the word 'Chit' or knowledge is associated with the name of God. And where there is true knowledge, there is always bliss (*ananda*). Sorrow has no place there. And even as Truth is eternal, so is the bliss derived from it. Hence we know God as 'Sat-chit-ananda', one who combined in Himself Truth, Knowledge and Bliss.

Devotion to this Truth is the sole reason for our existence. All our activities should be centred in Truth. Truth should be the very breath of our life. When once this stage in the pilgrim's progress is reached, all other rules of correct living will come without effort, and obedience to them will be instinctive. But without Truth it would be impossible to observe any principles or rules in life.

Generally speaking, observing the law of Truth is merely understood to mean that we must speak the truth. But we

1. Extract from *From Yeravda Mandir* by M. K. Gandhi, Ahmedabad, Navajivan Publishing House, 1932.

in the Ashram understand the word Satya or Truth in a much wider sense. There should be Truth in thought, Truth in speech, Truth in action. To the man who has realized this Truth in perfection, nothing else remains to be known, because all knowledge is necessarily included in it. What is not included in it is not Truth, and so not true knowledge; and there can be no inward peace without true knowledge. If we once learn how to apply this never-failing test of Truth, we will at once be able to find out what is worth doing, what is worth seeing, what is worth reading.

But how is one to realize this Truth, which may be likened to the philosopher's stone or the cow of plenty? By single-minded devotion (*abhyasa*) and indifference to every other interest in life (*vairagya*)—replies the Bhagavad Gita. In spite, however, of such devotion, what may appear as truth to one person will often appear as untruth to another person. But that need not worry the seeker. Where there is honest effort, it will be realized that what appear to be different truths are like apparently different countless leaves of the same tree. Does not God Himself appear to different individuals in different aspects? Still we know that He is one. But Truth is the right designation of God. Hence there is nothing wrong in every one following Truth according to one's lights. Indeed it is one's duty to do so. Then if there is a mistake on the part of any one so following Truth, it will be automatically set right. For the quest of Truth involves *tapas*—self-suffering, sometimes even unto death. There can be no place in it for even a trace of self-interest. In such selfless search for Truth nobody can lose his bearings for long. Directly one takes to the wrong path one stumbles, and is thus redirected to the right path. Therefore the pursuit of Truth is true *bhakti* (devotion). It is the path that leads to God, and therefore there is no place in it for cowardice, no place for defeat. It is the talisman by which death itself becomes the portal to life eternal.

NON-POSSESSION OR POVERTY

Civilization, in the real sense of the term, consists not in the multiplication, but in the deliberate and voluntary reduction of wants. This alone promotes real happiness and contentment, and increases the capacity for service.

From the standpoint of pure Truth, the body too is a

possession. It has been truly said, that desire for enjoyment creates bodies for the soul. When this desire vanishes, there remains no further need for the body, and man is free from the vicious cycle of births and deaths. The soul is omnipresent; why should she care to be confined within the cage-like body, or do evil and even kill for the sake of the cage? We thus arrive at the ideal of total renunciation, and learn to use the body for the purposes of service so long as it exists, so much so that service, and not bread, becomes with us the staff of life. We eat and drink, sleep and awake, for service alone. Such an attitude of mind brings us real happiness, and the beatific vision in the fullness of time. Let us all examine ourselves from this standpoint.

We should remember, that Non-possession is a principle applicable to thoughts, as well as to things. One, who fills his brain with useless knowledge, violates that inestimable principle. Thoughts, which turn us away from God, or do not turn us towards Him, constitute impediments in our way. In this connection we may consider the definition of knowledge contained in the 13th chapter of the Gita. We are there told, that humility (*amanitvam*) etc. constitute knowledge, and all the rest is ignorance. If this is true—and there is no doubt that it is true—much that we hug to-day as knowledge is ignorance pure and simple, and therefore, only does us harm, instead of conferring any benefit. It makes the mind wander, and even reduces it to a vacuity, and discontent flourishes in endless ramifications of evil. Needless to say, this is not a plea for inertia. Every moment of our life should be filled with activity, but that activity should be *sattvika*, tending to Truth. One, who has consecrated his life to service, cannot be idle for a single moment. But one has to learn to distinguish between good activity, and evil activity. This discernment goes naturally with a single-minded devotion to service.

FEARLESSNESS

Every reader of the Gita knows that fearlessness heads the list of the Divine Attributes enumerated in the 16th chapter. Whether this is merely due to the exigencies of metre, or whether the pride of place has been deliberately yielded to fearlessness, is more than I can say. In my opinion however, fearlessness richly deserves the first rank assigned to it there. For it is a *sine qua non* for the growth of the other noble qualities. How can one seek Truth, or cherish Love, without fearlessness? As Pritam has it, 'the path of Hari (the Lord) is the path of the brave, not of cowards'. Hari here means Truth, and the brave are those armed with fearlessness, not with the sword, the rifle and other carnal weapons, which, strictly speaking are affected only by cowards.

Fearlessness connotes freedom from all external fear— fear of disease, bodily injury and death, of dispossession, of losing one's nearest and dearest, of losing reputation or giving offence, and so on. One, who overcomes the fear of death, does not surmount all other fears, as is commonly but erroneously supposed. Some of us do not fear death, but flee from the minor ills of life. Some are ready to die themselves, but cannot bear their loved ones to be taken away from them. Some misers will put up with all this, will part even with their lives, but not their property; others will do any number of black deeds in order to uphold their supposed prestige. Some will swerve from the strait and narrow path, which lies clear before them, simply because they are afraid of incurring the world's odium. The seeker after Truth must conquer all these fears. He should be ready to sacrifice his all in the quest of Truth, even as Harishchandra did. The story of Harishchandra may be only a parable; but every seeker will bear witness to its truth from his personal experience, and therefore that story is more precious than any historical fact.

Perfect fearlessness can be attained only by him who has realized the Supreme, as it implies freedom from delusions. One can always progress towards this goal by determined and constant endeavour, and by cultivating self-confidence.

As I have stated at the very outset, we must give up all external fears. But the internal foes we must always fear. We are rightly afraid of animal passion, anger, and the like. External fears cease of their own accord, when once we have conquered these traitors within the camp. All fears revolve round the body as the centre, and would therefore disappear, as soon as one got rid of attachment for the body. We thus find, that all fear is the baseless fabric of our own vision. Fear has no place in our hearts, when we have shaken off the attachment for wealth, for family and for the body. 'Enjoy the things of the earth by renouncing them' is a noble precept. Wealth, family and body will be there, just the same; we have only to change our attitude towards them. All these are not ours, but God's. Nothing whatever in this world is ours. Even we ourselves are His. Why, then, should we entertain any fears? The Upanishad therefore directs us 'to give up attachment for things, while we enjoy them'. That is to say, we must be interested in them, not as proprietors, but as only trustees. He, on whose behalf we hold them, will give us the strength and the weapons requisite for defending them against all usurpers. When we thus cease to be masters and reduce ourselves to the rank of servants, humbler than the very dust under our feet, all fears will roll away like mists; we shall attain ineffable peace, and see Satyanarayan (the God of Truth) face to face.

TOLERANCE

I did not like this word, but could not think of a better one. Tolerance implies a gratuitous assumption of the inferiority of other faiths to one's own, whereas *ahimsa* teaches us to entertain the same respect for the religious faiths of others as we accord to our own, thus admitting the imperfection of the latter. This admission will be readily made by a seeker of Truth, who follows the law of Love. If we had attained the full vision of Truth, we would no longer be mere seekers, but become one with God, for Truth is God. But being only seekers, we prosecute our quest, and are conscious of our imperfection. And if we are imperfect ourselves, religion as conceived by us must also be imperfect. We have not realized religion in its perfection, even as we have not realized God. Religion of our conception, being thus imperfect, is always subject to a process of evolution and reinterpretation. Progress towards Truth, towards God, is possible only because of such evolution. And if all faiths outlined by men are imperfect, the question of comparative merit does not arise. All faiths constitute a revelation of Truth, but all are imperfect, and liable to error. Reverence for other faiths need not blind us to their faults. We must be keenly alive to the defects of our own faith, and must not leave it on that account, but try to overcome those defects. Looking at all religions with an equal eye, we would not only not hesitate, but would think it our duty, to adopt into our faith every acceptable feature of other faiths.

The question then arises: Why should there be so many different faiths? The Soul is one, but the bodies which she animates are many. We cannot reduce the number of bodies; yet we recognize the unity of the Soul. Even as a tree has a single trunk, but many branches and leaves, so is there one true and perfect Religion, but it becomes many, as it passes through the human medium. The one Religion is beyond all speech. Imperfect men put it into such language as they can command and their words are interpreted by other men equally imperfect. Whose interpretation is to be held to be the right one? Every one is right from his own standpoint, but it is not impossible that every one is wrong. Hence the necessity for tolerance, which does not mean indifference towards one's own faith but a more intelligent and purer love for it. Tolerance gives us spiritual insight, which is as far from fanaticism as the North Pole is from the South. True knowledge of religion breaks down the barriers between faith and faith. Cultivation of tolerance for other faiths will impart to us a truer understanding of our own.

Tolerance obviously does not disturb the distinction between right and wrong, or good and evil. The reference here throughout is naturally to the principal faiths of the world. They are all based on common fundamentals. They have all produced saintly men and women.

HUMILITY

Humility cannot be an observance by itself. For it does not lend itself to being practised. It is however an indispensable test of *ahimsa*. In one who has *ahimsa* in him it becomes part of his very nature.

But although humility is not one of the observances, it is certainly as essential as, and perhaps even more essential than, any one of them. Only it never came to any one by practice. Truth can be cultivated, as well as Love. But to cultivate humility is tantamount to cultivating hypocrisy. Humility must not be here confounded with mere manners or etiquette. One man will sometimes prostrate himself before another, although his heart is full of bitterness against the latter. This is not humility, but cunning. A man may repeat Ramanama, or tell his beads all day long, and move in society like a sage; but if he is selfish at heart, he is not meek, but only hypocritical.

A humble person is not himself conscious of his humility. Truth and the like perhaps admit of measurement, but not humility. Inborn humility can never remain hidden, and yet the possessor is unaware of its existence. The story of Vasishtha and Vishvamitra furnishes a very good case in point. Humility should make the possessor realize that he is as nothing. Directly one imagines oneself to be something, there is egotism. If a man who keeps observances is proud of keeping them, they will lose much, if not all of their values. And a man who is proud of his virtue often becomes a curse to society. Society will not appreciate it, and he himself will fail to reap any benefit out of it. Only a little thought will suffice to convince us, that all creatures are nothing more than a mere atom in this universe. Our existence as embodied beings is purely momentary; what are a hundred years in eternity? But if we shatter the chains of egotism, and are melted in the ocean of humanity, we share its dignity. To feel that we are something is to set up a barrier between God and ourselves. To cease feeling that we are something is to become one with God. A drop in the ocean partakes of the greatness of its parent, although it is unconscious of it. But it is dried up, as soon as it enters upon an existence independent of the ocean. We do not exaggerate when we say that life is a mere bubble.

A life of service must be one of humility. One, who would sacrifice his life for others, has hardly time to reserve for himself a place in the sun. Inertia must not be mistaken for humility, as it has been in Hinduism. True humility means most strenuous and constant endeavour entirely directed to the service of humanity. God is performing continuous action without resting for a single moment. If we would serve Him or become one with Him, our activity must be as unwearied as His. There may be rest in store for the drop which is separated from the ocean, but not for the drop in the ocean, which knows no rest. The same is the case with ourselves. As soon as we become one with the ocean in the shape of God, there is no more rest for us, nor indeed do we need rest any longer. Our very sleep is action. For we sleep with the thought of God in our hearts. This restlessness constitutes true rest. This never-ceasing agitation holds the key to peace ineffable. This supreme state of total surrender is difficult to describe, but not beyond the bounds of human experience.

THE DOCTRINE OF THE SWORD

I do believe that, where there is only a choice between cowardice and violence, I would advise violence. Thus when my eldest son asked me what he should have done, had he been present when I was almost fatally assaulted in 1908, whether he should have run away and seen me killed or whether he should have used his physical force which he could and wanted to use, and defended me, I told him that it was his duty to defend me even by using violence. Hence it was that I took part in the Boer War, the so-called Zulu Rebellion and the late war. Hence also do I advocate training in arms for those who believe in the method of violence. I would rather have India resort to arms in order to defend her honour than that she should, in a cowardly manner, become or remain a helpless witness to her own dishonour.

But I believe that non-violence is infinitely superior to violence, forgiveness is more manly than punishment. Forgiveness adorns a soldier. But abstinence is forgiveness only when there is the power to punish; it is meaningless when it pretends to proceed from a helpless creature. A mouse hardly forgives a cat when it allows itself to be torn to pieces by her. I therefore appreciate the sentiment of those who cry out for the condign punishment of General Dyer and his ilk. They would tear him to pieces, if they could. But I do not believe India to be helpless. I do not believe myself to be a helpless creature. Only I want to use India's and my strength for a better purpose.

Let me not be misunderstood. Strength does not come from physical capacity. It comes from an indomitable will. An average Zulu is any way more than a match for an average Englishman in bodily capacity. But he flees from an English boy, because he fears the boy's revolver or those who will use it for him. He fears death and is nerveless in spite of his burly figure. We in India may in a moment realize that one hundred thousand Englishmen need not frighten three hundred million human beings. A definite forgiveness would, therefore, mean a definite recognition of our strength. With enlightened forgiveness must come a mighty wave of strength in us, which would make it impossible for a Dyer and a Frank Johnson to heap affront on India's devoted head. It matters little to me that for the moment I do not drive my point home. We feel too downtrodden not to be angry and revengeful. But I must not refrain from saying that India can gain more by waiving the right of punishment. We have better work to do, a better mission to deliver to the world.

I am not a visionary. I claim to be a practical idealist. The religion of non-violence is not meant merely for the *rishis* and saints. It is meant for the common people as well. Non-violence is the law of our species as violence is the law of the brute. The spirit lies dormant in the brute, and he knows no law but that of physical might. The dignity of man requires obedience to a higher law—to the strength of the spirit.

I have therefore ventured to place before India the ancient law of self-sacrifice. For *satyagraha* and its offshoots, non-co-operation and civil resistance are nothing but new names for the law of suffering. The *rishis*, who discovered the law of non-violence in the midst of violence, were greater geniuses than Newton. They were themselves greater warriors than Wellington. Having themselves known the use of arms, they realized their uselessness, and taught a weary world that its salvation lay not through violence but through non-violence.

Non-violence in its dynamic condition means conscious suffering. It does not mean meek submission to the will of the evil-doer, but it means the pitting of one's whole soul against the will of the tyrant. Working under this law of our being, it is possible for a single individual to defy the whole might of an unjust empire to save his honour, his religion, his soul, and lay the foundation for that empire's fall or its regeneration.[2]

Not only did I offer my services at the time of the Zulu revolt but before that, at the time of the Boer War, and not only did I raise recruits in India during the late war, but I raised an ambulance corps in 1914 in London. If, therefore, I have sinned, the cup of my sins is full to the brim I lost no occasion of serving the Government at all times. Two questions presented themselves to me during all those crises.

[2]. Extract from *Non-Violence in Peace and War* by M. K. Gandhi, Ahmedabad, Navajivan Publishing House, 1942.

What was my duty as a citizen of the Empire as I then believed myself to be, and what was my duty as an out-and-out believer in the religion of *ahimsa*—non-violence?

I know now that I was wrong in thinking that I was a citizen of the Empire. But on those four occasions I did honestly believe that, in spite of the many disabilities that my country was labouring under, it was making its way towards freedom, and that on the whole the Government from the popular standpoint was not wholly bad, and that the British administrators were honest though insular and dense. Holding that view, I set about doing what an ordinary Englishman would do in the circumstances. I was not wise or important enough to take independent action. I had no business to judge or scrutinize ministerial decisions with the solemnity of a tribunal. I did not impute malice to the ministers either at the time of the Boer War, the Zulu revolt or the late war. I did not consider Englishmen, nor do I now consider them, as particularly bad or worse than other human beings. I considered and still consider them to be as capable of high motives and actions as any other body of men, and equally capable of making mistakes. I therefore felt that I sufficiently discharged my duty as a man and a citizen by offering my humble services to the empire in the hour of its need whether local or general. That is how I would expect every Indian to act by his country under Swaraj. I should be deeply distressed, if on every conceivable occasion every one of us were to be a law unto oneself and to scrutinize in golden scales every action of our future National Assembly. I would surrender my judgment in most matters to national representatives, taking particular care in making my choice of such representatives. I know that in no other manner would a democratic government be possible for one single day.

The whole situation is now changed for me. My eyes, I fancy, are opened. Experience has made me wiser. I consider the existing system of government to be wholly bad and requiring special national effort to end or mend it. It does not possess within itself any capacity for self-improvement. That I still believe many English administrators to be honest does not assist me, because I consider them to be as blind and deluded as I was myself. Therefore I can take no pride in calling the Empire mine or describing myself as a citizen. On the contrary, I fully realize that I am a *pariah* untouchable of the Empire. I must, therefore, constantly pray for its radical reconstruction or total destruction, even as a Hindu *pariah* would be fully justified in so praying about Hinduism or Hindu society.

The next point, that of *ahimsa*, is more abstruse. My conception of *ahimsa* impels me always to dissociate myself from almost every one of the activities I am engaged in. My soul refuses to be satisfied so long as it is a helpless witness of a single wrong or a single misery. But it is not possible for me—a weak, frail, miserable being—to mend every wrong or to hold myself free of blame for all the wrong I see. The spirit in me pulls one way, the flesh in me pulls in the opposite direction. There is freedom from the action of these two forces, but that freedom is attainable only by slow and painful stages. I can attain freedom not by a mechanical refusal to act, but only by intelligent action in a detached manner. This struggle resolves itself into an incessant crucifixion of the flesh so that the spirit may become entirely free.

I was, again, an ordinary citizen no wiser than my fellows, myself believing in *ahimsa* and the rest not believing in it at all but refusing to do their duty of assisting the Government because they were actuated by anger and malice. They were refusing out of their ignorance and weakness. As a fellow worker it became my duty to guide them aright. I therefore placed before them their clear duty, explained the doctrine of *ahimsa* to them, and let them make their choice, which they did. I do not repent of my action in terms of *ahimsa*. For, under Swaraj too I would not hesitate to advise those who would bear arms to do so and fight for the country.

That brings to me the second question. Under Swaraj of my dream there is no necessity for arms at all. But I do not expect that dream to materialize in its fullness as a result of the present effort, first because the effort is not directed to that end as an immediate goal, and secondly because I do not consider myself advanced enough to be able to prescribe a detailed course of conduct to the nation for such preparation. I am still myself too full of passion and other frailties of human nature to feel the call or the capacity. All I claim for myself is that I am incessantly trying to overcome every one of my weaknesses. I have attained great capacity, I believe, for suppressing and curbing my senses, but I have not become incapable of sin, i.e. of being acted upon by my senses. I believe it to be possible for every human being to attain that blessed and indescribably sinless state in which he feels within himself the presence of God to the exclusion of everything else. It is, I must confess, as yet a distant scene. And therefore it is not possible for me to show the nation a present way to complete non-violence in practice.[3]

My path is clear. Any attempt to use me for violent purposes is bound to fail. I have no secret methods. I know no diplomacy save that of Truth. I have no weapon but non-violence. I may be unconsciously led astray for a while but not for all time. I have therefore well-defined limitations, within which alone I may be used. Attempts have been made before now to use me unlawfully more than once. They have failed each time so far as I am aware.

I am yet ignorant of what exactly Bolshevism is. I have not been able to study it. I do not know whether it is for the good of Russia in the long run. But I do know that in so far as it is based on violence and denial of God, it repels me. I do not believe in short—violent—cuts to success. Those Bolshevik friends who are bestowing their attention on me should realize that, however much I may sympathize with and admire worthy motives, I am an uncompromising opponent of violent methods even to serve the noblest of causes. There is, therefore, really no meeting ground between the school of violence and myself. But my creed of non-violence not only does not preclude me but compels me even to associate with anarchists and all those who believe in violence. But that association is always with the sole object of weaning them from what appears to me to be their error. For experience convinces me that permanent good can never be the outcome of untruth and violence. Even if my belief is a fond delusion, it will be admitted that it is a fascinating delusion.[4]

I have not the capacity for preaching universal non-violence to the country. I preach, therefore, non-violence restricted strictly to the purpose of winning our freedom and therefore perhaps for preaching the regulation of international

3. Extract from *Non-Violence in Peace and War.*
4. Extract from *Non-Violence in Peace and War.*

relations by non-violent means. But my incapacity must not be mistaken for that of the doctrine of non-violence. I see it with my intellect in all its effulgence. My heart grasps it. But I have not yet the attainments of preaching universal non-violence with effect. I am not advanced enough for the great task. I have yet anger within me, I have yet the *dwaitabhava*—duality—in me. I can regulate my passions, I keep them under subjection, but before I can preach universal non-violence with effect, I must be wholly free from passions. I must be wholly incapable of sin. Let the revolutionary pray with and for me that I may soon become that. But meanwhile let him take with me the one step to it which I see as clearly as daylight, i.e. to win India's freedom with strictly non-violent means. And then under Swaraj you and I shall have a disciplined intelligent educated police force that would keep order within and fight raiders from without, if by that time I or someone else does not show a better way of dealing with either.[5]

From what will the masses be delivered? It will not do to have a vague generalization and to answer: 'from exploitation and degradation.' Is not the answer that, that they want to occupy the status that capital does to-day? If so, it can be attained only by violence. But if they want to shun the evils of capital, then they would strive to attain a juster distribution of the products of labour. This immediately takes us to contentment and simplicity, voluntarily adopted. Under the new outlook multiplicity of material wants will not be the aim of life, the aim will be rather their restriction consistently with comfort. We shall cease to think of getting what we can, but we shall decline to receive what all cannot get. It occurs to me that it ought not to be difficult to make a successful appeal to the masses of Europe in terms of economics, and a fairly successful working of such an experiment must lead to immense and unconscious spiritual results. I do not believe that the spiritual law works on a field of its own. On the contrary, it expresses itself only through the ordinary activities of life. It thus affects the economic, the social and the political fields. If the masses of Europe can be persuaded to adopt the view I have suggested, it will be found that violence will be wholly unnecessary to attain the aim, and that they

5. *Idem.*

can easily come to their own by following out the obvious corollaries of non-violence. It may even be that what seems to me to be so natural and feasible for India may take longer to permeate the inert Indian masses than the active European masses. But I must reiterate my confession that all my argument is based on suppositions and assumptions and must, therefore, be taken for what it is worth.[6]

I do justify entire non-violence, and consider it possible in relation between man and man and nation and nation; but it is not 'a resignation from all real fighting against wickedness'. On the contrary, the non-violence of my conception is a more active and more real fighting against wickedness than retaliation whose very nature is to increase wickedness. I contemplate a mental, and therefore a moral, opposition to immoralities. I seek entirely to blunt the edge of the tyrant's sword, not by putting up against it a sharper-edged weapon, but by disappointing his expectation that I should be offering physical resistance. The resistance of the soul that I should offer instead would elude him. It would at first dazzle him, and at last compel recognition from him, which recognition would not humiliate him but would uplift him. It may be urged that this again is an ideal state. And so it is. The propositions from which I have drawn my arguments are as true as Euclid's definitions, which are none the less true, because in practice we are unable even to draw Euclid's line on a blackboard. But even a geometrician finds it impossible to get on without bearing in mind Euclid's definitions. Nor may we, the German friend, his colleagues and myself, dispense with the fundamental propositions on which the doctrine of *satyagraha* is based.

I have often noticed that weak people have taken shelter under the Congress creed or under my advice, when they have simply, by reason of their cowardice, been unable to defend their own honour or that of those who were entrusted to their care. I recall the incident that happened near Bettiah when non-co-operation was at its height. Some villagers were looted. They had fled, leaving their wives, children and belongings to the mercy of the looters. When I rebuked them for their cowardice in thus neglecting their

6. *Idem.*

charge, they shamelessly pleaded non-violence. I publicly denounced their conduct and said that my non-violence fully accommodated violence offered by those who did not feel non-violence and who had in their keeping the honour of their womenfolk and little children. Non-violence is not a cover for cowardice, but it is the supreme virtue of the brave. Exercise of non-violence requires far greater bravery than that of swordsmanship. Cowardice is wholly inconsistent with non-violence. Translation from swordsmanship to non-violence is possible and, at times, even an easy stage. Non-violence, therefore, presupposes ability to strike. It is a conscious deliberate restraint put upon one's desire for vengeance. But vengeance is any day superior to passive, effeminate and helpless submission. Forgiveness is higher still. Vengeance too is weakness. The desire for vengeance comes out of fear of harm, imaginary or real. A dog barks and bites when he fears. A man who fears no one on earth would consider it too troublesome even to summon up anger against one who is vainly trying to injure him. The sun does not wreak vengeance upon little children who throw dust at him. They only harm themselves in the act.[7]

Non-resistance is restraint voluntarily undertaken for the good of society. It is, therefore, an intensely active, purifying, inward force. It is often antagonistic to the material good of the non-resister. It may even mean his utter material ruin. It is rooted in internal strength, never weakness. It must be consciously exercised. It therefore presupposes ability to offer physical resistance.[8]

The acquisition of the spirit of non-resistance is a matter of long training in self-denial and appreciation of the hidden forces within ourselves. It changes one's outlook upon life. It puts different values upon things and upsets previous calculations, and when once it is intensive enough can overtake the whole universe. It is the greatest force because it is the highest expression of the soul. All need not possess the same measure of conscious non-resistance for its full operations. It is enough for one person only to possess it, even as one general is enough to regulate and dispose of the energy of millions of soldiers who enlist under his banner, even though they know not the why and the where-

7. Idem.   8. Idem.

fore of his dispositions. The monkeys of one Rama were
enough to confound the innumerable hosts armed from head
to foot of the ten-headed Ravana.[9]

A friend sends me the following cutting from the New
York *Nation*:

'Some time ago (either in the latter part of 1924, or early
in 1925) a band of twenty-five American missionaries in
China addressed the following appeal to the American
Minister at Peking:

' "The undersigned American missionaries are in China
as messengers of the gospel of brotherhood and peace.
Our task is to lead men and women into a new life in
Christ, which promotes brotherhood and takes away all
occasions of war. We therefore express our earnest
desire that no form of military pressure, especially no
foreign military force, be exerted to protect us or our
property; and that, in the event of our capture by lawless persons or our death at their hands, no money be
paid for our release, no punitive expedition be sent out,
and no indemnities be exacted. We take this stand
believing that the way to establish righteousness and
peace is through bringing the spirit of personal goodwill
to bear on all persons under all circumstances, even
though suffering wrong without retaliation."

'The American Legation, however, replied that this
petition was inconsistent with the necessity that exists
for safeguarding Americans in China, and that therefore
no exception could or would be made in the procedure in
case of emergencies with regard to the signers of the
petition.'

This is one of those instances in which two apparently
contradictory positions are right at the same time. For the
brave missionaries there was no other attitude possible,
though nowadays very few adopt it. Was it not about
China that a missionary deputation some thirty years ago
waited on the late Lord Salisbury and asked the protection
of the British gunboats for carrying their message to the
unwilling Chinese? Then the late noble Marquess had to tell
the missionaries that, if they sought the protection of the
British arms, they must submit to international obligations
and curb their missionary ardour. He reminded them that

9. *Idem.*

the Christians of old, if they penetrated the remotest regions of the earth, expected no protection save from God and put their lives in constant danger. In the case quoted by the New York *Nation*, the missionaries, according to the report, have reverted to the ancient practice.

The American Government, however, so long as it retains its present character, can only give the answer they are reported to have given. That the answer betrays the evil of the modern system is another matter. The American prestige depends not upon its moral strength but upon force. But why should the whole armed force of America be mobilized for the so-called vindication of its honour or name? What harm can accrue to the honour of America if twenty-five missionaries choose to go to China uninvited for the sake of delivering their message and get killed in the act? Probably it would be the best thing for their mission. The American Government by its interference could only interrupt the full working of the law of suffering. But self-restraint of America would mean a complete change of outlook. To-day defence of citizenship is a defence of national commerce, i.e. exploitation. That exploitation presupposes the use of force for imposing commerce upon an unwilling people. Nations have, in a sense, therefore, almost become gangs of robbers, whereas they should be a peaceful combination of men and women united for the common good of mankind. In the latter case, their strength will lie not in their skill in the use of gunpowder, but in the possession of superior moral fibre. The action of the twenty-five missionaries is a dim shadow of reconstructed society or even reconstructed nations. I do not know whether they carried their principle into practice in every department of life. I need hardly point out that, in spite of the threat of the American Government to protect them against themselves, they could neutralize, indeed even frustrate, any effort at retaliation. But that means complete self-effacement. And if one is to combat the fetish of force, it will only be by means totally different from those in vogue among the pure worshippers of brute force.

It must not be forgotten that after all there is a philosophy behind the modern worship of brute force with a history to back it. The microscopic non-militant minority has indeed nothing to fear from it, if only it has immovable faith behind it. But faith in the possibility of holding together society without brute force seems somehow to be lacking. Yet if one person can pit himself against the whole world, why cannot two or more do likewise together? I know the answer that has been given. Time alone can show the possibilities of the revolution that is silently creeping upon us. Speculation is waste of effort where action is already afoot. Those who have faith will join the initial effort in which demonstrable results cannot be shown.[10]

Language at best is but a poor vehicle for expressing one's thoughts in full. For me non-violence is not a mere philosophical principle. It is the rule and the breath of my life. I know I fail often, sometimes consciously, more often unconsciously. It is a matter not of the intellect but of the heart. True guidance comes by constant waiting upon God, by utmost humility, self-abnegation, by being ever ready to sacrifice one's self. Its practice requires fearlessness and courage of the highest order. I am painfully aware of my failings.

But the Light within me is steady and clear. There is no escape for any of us save through Truth and non-violence. I know that war is wrong, is an unmitigated evil. I know too that it has got to go. I firmly believe that freedom won through bloodshed or fraud is no freedom. Would that all the acts alleged against me were found to be wholly indefensible rather than that by any act of mine non-violence was held to be compromised or that I was ever thought to be in favour of violence or untruth in any shape or form. Not violence, not untruth, but non-violence, Truth is the law of our being.[11]

Ahimsa is not the way of the timid or the cowardly. It is the way of the brave ready to face death. He who perishes sword in hand is no doubt brave, but he who faces death without raising his little finger and without flinching is braver. But he who surrenders his rice bags for fear of being beaten is a coward and no votary of ahimsa. He is innocent of ahimsa. He who, for fear of being beaten, suffers the women of his household to be insulted, is not manly but just the reverse. He is fit to be neither a husband nor a father nor a brother. Such people have no right to complain.

10. Idem.   11. Idem.

These cases have nothing to do with inveterate enmity between the Hindus and Mussulmans. Where there are fools there are bound to be knaves, where there are cowards there are bound to be bullies, whether they are Hindus or Mussulmans. Such cases used to happen before the outbreak of these communal hostilities. The question here, therefore, is not how to teach one of the two communities a lesson or how to humanize it, but how to teach a coward to be brave.

If the thinking sections of both the communities realize the cowardice and folly at the back of the hostilities, we can easily end them. Both have to be brave, both have to be wise. If both or either deliberately get wise, theirs will be the way of non-violence. If both fight and learn wisdom only by bitter experience, the way will be one of violence. Either way there is no room for cowards in a society of men, i.e. in a society which loves freedom. Swaraj is not for cowards.

It is idle, therefore, to denounce *ahimsa* or to be angry with me on the strength of the cases cited. Ever since my experience of the distortion of *ahimsa* in Bettiah in 1921 I have been repeating over and over again that he who cannot protect himself or his nearest and dearest or their honour by non-violently facing death, may and ought to do so by violently dealing with the oppressor. He who can do neither of the two is a burden. He has no business to be the head of a family. He must either hide himself, or must rest content to live for ever in helplessness and be prepared to crawl like a worm at the bidding of a bully.

I know only one way—the way of *ahimsa*. The way of *himsa* goes against my grain. I do not want to cultivate the power to inculcate *himsa*. As *ahimsa* has no place in the atmosphere of cowardice prevailing to-day, I must needs be reticent over the riots we hear of from day to day. This exhibition of my helplessness cannot be to my liking. But God never ordains that only things that we like should happen and things that we do not like should not happen. In spite of the helplessness, the faith sustains me that He is the Help of the helpless, that He comes to one's succour only when one throws oneself on His mercy. It is because of this faith that I cherish the hope that God will one day show me a path which I may confidently commend to the people. With me the conviction is as strong as ever that willy-nilly Hindus and Mussulmans must be friends one day. No one can say how and when that will happen. The future is entirely in the hands of God. But He has vouch-safed to us the ship of Faith which alone can enable us to cross the ocean of Doubt.

Not to believe in the possibility of permanent peace is to disbelieve in godliness of human nature. Methods hitherto adopted have failed because rock-bottom sincerity on the part of those who have striven has been lacking. Not that they have realized this lack. Peace is unattainable by part performance of conditions, even as chemical combination is impossible without complete fulfilment of conditions of attainment thereof. If recognized leaders of mankind who have control over engines of destruction were wholly to renounce their use with full knowledge of implications, permanent peace can be obtained. This is clearly impossible without the great powers of the earth renouncing their imperialistic designs. This again seems impossible without these great nations ceasing to believe in soul-destroying competition and to desire to multiply wants and therefore increase their material possessions. It is my conviction that the root of the evil is want of a living faith in a living God. It is a first-class human tragedy that peoples of the earth who claim to believe in the message of Jesus whom they describe as the Prince of Peace show little of that belief in actual practice. It is painful to see sincere Christian divines limiting the scope of Jesus's message to select individuals. I have been taught from my childhood, and I have tested the truth by experience, that primary virtues of mankind are possible of cultivation by the meanest of the human species. It is this undoubted universal possibility that distinguishes the human from the rest of God's creation. If even one great nation were uncondition-ally to perform the supreme act of renunciation, many of us would see in our lifetime visible peace established on earth.[12]

Arjuna believed in war. He had fought the Kaurava Hosts many times before. But he was unnerved when the two armies were drawn up in battle array and when he suddenly realized that he had to fight his nearest kinsmen and

12. *Idem.*

revered teachers. It was not love of man or the hatred of war that had actuated the questioner. Krishna could give no other answer than he did. The immortal author of the Mahabharata, of which the Gita is one—no doubt the brightest—of the many gems contained in that literary mine, has shown to the world the futility of war by giving the victors an empty glory, leaving but seven victors alive out of millions said to have been engaged in the fight in which unnamable atrocities were used on either side. But the Mahabharata has a better message even than the demonstration of war as a delusion and folly. It is the spiritual history of man considered as an immortal being and has used with a magnifying lens an historical episode considered in his times of moment for the tiny world round him, but in terms of present-day values of no significance. In those days the globe had not shrunk to a pinhead, as it has to-day, on which the slightest movement on one spot affects the whole. The Mahabharata depicts for all time the eternal struggle that goes on daily between the forces of good and evil in the human breast and in which though good is ever victorious evil does put up a brave show and baffles even the keenest conscience. It shows also the only way to right action.

But whatever the true message of the Bhagavad Gita may be, what matters to the leaders of the peace movement is not what the Gita says but what the Bible, which is their spiritual dictionary, says, and then too not what meaning the Church authorities give to it, but what meaning a prayerful reading of it yields to the reader. What matters most of all is the objectors' knowledge of the implications of the law of love or *ahimsa*, inadequately rendered in English as non-violence.[13]

A LETTER FROM TOLSTOY TO GANDHI

Kotchety, Russia
7 September 1910

I received your journal and was pleased to learn all contained therein concerning the passive resisters. And I felt like telling you all the thoughts which that reading called up in me.

13. *Idem.*

The longer I live and especially now, when I vividly feel the nearness of death, I want to tell others what I feel so particularly clearly and what to my mind is of great importance—namely, that which is called passive resistance, but which is in reality nothing else than the teaching of love, uncorrupted by false interpretations. That love—i.e. the striving for the union of human souls and the activity derived from this striving—is the highest and only law of human life, and in the depth of his soul every human being (as we most clearly see in children) feels and knows this; he knows this until he is entangled by the false teachings of the world. This law was proclaimed by all—by the Indian as by the Chinese, Hebrew, Greek and Roman sages of the world. I think this law was most clearly expressed by Christ, who plainly said that 'in this only is all the law and the prophets'. But besides this, foreseeing the corruption to which this law is and may be subject, he straightway pointed out the danger of its corruption, which is natural to people who live in worldly interests, the danger, namely, which justifies the defences of these interests, by the use of force or, as he said, 'with blows to answer blows, by force to take back things usurped', etc. He knew, as every sensible man must know, that the use of force is incompatible with love as the fundamental law of life, that as soon as violence is permitted, in whichever case it may be, the insufficiency of the law of love is acknowledged, and by this the very law is denied. The whole Christian civilization, so brilliant outwardly, grew upon this self-evident and strange misunderstanding and contradiction, sometimes conscious, but mostly unconscious.

In reality, as soon as force was admitted into love it was no more, and there could be no love as the law of life, and as there was no law of life, there was no law at all except violence—i.e. the power of the strongest. So lived Christian humanity for nineteen centuries. It is true that in all times people were guided by violence in arranging their lives. The difference between the Christian nations and all other nations is only that in the Christian world the law of love was expressed clearly and definitely, whereas it was so expressed in the religious teaching, and that the people of the Christian world have solemnly accepted this law, whilst at the same time they have permitted violence, and built their lives on violence, and that is why the whole life of the Christian peoples is a continuous contradiction between that which they profess and the principles on which they order their lives—a contradiction between love accepted as the law of life and violence which is recognized and praised, acknowledged even as a necessity in different phases of life, such as the power of the rulers, courts and armies. This contradiction always grew with the development of the people of the Christian world, and lately it reached the highest stage. The question now evidently stands thus: either to admit that we do not recognize any religio-moral teaching, and we guide ourselves in arranging our lives only by power of the stronger, or that all our compulsory taxes, court and police establishments, but mainly our armies, must be abolished.

This year, in spring, at a Scripture examination in a girls' high school in Moscow, the teacher and the bishop present asked the girls questions on the Commandments, and especially on the sixth. After a correct answer the bishop generally put another question, whether murder was always in all cases forbidden by God's law and the unhappy young ladies were forced by previous instruction to answer 'Not always'—that murder was permitted in war and in execution of criminals. Still, when one of these unfortunate young ladies (what I am telling is not an invention, but a fact told me by an eye-witness) after her first answer, was asked the usual question, if killing was always sinful, she, agitated and blushing, decisively answered, 'Always', and to all the usual sophisms of the bishop, she answered with decided conviction that killing always was forbidden in the Old Testament and forbidden by Christ, not only killing, but even wrong against a brother. Notwithstanding all his grandeur and arts of speech, the bishop became silent and the girl remained victorious.

Yes, we can talk in our newspapers of the progress of aviation, of complicated diplomatic relations, of different clubs and conventions, of unions of different kinds, of so-called productions of art, and keep silent about what that young lady said. But it cannot be passed over in silence because it is felt, more or less dimly, but always felt by every man in the Christian world. Socialism, Communism, Anarchism, Salvation Army, increasing crime, unemployment, the growing insane luxury of the rich and misery of the poor, the alarmingly increasing number of suicides—

all these are the signs of that 'internal contradiction which must be solved and cannot remain unsolved'. And of course solved in the sense of acknowledging the law of love and denying violence. And so your activity in the Transvaal, as it seems to us, at the end of the world, is the most essential work, the most important of all the work now being done in the world, and in which not only the nations of the Christians, but of all the world, will unavoidably take part.

I think that you will be pleased to know that here, in Russia, this activity is also fast developing in the way of refusals to serve in the Army, the number of which increases from year to year. However insignificant is the number of our people who are passive resisters in Russia, who refuse to serve in the Army, these and the others can boldly say that God is more powerful than man.

In acknowledging Christianity, even in the corrupt form in which it is professed amongst the Christian nations and at the same time in acknowledging the necessity of armies and armaments for killing on the greatest scale in wars, there is such a clear clamouring contradiction, that it must sooner or later, possibly very soon, inevitably reveal itself and annihilate either the professing of the Christian religion, which is indispensable in keeping up these forces or the existence of armies and all the violence kept up by them, which is not less necessary for power. This contradiction is felt by all governments, by your British as well as by our Russian Government, and out of a general feeling of self-preservation the persecution of them (as seen in Russia and in the journal sent by you) against such anti-government activity as those above-mentioned, is carried on with more energy than against any other form of opposition. The governments know where their chief danger lies, and they vigilantly guard in this question, not only their interests, but the question: 'To be or not to be?'

Yours very faithfully,

LEO TOLSTOY

(Translated from the Russian by Pauline Padlashuk)

PART III

*The Practice of Satyagraha or Civil Disobedience:
the Passive Resister's Discipline and Method, the
Growth of Congress, Satyagraha and Nazism,
Satyagraha as a Means of National Defence, an
Appeal to Every Briton, Ahimsa and Himsa,
Fasting as a Means of Passive Resistance*

For the past thirty years, I have been preaching and practising *satyagraha*. The principles of *satyagraha*, as I know
it to-day, constitute a gradual evolution.[1]

Satyagraha differs from Passive Resistance as the North
Pole from the South. The latter has been conceived as a
weapon of the weak and does not exclude the use of physical force or violence for the purpose of gaining one's end,
whereas the former has been conceived as a weapon of
the strongest and excludes the use of violence in any shape
or form.

The term *satyagraha* was coined by me in South Africa
to express the force that the Indians there used for full
eight years, and it was coined in order to distinguish it
from the movement then going on in the United Kingdom
and South Africa under the name of Passive Resistance.

On the political field, the struggle on behalf of the people
mostly consists in opposing error in the shape of unjust
laws. When you have failed to bring the error home to the
law-giver by way of petitions and the like, the only
remedy open to you, if you do not wish to submit to error,
is to compel him by physical force to yield to you or by
suffering in your own person by inviting the penalty for
the breach of the law. Hence *satyagraha* largely appears
to the public as Civil Disobedience or Civil Resistance. It is
civil in the sense that it is not criminal.

The law-breaker breaks the law surreptitiously and
tries to avoid the penalty; not so the civil resister. He ever

1. Extract from *Young India*, Vol. I by M. K. Gandhi, Madras,
Ganesan Ltd, 1922.

obeys the laws of the state to which he belongs, not out of fear of the sanctions, but because he considers them to be good for the welfare of society. But there come occasions, generally rare, when he considers certain laws to be so unjust as to render obedience to them a dishonour. He then openly and civilly breaks them and quietly suffers the penalty for their breach. And in order to register his protest against the action of the law-givers, it is open to him to withdraw his co-operation from the state by disobeying such other laws whose breach does not involve moral turpitude.

In my opinion, the beauty and efficacy of *satyagraha* are so great and the doctrine so simple that it can be preached even to children. It was preached by me to thousands of men, women and children commonly called indentured Indians with excellent results.

The spirit of non-violence necessarily leads to humility. Non-violence means reliance on God, the Rock of Ages. If we would seek His aid, we must approach Him with a humble and a contrite heart. Non-co-operationists may not trade upon their amazing success at the Congress. We must act, even as the mango tree which droops as it bears fruit. Its grandeur lies in its majestic lowliness.

Non-co-operation is not a movement of brag, bluster, or bluff. It is a test of our sincerity. It requires solid and silent self-sacrifice. It challenges our honesty and our capacity for national work. It is a movement that aims at translating ideas into action. And the more we do, the more we find that much more must be done than we had expected. And this thought of our imperfection must make us humble.

A non-co-operationist strives to compel attention and to set an example not by his violence, but by his unobtrusive humility. He allows his solid action to speak for his creed. His strength lies in his reliance upon the correctness of his position. And the conviction of it grows most in his opponent when he least interposes his speech between his action and his opponent. Speech, especially when it is haughty, betrays want of confidence and it makes one's opponent sceptical about the reality of the act itself. Humility therefore is the key to quick success. I hope that every non-co-operationist will recognize the necessity of being humble and self-restrained. It is because so little is really required to be done and because all of that little depends entirely upon ourselves that I have ventured the belief that Swaraj is attainable in less than one year.

I am sorry that I find a nervous fear among some Hindus and Mohammedans that I am undermining their faith, and that I am even doing irreparable harm to India by my uncompromising preaching of non-violence. They seem almost to imply that violence is their creed. I touch a tender spot if I talk about extreme non-violence in their presence. They confound me with texts from the Mahabharata and the Koran eulogizing or permitting violence. Of the Mahabharata I can write without restraint, but the most devoted Mohammedan will not, I hope, deny me the privilege of understanding the message of the Prophet. I make bold to say that violence is the creed of no religion and that, whereas non-violence in most cases is obligatory in all, violence is merely permissible in some cases. But I have not put before India the final form of non-violence. The non-violence that I have preached from Congress platforms is non-violence as a policy. But even policies require honest adherence in thought, word and deed. If I believe that honesty is the best policy, surely whilst I so believe, I must be honest in thought, word and deed; otherwise I become an impostor. Non-violence being a policy means that it can upon due notice be given up when it proves unsuccessful or ineffective. But simple morality demands that, whilst a particular policy is pursued, it must be pursued with all one's heart. It is simple policy to march along a certain route, but the soldier who marches with an unsteady step along that route is liable to be summarily dismissed. I become therefore incredulous when people talk to me sceptically about non-violence or are seized with fright at the very mention of the word non-violence. If they do not believe in the expedient of non-violence, they must denounce it but not claim to believe in the expedient when their heart resists it. How disastrous it would be, if, not believing in violence even as an expedient, I joined, say a violence party and approached a gun with a perturbed heart! The reader will believe me when I say that I have the capacity for killing a fly. But I do not believe in killing even flies. Now suppose I joined an expedition for fly-killing as an expedient.

Will I not be expected, before being permitted to join the expedition, to use all the available engines of destruction, whilst I remained in the army of fly-killers? If those who are in the Congress and the Khilafat committees will perceive this simple truth, we shall certainly either finish the struggle this year to a successful end, or be so sick of non-violence as to give up the pretension and set about devising some other programme.

I hold that Swami Shraddhanandji has been needlessly criticized for the proposition he intended to move. His argument is absolutely honest. He thinks that we, as a body, do not really believe in non-violence even as a policy. Therefore, we shall never fulfil the programme of non-violence. Therefore, he says, let us go to the councils and get what crumbs we may. He was trying to show the unreality of the position of those who believe in the policy with their lips, whereas they are looking forward to violence for final deliverance. I do say that, if Congressmen do not fully believe in the policy, they are doing an injury to the country by pretending to follow it. If violence is to be the basis of future government, the councillors are undoubtedly the wisest. For it is through the councils that, by the same devices by which the present administrators rule us, the councillors hope to seize power from the former's hands. I have little doubt that those who nurse violence in their bosoms will find no benefit from the lip-profession of non-violence. I urge, therefore, with all the vehemence at my command, that those who do not believe in non-violence should secede from the Congress and from non-co-operation and prepare to seek election or rejoin law courts or Government colleges as the case may be. Let there be no manner of doubt that Swaraj established by non-violent means will be different in kind from the Swaraj that can be established by armed rebellion. Police and punishments there will be, even under such Swaraj. But there would be no room for brutalities such as we witness to-day both on the part of the people and the Government. And those, whether they call themselves Hindus or Mussulmans, who do not fully believe in the policy of non-violence, should abandon both non-co-operation and non-violence.

For me, I am positive that neither in the Koran nor in the Mahabharata is there any sanction for and approval of the triumph of violence. Though there is repulsion enough in Nature, she lives by attraction. Mutual love enables Nature to persist. Man does not live by destruction. Self-love compels regard for others. Nations cohere, because there is mutual regard among the individuals composing them. Some day we must extend the national law to the universe, even as we have extended the family law to form nations—a larger family. God had ordained that India should be such a nation. For so far as reason can perceive, India cannot become free by armed rebellion for generations. India can become free by refraining from national violence. India has now become tired of rule based upon violence. That to me is the message of the plains. The people of the plains do not know what it is to put up an organized armed fight. And they must become free, for they want freedom. They have realized that power seized by violence will only result in their greater grinding.

Such, at any rate, is the reasoning that has given birth to the policy, not the *dharma*, of non-violence. And even as a Mussulman or a Hindu, believing in violence, applies the creed of non-violence in his family, so are both called upon without question to apply the policy of non-violence in their mutual relations and in their relation to other races and classes, not excluding Englishmen. Those who do not believe in this policy and do not wish to live up to it in full, retard the movement by remaining in it.

When a person claims to be non-violent, he is expected not to be angry with one who has injured him. He will not wish him harm; he will wish him well; he will not swear at him; he will not cause him any physical hurt. He will put up with all the injury to which he is subjected by the wrong-doer. Thus non-violence is complete innocence. Complete non-violence is complete absence of ill-will against all that lives. It therefore embraces even sub-human life, not excluding noxious insects or beasts. They have not been created to feed our destructive propensities. If we only knew the mind of the Creator, we should find their proper place in His creation. Non-violence is therefore in its active form good will towards all life. It is pure Love. I read it in the Hindu scriptures, in the Bible, in the Koran.

Non-violence is a perfect state. It is a goal towards which all mankind moves naturally though unconsciously. Man does not become divine when he personifies innocence in himself. Only then does he become truly man. In our present state, we are partly men and partly beasts and in our ignorance and even arrogance say that we truly fulfil the purpose of our species, when we deliver blow for blow and develop the measure of anger required for the purpose. We pretend to believe that retaliation is the law of our being, whereas in every scripture we find that retaliation is nowhere obligatory but only permissible. It is restraint that is obligatory. Retaliation is indulgence requiring elaborate regulating. Restraint is the law of our being. For highest perfection is unattainable without highest restraint. Suffering is thus the badge of the human tribe.

The goal ever recedes from us. The greater the progress, the greater the recognition of our unworthiness. Satisfaction lies in the effort, not in the attainment. Full effort is full victory.

Therefore though I realize more than ever how far I am from that goal, for me the Law of Complete Love is the law of my being. Each time I fail, my effort shall be all the more determined for my failure.

I know my own limitations only too well. I know that any such attempt is foredoomed to failure. To expect a whole mass of men and women to obey that law all at once is not to know its working. But I do preach from the Congress platform the deductions of the law. What the Congress and the Khilafat organizations have accepted is but a fragment of the implications of that law. Given true workers, the limited measure of its application can be realized in respect of vast masses of people within a short time. But the little measure of it to be true must satisfy the same test as the whole. A drop of water must yield to the analyst the same results as a lakeful. The nature of my non-violence towards my brother cannot be different from that of my non-violence to the universe. When I extend the love for my brother to the whole universe, it must still satisfy the same test.

A particular practice is a policy when its application is limited to time or space. Highest policy is therefore fullest practice. But honesty as policy while it lasts is not anything different from honesty as a creed. A merchant believing in honesty as a policy will sell the same measure and quality of cloth to the yard as a merchant with honesty as a creed. The difference between the two is that, while the political merchant will leave his honesty when it does not pay, the believing one will continue it, even though he should lose his all.

The political non-violence of the non-co-operator does not stand this test in the vast majority of cases. Hence the prolongation of the struggle. Let no one blame the unbending English nature. The hardest fibre must melt in the fire of love. It cannot be dislodged from that position because I know it. When British or other nature does not respond, the fire is not strong enough, if it is there at all.

Our non-violence need not be of the strong, but it has to be of the truthful. We must not intend harm to the English or to our co-operating countrymen, if and whilst we claim to be non-violent. But the majority of us have intended harm, and we have refrained from doing it because of our weakness or under the ignorant belief that mere refraining from physical hurt amounted to a due fulfilment of our pledge. Our pledge of non-violence excludes the possibility of future retaliation. Some of us seem unfortunately to have merely postponed the date of revenge.

Let me not be misunderstood. I do not say that the policy of non-violence excludes the possibility of revenge when the policy is abandoned. But it does most emphatically exclude the possibility of future revenge after a successful termination of the struggle. Therefore, whilst we are pursuing the policy of non-violence, we are bound to be actively friendly to English administrators and their co-operators. I felt ashamed when I was told that in some parts of India it was not safe for Englishmen or well-known co-operators to move about safely. The disgraceful scenes that took place at a recent Madras meeting were a complete denial of non-violence. Those who howled down the chairman because he was supposed to have insulted me, disgraced themselves and their policy. They wounded the heart of their friend and helper, Mr Andrews. They injured their own cause. If the chairman believed that I was a scoundrel, he had a perfect right to say so.

We must try patiently to convert our opponents. If we wish to evolve the spirit of democracy out of slavery, we must be scrupulously exact in our dealings with opponents. We may not replace the slavery of the Government by that of the non-co-operationists. We must concede to our opponents the freedom we claim for ourselves and for which we are fighting. The stoutest co-operationist will bend to the stern realities of practice if there is real response from the people.

But there is a non-violent boycott which we shall be bound to practise, if we are to make any impression. We must not compromise with what we believe to be an untruth, whether it resides in a white skin or a brown. Such boycott is political boycott. We may not receive favours from the new councillors. The voters, if they are true to their pledge, will be bound to refrain from making use of the services of those whom they have declined to regard as their representatives. They must ratify their verdict by complete abstention from any encouragement of the so-called respresentatives.

The public will be bound, if they are non-co-operationists, to refrain from giving these representatives any prestige by attending their political functions or parties.

I can conceive the possibility of non-violent social ostracism under certain extreme conditions, when a defiant minority refuses to bend to the majority, not out of any regard for principle, but from sheer defiance or worse. But that time has certainly not arrived. Ostracism of a violent character, such as the denial of the use of public wells is a species of barbarism, which I hope will never be practised by any body of men having any desire for national self-respect and national uplift. We will free neither Islam nor India by processes of coercion, whether among ourselves or against Englishmen.

Non-co-operation being a movement of purification is bringing to the surface all our weaknesses as also excesses of even our strong points. Social boycott is an age-old institution. It is coeval with caste. It is the one terrible sanction exercised with great effect. It is based upon the notion that a community is not bound to extend its hospitality or service to an excommunicate. It answered when every village was a self-contained unit, and the occasions of recalcitrancy were rare. But when opinion is divided, as it is to-day, on the merits of non-co-operation, when its new application is having a trial, a summary use of social boycott in order to bend a minority to the will of the majority is a species of unpardonable violence. If persisted in, such boycott is bound to destroy the movement. Social boycott is applicable and effective when it is not felt as a punishment and accepted by the object of boycott as a measure of discipline. Moreover, social boycott to be admissible in a campaign of non-violence must never savour of inhumanity. It must be civilized. It must cause pain to the party using it, if it causes inconvenience to its object. Thus, depriving a man of the services of a medical man, as is reported to have been done in Jhansi, is an act of inhumanity tantamount in the moral code to an attempt to murder. I see no difference in murdering man and withdrawing medical aid from a man who is on the point of dying. Even the laws of war, I apprehend, require the giving of medical relief to the enemy in need of it. To deprive a man of the use of an only village well is notice to him to quit that village. Surely, non-co-operators have acquired no right to use that extreme pressure against those who do not see eye to eye with them. Impatience and intolerance will surely kill this great religious movement. We may not make people pure by compulsion. Much less may we compel them by violence to respect our opinion.[2] It

2. In *Young India* of 9th March 1922, commenting on a letter received by him from a well-known resident of Feni in the Noakhali district alleging that the Congress Volunteer Corps had become an organization for bad characters, that the whole country thereabout was under it and that these were guilty of extortion, terrorism and humiliating rowdyism, Mr Gandhi wrote asking the Congress Committee to inquire.

'An inquiry therefore is a simple matter. Meanwhile, as I know that publication is also half the remedy, I gladly place the columns of *Young India* at the disposal of those who can send authentic instances of intimidation, coercion, assaults, social boycott by or on behalf of non-co-operators whether Congressmen or Khilafatists. Indeed every Congressman is a Khilafatist, and every Khilafatist is a Congressman, but since we have two organizations in the country I appeal to both to be merciless in exposing our own wrong-doing. I could find a thousand excuses for the wrong-doing of the administrators if only because we impute to them nothing better, whereas we claim to be immaculate so far as non-violence and honesty are concerned. We shall bring the struggle to a successful issue far more quickly by being strict with ourselves. There is no excuse whatsoever for intimidation, coercion, assault or social boycott on our part. I would urge the correspondents, who may send me letters of complaints, to be brief, strictly accurate and to write

is utterly against the spirit of democracy we want to cultivate.

There are no doubt serious difficulties in our way. The temptation to resort to social boycott is irresistible when a defendant, who submits to private arbitration, refuses to abide by its award. Yet it is easy to see that the application of social boycott is more than likely to arrest the splendid movement to settle disputes by arbitration which, apart from its use as a weapon in the armoury of non-co-operation is a movement fraught with great good to the country. People will take time before they accommodate themselves to private arbitration. Its very simplicity and inexpensiveness will repel many people even as palates jaded by spicy foods are repelled by simple combinations. All awards will not always be above suspicion. We must therefore rely upon the intrinsic merits of the movement and the correctness of awards to make themselves felt.

It is much to be desired if we can bring about a complete voluntary boycott of law courts. That one event can bring about Swaraj. But it was never expected that we would reach completion in any single item of non-co-operation. Public opinion has been so far developed as to recognize the courts as signs not of our liberty but of our slavery. It has made it practically impossible for lawyers to practise their profession and be called popular leaders.

Non-co-operation has greatly demolished the prestige of law courts and to that extent of the Government. The disintegrating process is slowly but surely going on. Its velocity will suffer diminution if violent methods are adopted to hasten it. This Government of ours is armed to the teeth to meet and check forces of non-violence. How can a handful of Englishmen resist a voluntary expression of opinion accompanied by the voluntary self-denial of thirty crores of people?

I hope, therefore, that non-co-operation workers will beware of the snares of social boycott. But the alternative

---

in a clear hand on one side of the paper only. It is not an easy matter to go through the heavy correspondence pouring in from day to day. Compliance with this simple request will ensure quicker attention. Correspondents will take care to avoid vague generalizations. Specific details as in the Noakhali letter are absolutely necessary to inspire belief and to assist inquiry.

to social boycott is certainly not social intercourse. A man who defies strong clear public opinion on vital matters is not entitled to social amenities and privileges. We may not take part in his social functions such as marriage feasts, we may not receive gifts from him. But we dare not deny social service. The latter is a duty. Attendance at dinner parties and the like is a privilege which it is optional to withhold or extend. But it would be wisdom to err on the right side and to exercise the weapon even in the limited sense described by me on rare and well-defined occasions. And in every case the user of the weapon will use it at his own risk. The use of it is not as yet in any form a duty. No one is entitled to its use, if there is any danger of hurting the movement.

Popular imagination has pictured *satyagraha* as purely and simply civil disobedience, if not in some cases even criminal disobedience. The latter is the very opposite of *satyagraha.* The former, i.e. civil disobedience, is undoubtedly an important branch but by no means always the main part of *satyagraha.* To-day, for instance, on the question of Rowlatt legislation civil disobedience has gone into the background. As *satyagraha* is being brought into play on a large scale in the political field for the first time, it is in an experimental stage. I am therefore ever making new discoveries. And my error in trying to let civil disobedience take the people by storm, appears to me to be Himalayan because of the discovery I have made, namely, that he only is able and attains the right to offer civil disobedience who has known how to offer voluntary and deliberate obedience to the laws of the state in which he is living. It is only after one has voluntarily obeyed such laws a thousand times that an occasion rightly comes to him civilly to disobey certain laws. Nor is it necessary for voluntary obedience that the laws to be obeyed must be good. There are many unjust laws which a good citizen obeys so long as they do not hurt his self-respect or the moral being, and when I look back upon my life, I cannot recall a single occasion when I have obeyed a law whether of society or the state because of the fear of punishment. I have obeyed bad laws of the society as well as of the state, believing that it was good for me and the state or the society to which I belonged to do so, and I feel that having regularly and in a disciplined manner done so, the call for disobedience to a law of society came when I went to England in 1888, and to a law of the state in South Africa when the Asiatic Registration Act was passed by the Transvaal Government. I have therefore come to the conclusion that civil disobedience, if it has to be renewed, shall be offered in the first instance only by me as being the fittest to do so, and the duty of fellow *satyagrahis* will be to assimilate for the time being the first essential just mentioned of civil disobedience. In the instruction I have drawn up, I have suggested that civil disobedience by the others should not be taken up for at least one month after I have been taken charge of by the Government. And then too by one or two chosen *satyagrahis*, chosen in the sense above mentioned, and only if it is found that no violence has been offered after my incarceration by the *satyagrahis* so-called or others acting in co-operation with them. The next duty then is for the remaining *satyagrahis* themselves to observe perfect calm and quiet and to see that others do likewise. You will, therefore, see to it that after I have offered civil disobedience, if I do, there is no *hartal*, no public meetings and no demonstrations of any kind whatsoever so as to give excitement. And I feel sure that if perfect peace is observed after my incarceration, Rowlatt legislation will go, by reason of that very fact. But it is quite likely that the Government may remain perfectly obstinate. In that event, under the conditions I have already mentioned, it will be open to the *satyagrahis* to offer further civil disobedience and continue to do so till every *satyagrahi* has rendered a good account of himself.[8]

THE GROWTH OF CONGRESS

The communal riots in Allahabad—the headquarters of the Congress, and the necessity of summoning the assistance of the police and even the military show that the Congress has not yet become fit to substitute the British authority. It is best to face this naked truth, however unpleasant it may be.

The Congress claims to represent the whole of India, not merely those few who are on the Congress register. It should represent even those who are hostile to it and who will even crush it, if they can. Not until we make good that

3. Extract from *Young India*, Vol. III.

claim, shall we be in a position to displace the British Government and function as an independent nation.

This proposition holds good whether we seek to displace British rule by violent action or non-violent.

Most probably by the time these lines appear in print peace will have been established in Allahabad and the other parts. That, however, will not take us further in our examination of the fitness of the Congress as an organization ready to displace British authority in its entirety.

No Congressman will seriously doubt that the Congress is not at the present moment capable of delivering the goods if it was called upon to do so. If it was capable, it would not wait for the call. But every Congressman believes that the Congress is fast becoming such a body. The brilliant success at Haripura will be cited as the most conclusive proof of the fact.

The riots and certain other things I can mention should make us pause and ask ourselves whether the Congress is really growing from strength to strength. I must own that I have been guilty of laying that claim. Have I been over-hasty in doing so?

It is my conviction that the phenomenal growth of the Congress is due to its acceptance and enforcement, however imperfect, of the policy of non-violence. Time has arrived to consider the nature of Congress non-violence. Is it non-violence of the weak and the helpless, or of the strong and the powerful? If it is the former, it will never take us to our goal and, if long practised, may even render us for ever unfit for self-government. The weak and helpless are non-violent in action because they must be. But in reality they harbour violence in their breasts and simply await opportunity for its display. It is necessary for Congressmen individually and collectively to examine the quality of their non-violence. If it does not come out of real strength, it would be best and honest for the Congress to make such a declaration and make the necessary changes in its behaviour.

By this time, i.e. after seventeen years' practice of non-violence, the Congress should be able to put forth a non-violent army of volunteers numbering not a few thousands but lacs who would be equal to every occasion where the police and the military are required. Thus, instead of one brave Pashupatinath Gupta who died in the attempt to secure peace, we should be able to produce hundreds. And a non-violent army acts unlike armed men, as well in times of peace as of disturbances. They would be constantly engaged in constructive activities that make riots impossible. Theirs will be the duty of seeking occasions for bringing warring communities together, carrying on peace propaganda, engaging in activities that would bring and keep them in touch with every single person, male and female, adult and child, in their parish or division. Such an army should be ready to cope with any emergency, and in order to still the frenzy of mobs should risk their lives in numbers sufficient for the purpose. A few hundred, maybe a few thousand, such spotless deaths will once for all put an end to the riots. Surely a few hundred young men and women giving themselves deliberately to mob fury will be any day a cheap and braver method of dealing with such madness than the display and use of the police and the military.

It has been suggested that when we have our independence, riots and the like will not occur. This seems to me to be an empty hope, if in the course of the struggle for freedom we do not understand and use the technique of non-violent action in every conceivable circumstance. To the extent that the Congress ministers have been obliged to make use of the police and the military, to that extent, in my opinion, we must admit our failure. That the ministers could not have done otherwise is unfortunately only too true. I should like every Congressman, I should like the working committee, to ask themselves why we have failed, if they think with me that we have.

(*Harijan*, 26th March 1938)

SATYAGRAHA AND NAZISM

One must feel happy that the danger of war has been averted for the time being. Is the price paid likely to be too great? Is it likely that honour has been sold? Is it a triumph of organized violence? Has Herr Hitler discovered a new technique of organizing violence which enables him to gain his end without shedding blood? I do not profess to know European politics. But it does appear to me that small nationalities cannot exist in Europe with their heads erect. They must be absorbed by their larger neighbours. They must become vassals.

Europe has sold her soul for the sake of a seven-days' earthly existence. The peace Europe gained at Munich is a triumph of violence; it is also its defeat. If England and France were sure of victory, they would certainly have fulfilled their duty of saving Czechoslovakia or of dying with it. But they quailed before the combined violence of Germany and Italy. But what have Germany and Italy gained? Have they added anything to the moral wealth of mankind?

In penning these lines my concern is not with the great powers. Their height dazes me. Czechoslovakia has a lesson for me and us in India. The Czechs could not have done anything else when they found themselves deserted by their two powerful allies. And yet I have the hardihood to say that, if they had known the use of non-violence as a weapon for the defence of national honour, they would have faced the whole might of Germany with that of Italy thrown in. They would have spared England and France the humiliation of suing for a peace which was no peace; and to save their honour they would have died to a man without shedding the blood of the robber. I must refuse to think that such heroism, or call it restraint, is beyond human nature. Human nature will only find itself when it fully realizes that to be human it has to cease to be beastly or brutal. Though we have the human form, without the attainment of the virtue of non-violence, we still share the qualities of our remote reputed ancestor, the orang-outang.

(*Harijan*, 8th October 1938)

If I have called the arrangement with Herr Hitler 'peace without honour', it was not to cast any reflection on British or French statesmen. I have no doubt that Mr Chamberlain could not think of anything better. He knew his nation's limitations. He wanted to avoid war, if it could be avoided at all. Short of going to war, he pulled his full weight in favour of the Czechs. That it could not save honour was no fault of his. It would be so every time there is a struggle with Herr Hitler or Signor Mussolini.

It cannot be otherwise. Democracy dreads to spill blood. The philosophy for which the two dictators stand calls it cowardice to shrink from carnage. They exhaust the resources of poetic art in order to glorify organized murder. There is no humbug about their word or deed. They are ready for war. There is nobody in Germany or Italy to cross their path. Their word is law.

It is different with Mr Chamberlain or M Daladier. They have their Parliaments and Chambers to please. They have parties to confer with. They cannot maintain themselves on a perpetual war footing, if their language is to have a democratic accent about it.

Science of war leads one to dictatorship pure and simple. Science of non-violence can alone lead one to pure democracy. England, France and America have to make their choice. That is the challenge of the two dictators.

Russia is out of the picture just now. Russia has a dictator who dreams of peace and thinks he will wade to it through a sea of blood. No one can say what Russian dictatorship will mean to the world.

It was necessary to give this introduction to what I want to say to the Czechs and through them to all those nationalities which are called 'small' or 'weak'. I want to speak to the Czechs because their plight moved me to the point of physical and mental distress, and I felt that it would be cowardice on my part not to share with them the thoughts that were welling up within me. It is clear that the small nations must either come or be ready to come under the protection of the dictators or be a constant menace to the peace of Europe. In spite of all the goodwill in the world England and France cannot save them. Their intervention can only mean bloodshed and destruction such as has never been seen before. If I were a Czech, therefore, I would free these two nations from the obligation to defend my country. And yet I must live. I would not be a vassal to any nation or body. I must have absolute independence or perish. To seek to win in a clash of arms would be pure bravado. Not so, if in defying the might of one who would deprive me of my independence I refuse to obey his will and perish unarmed in the attempt. In so doing, though I lose the body, I save my soul, i.e. my honour.

This inglorious peace should be my opportunity. I must live down the humiliation and gain real independence.

But, says a comforter, 'Hitler knows no pity. Your spiritual effort will avail nothing before him.'

My answer is: 'You may be right. History has no record of a nation having adopted non-violent resistance. If Hitler is unaffected by my suffering, it does not matter. For I shall have lost nothing worth. My honour is the only thing worth preserving. That is independent of Hitler's pity. But as a believer in non-violence I may not limit its possibilities. Hitherto he and his likes have built upon their invariable experience that men yield to force. Unarmed men, women and children offering non-violent resistance without any bitterness in them will be a novel experience for them. Who can dare say it is not in their nature to respond to the higher and finer forces? They have the same soul that I have.'

But says another comforter, 'What you say is all right for you. But how do you expect your people to respond to the novel call? They are trained to fight. In personal bravery they are second to none in the world. For you now to ask them to throw away their arms and be trained for non-violent resistance seems to me to be a vain attempt.'

'You may be right. But I have a call I must answer. I must deliver my message to my people. This humiliation has sunk too deep in me to remain without an outlet. I, at least, must act up to the light that has dawned on me.'

This is how I should, I believe, act if I was a Czech. When I first launched out on *satyagraha*, I had no companion. We were thirteen thousand men, women and children against a whole nation capable of crushing the existence out of us. I did not know who would listen to me. It all came as in a flash. All the 13,000 did not fight. Many fell back. But the honour of the nation was saved. New history was written by the South African *satyagraha*.

A more apposite instance, perhaps, is that of Khansaheb Abdul Gaffar Khan, the servant of God as he calls himself, the pride of Afghan as the Pathans delight to call him. He is sitting in front of me as I pen these lines. He has made several thousands of his people throw down their arms. He thinks he has imbibed the lesson of non-violence. He is not sure of his people. I have come to the Frontier province, or rather he has brought me, to see with my own eyes what his men here are doing. I can say in advance and at once that these men know very little of non-violence. All the treasure they have on earth is their faith in their leader. I do not cite these soldiers of peace as at all a finished illustration. I cite them as an honest attempt being made by a soldier to convert fellow-soldiers to the ways of peace. I can testify that it is an honest attempt, and whether in the end it succeeds or fails, it will have its lessons for *satya-grahis* of the future. My purpose will be fulfilled, if I succeed in reaching these men's hearts and making them see that, if their non-violence does not make them feel much braver than the possession of arms and the ability to use them, they must give up their non-violence, which is another name for cowardice, and resume their arms, which there is nothing but their own will to prevent them from taking back.

I present Dr Beneš with a weapon not of the weak but of the brave. There is no bravery greater than a resolute refusal to bend the knee to an earthly power, no matter how great, and that without bitterness of spirit and in the fullness of faith that the spirit alone lives, nothing else does.

(*Harijan*, 15th October 1938)

PASSIVE RESISTANCE AND ANTI-SEMITISM

Several letters have been received by me asking me to declare my views about the Arab-Jew question in Palestine and the persecution of the Jews in Germany. It is not without hesitation that I venture to offer my views on this very difficult question.

My sympathies are all with the Jews. I have known them intimately in South Africa. Some of them became lifelong companions. Through these friends I came to learn much of their age-long persecution. They have been the untouchables of Christianity. The parallel between their treatment by Christians and the treatment of untouchables by Hindus is very close. Religious sanction has been invoked in both cases for the justification of the inhuman treatment meted out to them. Apart from the friendships, therefore, there is the more common universal reason for my sympathy for the Jews.

But my sympathy does not blind me to the requirements of justice. The cry for the national home for the Jews does not make much appeal to me. The sanction for it is sought in the Bible and the tenacity with which the Jews have hankered after return to Palestine. Why should they not, like other peoples of the earth, make that country their home where they are born and where they earn their livelihood?

Palestine belongs to the Arabs in the same sense that England belongs to the English or France to the French.

It is wrong and inhuman to impose the Jews on the Arabs. What is going on in Palestine to-day cannot be justified by any moral code of conduct. The mandates have no sanction but that of the last war. Surely it would be a crime against humanity to reduce the proud Arabs so that Palestine can be restored to the Jews partly or wholly as their national home.

The nobler cause would be to insist on a just treatment of the Jews wherever they are born and bred. The Jews born in France are French in precisely the same sense that Christians born in France are French. If the Jews have no home but Palestine, will they relish the idea of being forced to leave the other parts of the world in which they are settled? Or do they want a double home where they can remain at will? This cry for the national home affords a colourable justification for the German expulsion of the Jews.

But the German persecution of the Jews seems to have no parallel in history. The tyrants of old never went so mad as Hitler seems to have gone. And he is doing it with religious zeal. For, he is propounding a new religion of exclusive and militant nationalism in the name of which any inhumanity becomes an act of humanity to be rewarded here and hereafter. The crime of an obviously mad but intrepid youth is being visited upon his whole race with unbelievable ferocity. If there ever could be a justifiable war in the name of and for humanity, a war against Germany, to prevent the wanton persecution of a whole race would be completely justified. But I do not believe in any war. A discussion of the pros and cons of such a war is, therefore, outside my horizon or province.

But if there can be no war against Germany, even for such a crime as is being committed against the Jews, surely there can be no alliance with Germany. How can there be alliance between a nation which claims to stand for justice and democracy and one which is the declared enemy of both? Or is England drifting towards armed dictatorship and all it means?

Germany is showing to the world how efficiently violence can be worked when it is not hampered by any hypocrisy or weakness masquerading as humanitarianism. It is also showing how hideous, terrible and terrifying it looks in its nakedness.

Can the Jews resist this organized and shameless persecution? Is there a way to preserve their self-respect, and not to feel helpless, neglected and forlorn? I submit there is. No person who has faith in a living God need feel helpless or forlorn. Jehovah of the Jews is a God more personal than the God of the Christians, the Mussulmans or the Hindus, though as a matter of fact, in essence, He is common to all and one without a second and beyond description. But as the Jews attribute personality to God and believe that He rules every action of theirs, they ought not to feel helpless. If I were a Jew and were born in Germany and earned my livelihood there, I would claim Germany as my home even as the tallest gentile German might, and challenge him to shoot me or cast me in the dungeon; I would refuse to be expelled or to submit to discriminating treatment. And for doing this I should not wait for the fellow-Jews to join me in civil resistance, but would have confidence that in the end the rest were bound to follow my example. If one Jew or all the Jews were to accept the prescription here offered, he or they cannot be worse off than now. And suffering voluntarily undergone will bring them an inner strength and joy which no number of resolutions of sympathy passed in the world outside Germany can. Indeed, even if Britain, France and America were to declare hostilities against Germany, they can bring no inner joy, no inner strength. The calculated violence of Hitler may even result in a general massacre of the Jews by way of his first answer to the declaration of such hostilities. But if the Jewish mind could be prepared for voluntary suffering, even the massacre I have imagined could be turned into a day of thanksgiving and joy that Jehovah had wrought deliverance of the race even at the hands of the tyrant. For to the God-fearing, death has no terror. It is a joyful sleep to be followed by a waking that would be all the more refreshing for the long sleep.

It is hardly necessary for me to point out that it is easier for the Jews than for the Czechs to follow my prescription. And they have in the Indian *satyagraha* campaign in South Africa an exact parallel. There the Indians occupied precisely the same place that the Jews occupy in Germany. The persecution had also a religious tinge. President Kruger used to say that the White Christians were the chosen of God and Indians were inferior beings created to serve the

Whites. A fundamental clause in the Transvaal constitution was that there should be no equality between the Whites and coloured races including Asiatics. There, too, the Indians were consigned to ghettoes described as locations. The other disabilities were almost of the same type as those of the Jews in Germany. The Indians, a mere handful, resorted to *satyagraha* without any backing from the world outside or the Indian Government. Indeed the British officials tried to dissuade the *satyagrahis* from their contemplated step. World opinion and the Indian Government came to their aid after eight years of fighting. And that too was by way of diplomatic pressure, not of a threat of war.

But the Jews of Germany can offer *satyagraha* under infinitely better auspices than the Indians of South Africa. The Jews are a compact, homogeneous community in Germany. They are far more gifted than the Indians of South Africa. And they have organized world opinion behind them. I am convinced that, if someone with courage and vision can arise among them to lead them in non-violent action, the winter of their despair can in the twinkling of an eye be turned into the summer of hope. And what has to-day become a degrading man-hunt can be turned into a calm and determined stand offered by unarmed men and women possessing the strength of suffering given to them by Jehovah. It will be then a truly religious resistance offered against the godless fury of dehumanized man. The German Jews will score a lasting victory over the German gentiles in the sense that they will have converted the latter to an appreciation of human dignity. They will have rendered service to fellow-Germans and proved their title to be the real Germans as against those who are to-day dragging, however unknowingly, the German name into the mire.

And now a word to the Jews in Palestine. I have no doubt that they are going about things in the wrong way. The Palestine of the Biblical conception is not a geographical tract. It is in their hearts. But if they must look to the Palestine of geography as their national home, it is wrong to enter it under the shadow of the British gun. A religious act cannot be performed with the aid of the bayonet or the bomb. They can settle in Palestine only by the goodwill of the Arabs. They should seek to convert the Arab heart. The same God rules the Arab heart who rules the Jewish heart. They can offer *satyagraha* in front of the Arabs and offer themselves to be shot or thrown into the Dead Sea without raising a little finger against them. They will find the world opinion in their favour in their religious aspiration. There are hundreds of ways of reasoning with the Arabs, if they will only discard the help of. the British bayonet. As it is, they are co-sharers with the British in despoiling a people who have done no wrong to them.

I am not defending the Arab excesses. I wish they had chosen the way of non-violence in resisting what they rightly regarded as an unwarrantable encroachment upon their country. But according to the accepted canons of right and wrong, nothing can be said against the Arab resistance in the face of overwhelming odds.

Let the Jews who claim to be the chosen race prove their title by choosing the way of non-violence for vindicating their position on earth. Every country is their home, including Palestine, not by aggression but by loving service. A Jewish friend has sent me a book called *The Jewish Contribution to Civilization* by Cecil Rhoth. It gives a record of what the Jews have done to enrich the world's literature, art, music, drama, science, medicine, agriculture, etc. Given the will, the Jew can refuse to be treated as the outcast of the West to be despised or patronized. He can command the attention and respect of the world by being man, the chosen creation of God, instead of being man who is fast sinking to the brute and forsaken by God. They can add to their many contributions the surpassing contribution of non-violent action.

(*Harijan*, 26th November 1938)

I do not think that the sufferings of Pastor Niemoeller and others have been in vain. They have preserved their self-respect intact. They have proved that their faith was equal to any suffering. That they have not proved sufficient for melting Herr Hitler's heart merely shows that it is made of harder material than stone. But the hardest metal yields to sufficient heat. Even so must the hardest heart melt before sufficiency of the heat of non-violence. And there is no limit to the capacity of non-violence to generate heat.

Every action is a resultant of a multitude of forces even of a contrary nature. There is no waste of energy. So we learn in the books on mechanics. This is equally true of human actions. The difference is that in the one case we generally know the forces at work, and when we do, we can mathematically foretell the resultant. In the case of human actions, they result from a concurrence of forces, of most of which we have no knowledge. But our ignorance must not be made to serve the cause of disbelief in the power of these forces. Rather is our ignorance a cause for greater faith. And non-violence being the mightiest force in the world and also the most elusive in its working, it demands the greatest exercise of faith. Even as we believe in God in faith, so have we to believe in non-violence in faith.   (*Harijan*, 7th January 1939)

SATYAGRAHA AS A MEANS OF NATIONAL DEFENCE

In the course of the conversation with the members of the working committee, I discovered that their non-violence had never gone beyond fighting the British Government with that weapon. I had hugged the belief that Congressmen had appreciated the logical result of the practice of non-violence for the past twenty years in fighting the biggest imperialist power in the world. But in great experiments like that of non-violence, hypothetical questions have hardly any play. I myself used to say in answer to questions that when we had actually acquired independence we would know whether we could defend ourselves non-violently or not. But to-day the question is no longer hypothetical. Whether there is on the part of the British Government a favourable declaration or not, the Congress has to decide upon the course it would adopt in the event of an invasion of India. For though there may be no settlement with the Government, the Congress has to declare its policy and say whether it would fight the invading host violently or non-violently.

So far as I can read the working committee's mind after a fairly full discussion, the members think that Congressmen are unprepared for non-violent defence against armed invasion.

This is tragic. Surely the means adopted for driving an enemy from one's house must, more or less, coincide with those to be adopted for keeping him out of the house. If anything, the latter process must be easier. The fact, however, is that our fight has not been one of non-violent resistance of the strong. It has been one of passive resistance of the weak. Therefore there is no spontaneous response in our hearts, at this supreme moment, to an undying faith in the efficacy of non-violence. The working committee, therefore, wisely said that they were not ready for the logical step. The tragedy of the situation is that, if the Congress is to throw in its lot with those who believe in the necessity of armed defence of India, the past twenty years will have been years of gross neglect of the primary duty of Congressmen to learn the science of armed warfare. And I fear that history will hold me, as the general of the fight, responsible for the tragedy. The future historian will say that I should have perceived that the nation was learning not non-violence of the strong but merely passivity of the weak, and that I should have, therefore, provided for Congressmen's military training.

Being obsessed with the idea that somehow or other India will learn true non-violence, it would not occur to me to invite my co-workers to train themselves for armed defence. On the contrary, I used to discountenance all sword-play and the display of stout *lathis*. Nor am I even now repentant for the past. I have the unquenchable faith that, of all the countries in the world, India is the only country which can learn the art of non-violence, that if the test were applied even now, there would be found, perhaps, thousands of men and women who would be willing to die without harbouring malice against their persecutors. I have harangued crowds and told them repeatedly that they might have to suffer much, including death by shooting. Did not thousands of men and women brave hardships during the salt campaign equal to any that soldiers are called upon to bear? No different capacity is required from what has been already evinced, if India has to contend against an invader. Only it will have to be on vaster scale.

One thing ought not to be forgotten. India unarmed would not require to be destroyed through poison gas or bombardment. It is the Maginot Line that has made the Siegfried Line necessary. And vice versa. Defence of India by the present methods has been necessary because she is an appendage of Britain. Free India can have no enemy. And if her people have learnt the art of saying resolutely

'No' and acting up to it, I daresay no one would want to invade her. Our economy would be so modelled as to prove no temptation for the exploiter.

But some Congressmen will say: 'Apart from the British, India has so many martial races within her border that they will want to put up a fight for the country which is as much theirs as ours.' This is perfectly true. I am therefore talking, for the moment, only of Congressmen. How would they act in the event of an invasion? We shall never convert the whole of India to our creed unless we are prepared to die for it.

The opposite course appeals to me. Already, the bulk of the Army is manned by the Mussulmans of the North, Sikhs and Gurkhas. If the masses of the South and Centre wish to become militarized, the Congress, which is supposed to represent them, will have to enter into competition with the former. The Congress will then have to be party to an enormous military budget. There may be all these things without the Congress consent. It will make all the difference in the world whether the Congress is party to them or not. The world is looking for something new and unique from India. The Congress will be lost in the crowd, if it wears the same old outworn armour that the world is wearing to-day. The Congress has a name because it represents non-violence as a political weapon *par excellence*. If the Congress helps the Allies as a representative of non-violence, it will give to the Allied cause a prestige and a power which will be invaluable in deciding the ultimate fate of the war. But the members of the working committee have honestly and bravely not made the profession of such non-violence.

My position is, therefore, confined to myself alone. I have to find out whether I have any fellow-traveller along the lonely path. If I am in the minority of one, I must try to make converts. Whether one or many, I must declare my faith that it is better for India to discard violence altogether even for defending her borders. For India to enter into the race for armaments is to court suicide. With the loss of India to non-violence the last hope of the world will be gone. I must live up to the creed I have professed for the last half-century, and hope to the last breath that India will make non-violence her creed, preserve man's dignity, and prevent him from reverting to the type from which he is supposed to have raised himself.

(Harijan, 14th October 1939)

AN APPEAL TO EVERY BRITON

In 1896 I addressed an appeal to every Briton in South Africa on behalf of my countrymen who had gone there as labourers or traders and their assistants. It had its effect. However important it was from my viewpoint, the cause which I pleaded then was insignificant compared with the cause which prompts this appeal. I appeal to every Briton, wherever he may be now, to accept the method of non-violence instead of that of war, for the adjustment of relations between nations and other matters. Your statesmen have declared that this is a war on behalf of democracy. There are many other reasons given in justification. You know them all by heart. I suggest that, at the end of the war, whichever way it ends, there will be no democracy left to represent democracy. This war has descended upon mankind as a curse and a warning. It is a curse inasmuch as it is brutalizing man on a scale hitherto unknown. All distinctions between combatants and non-combatants have been abolished. No one and nothing is to be spared. Lying has been reduced to an art. Britain was to defend small nationalities. One by one they have vanished, at least for the time being. It is also a warning. It is a warning that, if nobody reads the writing on the wall, man will be reduced to the state of the beast, whom he is shaming by his manners. I read the writing when the hostilities broke out. But I had not the courage to say the word. God has given me the courage to say it before it is too late.

I appeal for cessation of hostilities, not because you are too exhausted to fight, but because war is bad in essence. You want to kill Nazism. You will never kill it by its indifferent adoption. Your soldiers are doing the same work of destruction as the Germans. The only difference is that perhaps yours are not as thorough as the Germans. If that be so, yours will soon acquire the same thoroughness as theirs, if not much greater. On no other condition can you win the war. In other words, you will have to be more ruthless than the Nazis. No cause, however just, can warrant the indiscriminate slaughter that is going on minute by minute. I suggest that a cause that demands the inhumanities that are being perpetrated to-day cannot be called just.

I do not want Britain to be defeated, nor do I want her to be victorious in a trial of brute strength, whether expressed through the muscle or the brain. Your muscular bravery is an established fact. Need you demonstrate that your brain is also as unrivalled in destructive power as your muscle? I hope you do not wish to enter into such an undignified competition with the Nazis. I venture to present you with a nobler and braver way, worthy of the bravest soldier. I want you to fight Nazism without arms, or, if I am to retain the military terminology, with non-violent arms. I would like you to lay down the arms you have as being useless for saving you or humanity. You will invite Herr Hitler and Signor Mussolini to take what they want of your beautiful island, with your many beautiful buildings. You will give all these but neither your souls, nor your minds. If these gentlemen choose to occupy your homes, you will vacate them. If they do not give you free passage out, you will allow yourselves man, woman and child, to be slaughtered, but you will refuse to owe allegiance to them.

This process or method, which I have called non-violent non-co-operation, is not without considerable success in its use in India. Your representatives in India may deny my claim. If they do, I shall feel sorry for them. They may tell you that our non-co-operation was not wholly non-violent, that it was born of hatred. If they give that testimony, I will not deny it. Had it been wholly non-violent, if all the non-co-operators had been filled with goodwill towards you, I make bold to say that you who are India's masters would have become her pupils and, with much greater skill than we have, perfected this matchless weapon and met the German and Italian friends' menace with it. Indeed the history of Europe during the past few months would then have been written differently. Europe would have been spared seas of innocent blood, the rape of so many small nations, and the orgy of hatred.

This is no appeal made by a man who does not know his business. I have been practising with scientific precision non-violence and its possibilities for an unbroken period of over fifty years. I have applied it in every walk of life, domestic, institutional, economic and political. I know of no single case in which it has failed. Where it has seemed sometimes to have failed, I have ascribed it to my imperfections. I claim no perfection for myself. But I do claim to be a passionate seeker after Truth, which is but another name for God. In the course of that search the discovery of non-violence came to me. Its spread is my life mission. I have no interest in living except for the prosecution of that mission.

I claim to have been a lifelong and wholly disinterested friend of the British people. At one time I used to be also a lover of your empire. I thought that it was doing good to India. When I saw that in the nature of things it could do no good, I used, and am still using, the non-violent method to fight imperialism. Whatever the ultimate fate of my country, my love for you remains, and will remain, undiminished. My non-violence demands universal love, and you are not a small part of it. It is that love which has prompted my appeal to you.

May God give power to every word of mine. In His name I began to write this, and in His name I close it. May your statesmen have the wisdom and courage to respond to my appeal. I am telling His Excellency the Viceroy that my services are at the disposal of His Majesty's Government, should they consider them of any practical use in advancing the object of my appeal.   (*Harijan*, 6th July 1940)

By writing that 'Appeal to Every Briton' I have invited upon my head an extra load of work which without God's help I would be ill able to bear. If it is His will that I should shoulder it, He will give me the strength to carry on.

When I decided to confine myself mostly to writing in Gujarati or Hindustani, I had no notion that I would have to write the appeal. It came to me like a flash, and the courage to write it came with it. I had resisted till then all pressure from English and American friends to give guidance. But I could not see my way. Now, having addressed that appeal, I must follow up the reactions to it. A large amount of correspondence is pouring in upon me. Save for one angry telegram, I had nothing but friendly criticism from Englishmen and even appreciation from some.

I was grateful to HE the Viceroy for forwarding my offer to His Majesty's Government. The correspondence with regard to it the readers have already seen or will see in this issue. Though no better response to the appeal was to be expected, I cannot help saying that it was the knowledge of the determination to carry the war to a victorious end that had prompted my appeal. No doubt the determination is natural and worthy of the best British tradition. Nevertheless the awful slaughter that the determination involves, should induce a search for a better and braver way to achieve the end. For peace has its victories more glorious than those of war. The non-violent method would have meant no abject surrender. It would have confounded all modern tactics of war, indeed rendered them of no use. The new world order, which all dream of, would surely have been found. I hold a new order to be impossible, if the war is fought to a finish or mutual exhaustion leads to a patched-up peace.

Let me, therefore, examine the argument advanced in a letter received from a friend. Here it is:

'Two English friends, who admire you, say your appeal to every Briton cannot have any effect *just now*. It is impossible to expect the man in the street to do a complete *volte face* with any degree of understanding—indeed it is impossible for the understanding to do, as you say, without a *heart*-belief in non-violence. The time to mould a new world on your lines will be *after* the war. They realize your way is the right one, but they say it needs endless preparation and instruction and *big* leadership—none of which they possess. Regarding India, they say the attitude of the present authority is deplorable. Long ago India should have been declared as independent as Canada, and her people should be allowed to work out their own constitution. But what they are extremely perplexed about now is that you want absolute independence straight away, and the next step you will take is "no further help to Britain in the prosecution of war, surrender to Germany, and opposition to her by non-violent means". You must explain what you mean in more detail so as to remove this misunderstanding. This is an honest reaction.'

The appeal was intended to produce the effect now. It could not come out of the mathematical calculation. If the conviction could have come, action was an easy matter. The mass mind responds under pressure. That the appeal has not produced the intended result shows that either my word has no power or that God has a purpose of which we have no knowledge. The appeal has come from an anguished heart. I could not suppress it. It was not written for the moment. I am quite sure that it enunciates a truth of eternal value.

If the ground is not prepared from now, there may be no time left after a dismal termination of the war for evolving a new order. Whatever the order, it will be in response to a conscious or unconscious effort from now. Indeed the effort began before my appeal. I hope that it has stimulated it, perhaps given it a definite direction. I suggest to the non-official leaders and moulders of British opinion, if they are convinced of the truth of my position, to work for its adoption. Compared to the big issue raised in my appeal, the question of Indian independence pales into insignificance. But I hold with the two Englishmen that the British Government's attitude is deplorable. The two friends are wholly wrong in the deduction they have drawn from the assumed recognition of India's independence. They forget that I am out of the picture. Those who are responsible for the working committee's last resolution have meant free India's co-operation with Britain. With them, there is no question of surrender to Germany or non-violent opposition.

But I must not here tarry on Indian independence and its implications, tempting though the subject is.

The cuttings and correspondence before me say that the Congress rejections of my advice to abstain from preparation for military defence of India precludes me from making the appeal to Britain or from expecting a favourable response. The argument is plausible, but only plausible. The critics say that, if I have failed with my people, I have no right to expect Britain whilst she is in the midst of a life and death struggle to listen to me. I am a man with a mission. India's millions have never tasted the bitters of war as the British have. Britain, if she is to fulfil her declared purpose, needs a radical change in her policy. I feel that I know the change that is needed. My inability to persuade the working committee is irrelevant to the theme under discussion. There is no analogy between India's case and Britain's. I am, therefore, wholly unrepentant, I maintain that in issuing my appeal I have acted wholly as a lifelong friend of Britain.

A writer, however, retorts: 'Address your appeal to Hitler.' In the first place, I did write to Herr Hitler. My letter was published in the Press some time after I addressed it. In the second place, there can be no meaning in my appeal to Herr Hitler to adopt non-violence. He is marching from victory to victory, I can only appeal to him to desist. That I have done. But to Britain, which is just now on the defensive, I can present the really effective weapon of non-violent non-co-operation. Let my method be rejected on merits, not by bringing inapt analogies or untenable arguments. The issue raised by me, I venture to think, is of universal importance. The usefulness of non-violent methods seems to be granted by all the critics. They gratuitously assume the impossibility of human nature, as it is constituted, responding to the strain involved in non-violent preparation. But that is begging the question. I say, 'You have never tried the method on any scale. In so far as it has been tried, it has shown promising results.'   (*Harijan*, 21st July 1940)

A friend quotes from a letter received from an English friend:

> 'Do you think that Mahatma's appeal to every Briton is going to produce right reactions in the mind or heart of a single Briton? That appeal has probably created more ill-will than anything else recently. We live in astonishing and critical times, and it is frightfully difficult to decide what should be done. At any rate we should try to avoid obvious dangers. So far as I can see, Mahatma's unadulterated policy must inevitably lead to disaster for India. How far he himself intends following it I do not know, for he has a wonderful way of adapting himself to his material.'

Well, I happen to know that many more than one single heart have been touched by my 'Appeal to Every Briton'. I know that many English friends were anxious for me to take some such step.

But I do not want to take comfort from the approbation, however pleasing in itself, of English friends. What is of value for me is to know that at least one Englishman thinks as stated in the extract. Such knowledge should put me on my guard. It should make me more careful, if possible, in the selection of the words I use to express my thought. But no displeasure even of the dearest friends can put me off the duty I see clearly in front of me. And this duty of making the appeal was so peremptory that it was impossible for me to put it off. As certain as I am writing this, the world has to come to the state to which I have invited Britain. Those who will be witnesses of that happy and not far-off event will recall my appeal with gladness. I know that the appeal has hastened its advent.

Why should a single Briton resent an appeal to him to be braver than he is, to be better than he is in every respect? He may plead inability, but he cannot be displeased by an appeal to his nobler nature.

Why should the appeal breed any ill-will at all? There is no cause given for it by the manner or the matter of the appeal. I have not advised cessation of fight. I have advised lifting it to a plane worthy of human nature, of the divinity man shares with God Himself. If the hidden meaning of the remarks is that by making the appeal I have strengthened Nazi hands, the suggestion does not bear scrutiny. Herr Hitler can only be confounded by the adoption by Britain of the novel method of fighting. At one single stroke he will find that all his tremendous armament has been put out of action. A warrior lives on his wars whether offensive or defensive. He suffers a collapse, if he finds that his warring capacity is unwanted.

My appeal is not from a coward to brave people to shed their bravery, nor is it a mockery from a fair-weather friend to one in distress. I suggest to the writer to re-read my appeal in the light of my explanation.

One thing Herr Hitler, as every critic, may say: I am a fool without any knowledge of the world or human nature. That would be a harmless certificate which need excite neither ill-will nor anger. It would be harmless because I have earned such certificates before now. This one would be the latest of the many editions, and I hope not the last, for my foolish experiments have not yet ended.

So far as India is concerned, my unadulterated policy can never harm her, if she adopts it. If India as a whole rejects it, there can be no harm accruing except to those who may foolishly pursue it. The correspondent has lighted upon my strong point when he says: 'Mahatma has a wonderful way of adapting himself to his material.' My instinctive knowledge of my material has given me a faith which cannot be moved. I feel within me that the material is ready. My instinct has not betrayed me once.

But I must not build much upon past experience. 'One step enough for me.' (*Harijan*, 28th July 1940)

AHIMSA AND HIMSA

If we turn our eyes to the time of which history has any record down to our own time, we shall find that man has been steadily progressing towards *ahimsa*. Our remote ancestors were cannibals. Then came a time when they were fed up with cannibalism and they began to live on chase. Next came a stage when man was ashamed of leading the life of a wandering hunter. He therefore took to agriculture and depended principally on mother earth for his food. Thus from being a nomad he settled down to civilized stable life, founded villages and towns, and from member of a family he became member of a community and a nation. All these are signs of progressive *ahimsa* and diminishing *himsa*. Had it been otherwise, the human species should have been extinct by now, even as many of the lower species have disappeared.

Prophets and *avatars* have also taught the lesson of *ahimsa* more or less. Not one of them has professed to teach *himsa*. And how should it be otherwise? *Himsa* does not need to be taught. Man as animal is violent, but as spirit is non-violent. The moment he awakes to the spirit within he cannot remain violent. Either he progresses towards *ahimsa* or rushes to his doom. That is why the prophets and *avatars* have taught the lessons of truth, harmony, brotherhood, justice, etc.—all attributes of *ahimsa*.

And yet violence seems to persist, even to the extent of thinking people like the correspondent regarding it as the final weapon. But, as I have shown, history and experience are against him.

If we believe that mankind has steadily progressed towards *ahimsa*, it follows that it has to progress towards it still further. Nothing in this world is static, everything is kinetic. If there is no progression, then there is inevitable retrogression. No one can remain without the eternal cycle, unless it be God Himself.

The present war is the saturation point in violence. It spells to my mind also its doom. Daily I have testimony of the fact that *ahimsa* was never before appreciated by mankind as it is to-day. All the testimony from the West that I continue to receive points in the same direction.

The Congress has pledged itself to *ahimsa* however limited.
I invite the correspondent and doubters like him to shed
their doubts and plunge confidently into the sacred sacrifi-
cial fire of *ahimsa*. Then I have little doubt that the Congress will retrace its step. 'It is always willing.' Well has
Pritan, our poet, sung:

> Happiest are those that plunge in the fire,
> The lookers-on are all but scorched by flames.

(*Harijan*, 11th August 1940)

FASTING IN NON-VIOLENT ACTION

If the struggle which we are seeking to avoid with all our
might has to come, and if it is to remain non-violent as it
must in order to succeed, fasting is likely to play an important part in it. It has its place in the tussle with authority
and with our own people in the event of wanton acts of
violence and obstinate riots, for instance.

There is a natural prejudice against it as part of a political
struggle. It has a recognized place in religious practice. But
it is considered a vulgar interpolation in politics by the
ordinary politician though it has always been resorted to
by prisoners in a haphazard way with more or less success.
By fasting, however, they have always succeeded in drawing public attention and disturbing the peace of jail authorities.

My own fasts have always, as I hold, been strictly
according to the law of *satyagraha*. Fellow *satyagrahis* too
in South Africa fasted partially or wholly. My fasts have
been varied. There was the Hindu-Muslim unity fast of
twenty-one days in 1924, started under the late Maulana
Mahomed Ali's roof in Delhi. The indeterminate fast against
the MacDonald Award was taken in the Yeravda prison in
1932. The twenty-one days' purificatory fast was begun in
the Yeravda prison and was finished at Lady Thakersey's, as
the Government would not take the burden of my being
in the prison in that condition. Then followed another fast
in the Yeravda prison in 1933 against the Government refusal to let me carry on anti-untouchability work through
Harijan (issued from prison) on the same basis as facilities
had been allowed me four months before. They would not
yield, but they discharged me when their medical advisers
thought I could not live many days if the fast was not given

up. Then followed the ill-fated Rajkot fast in 1939. A false step taken by me thoughtlessly during that fast thwarted the brilliant result that would otherwise certainly have been achieved. In spite of all these fasts, fasting has not been accepted as a recognized part of *satyagraha*. It has only been tolerated by the politicians. I have, however, been driven to the conclusion that fasting unto death is an integral part of *satyagraha* programme, and it is the greatest and most effective weapon in its armoury under given circumstances. Not every one is qualified for undertaking it without a proper course of training.

I may not burden this note with an examination of the circumstances under which fasting may be resorted to and the training required for it. Non-violence in its positive aspect as benevolence (I do not use the word love as it has fallen into disrepute) is the greatest force because of the limitless scope it affords for self-suffering without causing or intending any physical or material injury to the wrong-doer. The object always is to evoke the best in him. Self-suffering is an appeal to his better nature, as retaliation is to his baser. Fasting under proper circumstances is such an appeal *par excellence*. If the politician does not perceive its propriety in political matters, it is because it is a novel use of this very fine weapon.

To practise non-violence in mundane matters is to know its true value. It is to bring heaven upon earth. There is no such thing as the other world. All worlds are one. There is no 'here' and no 'there'. As Jeans has demonstrated, the whole universe including the most distant stars, invisible even through the most powerful telescope in the world, is compressed in an atom. I hold it therefore to be wrong to limit the use of non-violence to cave dwellers and for acquiring merit for a favoured position in the other world. All virtue ceases to have use if it serves no purpose in every walk of life. I would therefore plead with the purely political-minded people to study non-violence and fasting as its extreme manifestation with sympathy and under-standing.   (*Harijan*, 26th July 1942)

PART IV

The Call of Truth by Rabindranath Tagore, and Gandhi's Reply; Politics and Religion; Advice to Satyagrahis in an Industrial Strike; a Letter to the Viceroy Inaugurating the Non-Co-operative Movement; an Appeal to his Followers; the Swadeshi Movement

---

THE CALL OF TRUTH[1]
by Rabindranath Tagore

Parasites have to pay for their ready-made victuals by losing the power of assimilating food in its natural form. In the history of man this same sin of laziness has always entailed degeneracy. Man becomes parasitical, not only when he fattens on others' toil, but also when he becomes rooted to a particular set of outside conditions and allows himself helplessly to drift along the stream of things as they are; for the outside is alien to the inner self, and if the former be made indispensable by sheer habit, man acquires parasitical characteristics, and becomes unable to perform his true function of converting the impossible into the possible.

In this sense all the lower animals are parasites. They are carried along by their environment; they live or die by natural selection; they progress or retrogress as nature may dictate. Their mind has lost the power of growth. The bees, for millions of years, have been unable to get beyond the pattern of their hive. For that reason, the form of their cell has attained a certain perfection, but their mentality is confined to the age-long habits of their hive-life and cannot soar out of its limitations. Nature has developed a cautious timidity in the case of her lower types of life; she keeps them tied to her apron strings and has stunted their minds, lest they should stray into dangerous experiments.

But Providence displayed a sudden accession of creative courage when it came to man; for his inner nature has

1. From *The Modern Review* for October 1921, pp. 423-33.

not been tied down, though outwardly the poor human
creature has been left naked, weak and defenceless. In spite
of these disabilities, man in the joy of his inward freedom
has stood up and declared; 'I shall achieve the impossible.'
That is to say, he has consistently refused to submit to the
rule of things as they always have been, but is determined
to bring about happenings that have never been before. So
when, in the beginning of his history, man's lot was thrown
in with monstrous creatures, tusked and taloned, he did not,
like the deer, simply take refuge in flight, nor, like the tor-
toise, take refuge in hiding, but set to work with flints
to make even more efficient weapons. These, moreover,
being the creation of his own inner faculties, were not
dependent on natural selection, as were those of the other
animals, for their development. And so man's instruments
progressed from flint to steel. This shows that man's mind
has never been helplessly attached to his environment. What
came to his hand was brought under his thumb. Not content with the flint on the surface, he delved for the iron
beneath. Not satisfied with the easier process of chipping
flints, he proceeded to melt iron ore and hammer it into
shape. That which resisted more stubbornly was converted
into a better ally. Man's inner nature not only finds success
in its activity, but there it also has its joy. He insists on
penetrating further and further into the depths, from the
obvious to the hidden, from the easy to the difficult, from
parasitism to self-determination, from the slavery of his
passions to the mastery of himself. That is how he has won.

But if any section of mankind should say, 'The flint was
the weapon of our revered forefathers; by departing from
it we destroy the spirit of the race,' then they may succeed
in preserving what they call their race, but they strike at
the root of the glorious tradition of humanity which was
theirs also. And we find that those, who have steadfastly
stuck to their flints, may indeed have kept safe their pris-
tine purity to their own satisfaction, but they have been
outcast by the rest of mankind, and so have to pass their
lives slinking away in jungle and cave. They are, as I say,
reduced to a parasitic dependence on outside nature, driven
along blindfold by the force of things as they are. They
have not achieved Swaraj in their inner nature; and so are
deprived of Swaraj in the outside world as well. They have
ceased to be even aware, that it is man's true function to

make the impossible into the possible by dint of his own powers; that it is not for him to be confined merely to what has happened before; that he must progress towards what ought to be by rousing all his inner powers by means of the force of his soul.

Thirty years ago I used to edit the Sādhānā magazine, and there I tried to say this same thing. Then English-educated India was frightfully busy begging for its rights. And I repeatedly endeavoured to impress on my country-men, that man is not under any necessity to beg for rights from others, but must create them for himself; because man lives mainly by his inner nature, and there he is the master. By dependence on acquisition from the outside, man's inner nature suffers loss. And it was my contention, that man is not so hard oppressed by being deprived of his outward rights as he is by the constant bearing of the burden of prayers and petitions.

Then when the Bangadarshan magazine came into my hands, Bengal was beside herself at the sound of the sharpening of the knife for her partition. The boycott of Manchester, which was the outcome of her distress, had raised the profits of the Bombay mill-owners to a super-foreign degree. And I had then to say: 'This will not do, either; for it is also of the outside. Your main motive is hatred of the foreigner, not love of country.' It was then really necessary for our countrymen to be made conscious of the distinction, that the Englishman's presence is an external accident mere māyā—but that the presence of our country is an internal fact which is also an eternal truth. Māyā looms with an exaggerated importance, only when we fix our attention exclusively upon it, by reason of some infatuation—be it of love, or of hate. Whether in our passion we rush to embrace it, or attack it; whether we yearn for it, or spurn it; it equally fills the whole field of our blood-shot vision.

Māyā is like the darkness. No steed, however swift, can carry us beyond it; no amount of water can wash it away. Truth is like a lamp; even as it is lit māyā vanishes. Our shastras tell us that Truth, even when it is small, can rescue us from the terror which is great. Fear is the atheism of the heart. It cannot be overcome from the side of nega-tion. If one of its heads be struck off, it breeds, like the monster of the fable, a hundred others. Truth is positive:

it is the affirmation of the soul. If even a little of it be roused, it attacks negation at the very heart and overpowers it wholly.

Alien government in India is a veritable chameleon. To-day it comes in the guise of the Englishman; to-morrow perhaps as some other foreigner; the next day, without abating a jot of its virulence, it may take the shape of our own countrymen. However determinedly we may try to hunt this monster of foreign dependence with outside lethal weapons, it will always elude our pursuit by changing its skin, or its colour. But if we can gain within us the truth called our country, all outward _māyā_ will vanish of itself. The declaration of faith that my country _is_ there, to be realized, has to be attained by each one of us. The idea that our country is ours, merely because we have been born in it, can only be held by those who are fastened, in a parasitic existence, upon the outside world. But the true nature of man is his inner nature, with its inherent powers. Therefore that only can be a man's true country which he can help to create by his wisdom and will, his love and his actions. So, in 1905, I called upon my countrymen to _create_ their country by putting forth their own powers from within. For the act of creation itself is the realization of truth.

The Creator gains Himself in His universe. To gain one's own country means to realize one's own soul more fully expanded within it. This can only be done when we are engaged in building it up with our service, our ideas and our activities. Man's country being the creation of his own inner nature, when his soul thus expands within it, it is more truly expressed, more fully realized. In my paper called 'Swadeshi Samaj', written in 1905, I discussed at length the ways and means by which we could make the country of our birth more fully our own. Whatever may have been the shortcomings of my words then uttered, I did not fail to lay emphasis on the truth, that we must win our country, not from some foreigner, but from our own inertia, our own indifference. Whatever be the nature of the boons we may be seeking for our country at the door of the foreign Government, the result is always the same—it only makes our inertia more densely inert. Any public benefit done by the alien Government goes to their credit, not to ours. So whatever outside advantage such public benefit might mean for us, our country will only get more and more completely lost to us thereby. That is to say, we shall have to pay out in soul value for what we purchase as material advantage. The Rishi has said: 'The son is dear, not because we desire a son, but because we desire to realize our own soul in him.' It is the same with our country. It is dear to us, because it is the expression of our own soul. When we realize this, it will become impossible for us to allow our service of our country to wait on the pleasure of others.

These truths, which I then tried to press on my country-men, were not particularly new, nor was there anything therein which need have grated on their ears; but, whether anyone else remembers it or not, I at least am not likely to forget the storm of indignation which I roused. I am not merely referring to the hooligans of journalism whom it pays to be scurrilous. But even men of credit and courtesy were unable to speak of me in restrained language.

There were two root causes of this. One was anger, the second was greed.

Giving free vent to angry feelings is a species of self-indulgence. In those days there was practically nothing to stand in the way of the spirit of destructive revel, which spread all over the country. We went about picketing, burn-ing, placing thorns in the path of those whose way was not ours, acknowledging no restraints in language or be-haviour,—all in the frenzy of our wrath. Shortly after it was all over, a Japanese friend asked me: 'How is it you people cannot carry on your work with calm and deep determination? This wasting of energy can hardly be of assistance to your object.' I had no help but to reply: 'When we have the gaining of the object clearly before our minds, we can be restrained, and concentrate our ener-gies to serve it; but when it is a case of venting our anger, our excitement rises and rises till it drowns the object, and then we are spend-thrift to the point of bankruptcy.' However that may be, there were my countrymen encoun-tering, for the time being, no check to the overflow of their outraged feelings. It was like a strange dream. Everything seemed possible. Then all of a sudden it was my misfortune to appear on the scene with my doubts and my attempts to divert the current into the path of self-determination.

My only success was in diverting their wrath on to my own devoted head.

Then there was our greed. In history, all people have won valuable things by pursuing difficult paths. We had hit upon the device of getting them cheap, not even through the painful indignity of supplication with folded hands, but by proudly conducting our beggary in threatening tones. The country was in ecstasy at the ingenuity of the trick. It felt like being at a reduced price sale. Everything worth having in the political market was ticketed at half-price. Shabby-genteel mentality is so taken up with low prices that it has no attention to spare for quality, and feels inclined to attack anybody who has the hardihood to express doubts in that regard. It is like the man of worldly piety who believes that the judicious expenditure of coin can secure, by favour of a priest, a direct passage to heaven. The daredevil who ventures to suggest that not heaven but dreamland is likely to be his destination must beware of a violent end.

Anyhow, it was the outside *māyā* which was our dream and our ideal in those days. It was a favourite phrase of one of the leaders of the time that we must keep one hand at the feet and the other at the throat of the Englishman,— that is to say, with no hand left free for the country! We have since perhaps got rid of this ambiguous attitude. Now we have one party that has both hands down at his feet; but whichever attitude it may be, these methods still appertain to the outside *māyā*. Our unfortunate minds keep revolving round and round the British Government, now to the left, now to the right; our affirmations and denials alike are concerned with the foreigner.

In those days, the stimulus from every side was directed towards the heart of Bengal. But emotion by itself, like fire, only consumes its fuel and reduces it to ashes; it has no creative power. The intellect of man must busy itself, with patience, with skill, with foresight, in using this fire to melt that which is hard and difficult into the object of its desire. We neglected to rouse our intellectual forces, and so were unable to make use of this surging emotion of ours to create any organization of permanent value. The reason of our failure, therefore, was not in anything outside, but rather within us. For a long time past we have been in the habit, in our life and endeavour, of setting apart one place for our emotions and another for our practices. Our intellect has all the time remained dormant, because we have not dared to allow it scope. That is why, when we have to rouse ourselves to action, it is our emotion which has to be requisitioned, and our intellect has to be kept from interfering by the hypnotism of some magical formula,—that is to say we hasten to create a situation absolutely inimical to the free play of our intellect.

The loss which is incurred by this continual deadening of our mind cannot be made good by any other contrivance. In our desperate attempts to do so we have to invoke the magic of *māyā* and our impotence jumps for joy at the prospect of getting hold of Aladin's lamp. Of course everyone has to admit that there is nothing to beat Aladin's lamp, its only inconvenience being that it beats one to get hold of. The unfortunate part of it is that the person, whose greed is great, but whose powers are feeble, and who has lost all confidence in his own intellect, simply will not allow himself to dwell on the difficulties of bespeaking the services of some genie of the lamp. He can only be brought to exert himself at all by holding out the speedy prospect of getting at the wonderful lamp. If any one attempts to point out the futility of his hopes, he fills the air with wailing and imprecation, as at a robber making away with his all.

In the heat of the enthusiasm of the partition days, a band of youths attempted to bring about the millennium through political revolution. Their offer of themselves as the first sacrifice to the fire which they had lighted makes not only their own country, but other countries as well, bare the head to them in reverence. Their physical failure shines forth as the effulgence of spiritual glory. In the midst of their supreme travail, they realized at length that the way of bloody revolution is not the true way; that where there is no politics, a political revolution is like taking a short cut to nothing; that the wrong way may appear shorter, but it does not reach the goal, and only grievously hurts the feet. The refusal to pay the full price for a thing leads to the loss of the price without the gain of the thing. These impetuous youths offered their lives as the price of their country's deliverance; to them it meant the loss of their all, but alas! the price offered on behalf of the country was insufficient. I feel sure that those of them who still survive must have realized by now, that the country must be the creation of all its people, not of one section alone. It must be the expression of all their forces of heart, mind and will.

This creation can only be the fruit of that *yoga*, which gives outward form to the inner faculties. Mere political or economical *yoga* is not enough; for that all the human powers must unite.

When we turn our gaze upon the history of other countries, the political steed comes prominently into view; on it seems to depend wholly the progress of the carriage. We forget that the carriage also must be in a fit condition to move; its wheels must be in agreement with one another and its parts well fitted together; with which not only have fire and hammer and chisel been busy but much thought and skill and energy have also been spent in the process. We have seen some countries which are externally free and independent; when, however, the political carriage is in motion, the noise which it makes arouses the whole neighbourhood from slumber and the jolting produces aches and pains in the limbs of the helpless passengers. It comes to pieces in the middle of the road, and it takes the whole day to put it together again with the help of ropes and strings. Yet however loose the screws and however crooked the wheels, still it is a vehicle of some sort after all. But for such a thing as is our country,—a mere collection of jointed logs, that not only have no wholeness amongst themselves, but are contrary to one another,—for this, to be dragged along a few paces by the temporary pull of some common greed or anger, can never be called by the name of political progress. Therefore, is it not, in our case, wiser to keep for the moment our horse in the stable and begin to manufacture a real carriage?

From the writings of the young men, who have come back out of the valley of the shadow of death, I feel sure some such thoughts must have occurred to them. And so they must be realizing the necessity of the practice of *yoga* as of primary importance;—that form which is the union in a common endeavour of all the human faculties. This cannot be attained by any outside blind obedience, but only by the realization of self in the light of intellect. That which fails to illumine the intellect, and only keeps it in the obsession of some delusion, is its greatest obstacle.

The call to make the country our own by dint of our own creative power, is a great call. It is not merely inducing the people to take up some external mechanical exercise; for man's life is not in making cells of uniform pattern like the bee, nor in incessant weaving of webs like the spider; his greatest powers are within, and on these are his chief reliance. If by offering some allurement we can induce man to cease from thinking, so that he may go on and on with some mechanical piece of work, this will only result in prolonging the sway of *māyā*, under which our country has all along been languishing. So far, we have been content with surrendering our greatest right—the right to reason and to judge for ourselves—to the blind forces of shastric injunctions and social conventions. We have refused to cross the seas, because Manu has told us not to do so. We refuse to eat with the Mussulman, because prescribed usage is against it. In other words, we have systematically pursued a course of blind routine and habit, in which the mind of man has no place. We have thus been reduced to the helpless condition of the master who is altogether dependent on his servant. The real master, as I have said, is the internal man; and he gets into endless trouble, when he becomes his own servant's slave—a mere automaton, manufactured in the factory of servitude. He can then only rescue himself from one master by surrendering himself to another. Similarly, he who glorifies inertia by attributing to it a fanciful purity, becomes, like it, dependent on outside impulses, both for rest and motion. The inertness of mind, which is the basis of all slavery, cannot be got rid of by a docile submission to being hoodwinked, nor by going through the motions of a wound-up mechanical doll.

The movement, which has now succeeded the Swadeshi agitation, is ever so much greater and has moreover extended its influence all over India. Previously, the vision of our political leaders had never reached beyond the English-knowing classes, because the country meant for them only that bookish aspect of it which is to be found in the pages of the Englishman's history. Such a country was merely a mirage born of vapourings in the English language, in which flitted about thin shades of Burke and Gladstone, Mazzini and Garibaldi. Nothing resembling self-sacrifice or true feeling for their countrymen was visible. At this juncture, Mahatma Gandhi came and stood at the cottage door of the destitute millions, clad as one of themselves, and talking to them in their own language. Here was the truth at last, not a mere quotation out of a book. So the name of Mahatma, which was given to him, is his true name. Who else has felt so many men of India to be of his own flesh and blood? At the touch of Truth the pent-up forces of the soul are set free. As soon as true love stood at India's door, it flew open : all hesitation and holding back vanished. Truth awakened truth.

Stratagem in politics is a barren policy,—this was a lesson of which we were sorely in need. All honour to the Mahatma, who made visible to us the power of Truth. But reliance on tactics is so ingrained in the cowardly and the weak, that, in order to eradicate it, the very skin must be sloughed off. Even today, our worldly-wise men cannot get rid of the idea of utilizing the Mahatma as a secret and more ingenious move in their political gamble. With their minds corroded by untruth, they cannot understand what an important thing it is that the Mahatma's supreme love should have drawn forth the country's love. The thing that has happened is nothing less than the birth of freedom. It is the gain by the country of itself. In it there is no room for any thought, as to where the Englishman is, or is not. This love is self-expression. It is pure affirmation. It does not argue with negation : it has no need for argument.

Some notes of the music of this wonderful awakening of India by love, floated over to me across the seas. It was a great joy to me to think that the call of this festivity of awakening would come to each one of us; and that the true *shakti* of India's spirit, in all its multifarious variety, would at last find expression. This thought came to me because I have always believed that in such a way India would find its freedom. When Lord Buddha voiced forth the truth of compassion for all living creatures, which he had obtained as the fruit of his own self-discipline, the manhood of India was roused and poured itself forth in science and art and wealth of every kind True, in the matter of political unification the repeated attempts that were then made as often failed; nevertheless India's mind had awakened into freedom from its submergence in sleep, and its overwhelming force would brook no confinement within the petty limits of country. It overflowed across ocean and desert, scattering its wealth of the spirit over every land that it touched. No commercial or military exploiter, to-day, has ever been able to do anything like it. Whatever land these exploiters have touched, has been agonized with sorrow and insult, and the fair face of the world has been scarred and disfigured. Why? Because not greed but love is true. When love gives freedom it does so at the very centre of our life. When greed seeks unfettered power, it is forcefully impatient. We saw this during the partition agitation. We then compelled the poor to make sacrifices, not always out of the inwardness of love, but often by outward pressure. That was because greed is always seeking for a particular result within a definite time. But the fruit which love seeks is not of to-day or to-morrow, nor for a time only: it is sufficient unto itself.

So, in the expectation of breathing the buoyant breezes of this new found freedom, I came home rejoicing. But what I found in Calcutta when I arrived depressed me. An oppressive atmosphere seemed to burden the land. Some outside compulsion seemed to be urging one and all to talk in the same strain, to work at the same mill. When I wanted to inquire, to discuss, my well-wishers clapped their hands over my lips, saying: 'Not now, not now. To-day, in the atmosphere of the country, there is a spirit of persecution, which is not that of armed force, but some-thing still more alarming, because it is invisible.' I found, further, that those who had their doubts as to the present activities, if they happened to whisper them out, however cautiously, however guardedly, felt some admonishing hand clutching them within. There was a newspaper which one day had the temerity to disapprove, in a feeble way, of the burning of cloth. The very next day the editor was shaken out of his balance by the agitation of his readers. How long would it take for the fire which was burning cloth to reduce his paper to ashes? The sight that met my eye was, on the one hand, people immensely busy; on the other, intensely afraid. What I heard on every side was, that reason, and culture as well, must be closured. It was only necessary to cling to an unquestioning obedience. Obedience to whom? To some *mantra*, some unreasoned creed!

And why this obedience? Here again comes that same

greed, our spiritual enemy. There dangles before the country the bait of getting a thing of inestimable value, dirt cheap and in double-quick time. It is like the *faqir* with his gold-making trick. With such a lure men cast so readily to the winds their independent judgment and wax so mightily wroth with those who will not do likewise. So easy is it to overpower, in the name of outside freedom, the inner freedom of man. The most deplorable part of it is that so many do not even honestly believe in the hope that they swear by. 'It will serve to make our countrymen do what is necessary'—say they. Evidently, according to them, the India which once declared: 'In truth is Victory, not in untruth'—that India would not have been fit for Swaraj.

Another mischief is that the gain, with the promise of which obedience is claimed, is indicated by name, but is not defined. Just as when fear is vague it becomes all the more strong, so the vagueness of the lure makes it all the more tempting; inasmuch as ample room is left for each one's imagination to shape it to his taste. Moreover there is no driving it into a corner because it can always shift from one shelter to another. In short, the object of the temptation has been magnified through its indefiniteness, while the time and method of its attainment have been made too narrowly definite. When the reason of man has been overcome in this way, he easily consents to give up all legitimate questions and blindly follows the path of obedience. But can we really afford to forget so easily that delusion is at the root of all slavery—that all freedom means freedom from *māyā*? What if the bulk of our people have unquestioningly accepted the creed, that by means of sundry practices Swaraj will come to them on a particular date in the near future, and are also ready to use their clubs to put down all further argument,—that is to say, they have surrendered the freedom of their own minds and are prepared to deprive other minds of their freedom likewise,—is not this by itself a reason for profound misgiving? We were seeking the exorciser to drive out this very ghost; but if the ghost itself comes in the guise of exorciser then the danger is only heightened.

The Mahatma has won the heart of India with his love; for that we have all acknowledged his sovereignty. He has given us a vision of the *shakti* of truth; for that our gratitude to him is unbounded. We read about truth in books:

we talk about it: but it is indeed a red-letter day, when we see it face to face. Rare is the moment, in many a long year, when such good fortune happens. We can make and break Congresses every other day. It is at any time possible for us to stump the country preaching politics in English. But the golden rod which can awaken our country in Truth and Love is not a thing which can be manufactured by the nearest goldsmith. To the wielder of that rod our profound salutation! But if, having seen truth, our belief in it is not confirmed, what is the good of it all? Our mind must acknowledge the truth of the intellect, just as our heart does the truth of love. No Congress or other outside institution succeeded in touching the heart of India. It was roused only by the touch of love. Having had such a clear vision of this wonderful power of Truth, are we to cease to believe in it, just where the attainment of Swaraj is concerned? Has the truth, which was needed in the process of awakenment to be got rid of in the process of achievement?

Let me give an illustration. I am in search of a Vina player. I have tried East and I have tried West, but have not found the man of my quest. They are all experts, they can make the strings resound to a degree, they command high prices, but for all their wonderful execution they can strike no chord in my heart. At last I come across one whose very first notes melt away the sense of oppression within. In him is the fire of the shakti of joy which can light up all other hearts by its touch. His appeal to me is instant, and I hail him as Master. I then want a Vina made. For this, of course, are required all kinds of material and a different kind of science. If, finding me to be lacking in the means, my master should be moved to pity and say: 'Never mind, my son, do not go to the expense in workmanship and time which a Vina will require. Take rather this simple string tightened across a piece of wood and practise on it. In a short time you will find it to be as good as a Vina.' Would that do? I am afraid not. It would, in fact, be a mistaken kindness for the master thus to take pity on my circumstances. Far better if he were to tell me plainly that such things cannot be had cheaply. It is he who should teach me that merely one string will not serve for a true Vina; that the materials required are many and various; that the lines of its moulding must be shapely and precise; that if there be anything faulty, it will fail to make good music, so that all laws of science and technique of art must be rigorously and intelligently followed. In short, the true function of the master player should be to evoke a response from the depths of our heart, so that we may gain the strength to wait and work till the true end is achieved.

From our master, the Mahatma,—may our devotion to him never grow less!—we must learn the truth of love in all its purity, but the science and art of building up Swaraj is a vast subject. Its pathways are difficult to traverse and take time. For this task, aspiration and emotion must be there, but no less must study and thought be there likewise. For it, the economist must think, the mechanic must labour, the educationist and statesman must teach and contrive. In a word, the mind of the country must exert itself in all directions. Above all, the spirit of Inquiry throughout the whole country must be kept intact and untrammelled, its mind not made timid or inactive by compulsion, open or secret.

We know from past experience that it is not any and every call to which the Country responds. It is because no one has yet been able to unite in *Yoga* all the forces of the country in the work of its creation, that so much time has been lost over and over again. And we have been kept waiting and waiting for him who has the right and the power to make the call upon us. In the old forests of India, our *Gurus*, in the fulness of their vision of the Truth had sent forth such a call saying: 'As the rivers flow on their downward course, as the months flow on to the year, so let all seekers after truth come from all sides.' The initiation into Truth of that day has borne fruit, undying to this day, and the voice of its message still rings in the ears of the world.

Why should not our Guru of to-day, who would lead us on the paths of Karma, send forth such a call? Why should he not say: 'Come ye from all sides and be welcome. Let all the forces of the land be brought into action, for then alone shall the country awake. Freedom is in complete awakening, in full self-expression.' God has given the Mahatma the voice that can call, for in him there is the Truth. Why should this not be our long-awaited opportunity?

But his call came to one narrow field alone. To one and

all he simply says: Spin and weave, spin and weave. Is this
the call: 'Let all seekers after truth come from all sides'?
Is this the call of the New Age to new creation? When
nature called to the Bee to take refuge in the narrow life
of the hive, millions of bees responded to it for the sake
of efficiency, and accepted the loss of sex in consequence.
But this sacrifice by way of self-atrophy led to the opposite
of freedom. Any country, the people of which can agree to
become neuters for the sake of some temptation, or command, carries within itself its own prison-house. To spin is
easy, therefore for all men it is an imposition hard to bear.
The call to the ease of mere efficiency is well enough for the
Bee. The wealth of power, that is Man's, can only become
manifest when his utmost is claimed.

Sparta tried to gain strength by narrowing herself down
to a particular purpose, but she did not win. Athens sought
to attain perfection by opening herself out in all her fullness,—and she did win. Her flag of victory still flies at the
masthead of man's civilization. It is admitted that European
military camps and factories are stunting man, that their
greed is cutting man down to the measure of their own
narrow purpose, that for these reasons joylessness darkly
lowers over the West. But if man be stunted by big machines, the danger of his being stunted by small machines
must not be lost sight of. The *charka* in its proper place
can do no harm, but will rather do much good. But where,
by reason of failure to acknowledge the differences in
man's temperament, it is in the wrong place, there thread
can only be spun at the cost of a great deal of the mind
itself. Mind is no less valuable than cotton thread.

Some are objecting: 'We do not propose to curb our
minds for ever, but only for a time.' But why should it be
even for a time? Is it because within a short time spinning
will give us Swaraj? But where is the argument for this?
Swaraj is not concerned with our apparel only—it cannot
be established on cheap clothing; its foundation is in the
mind, which, with its diverse powers and its confidence
in those powers, goes on all the time creating Swaraj for
itself. In no country in the world is the building up of
Swaraj completed. In some part or other of every nation,
some lurking greed or illusion still perpetuates bondage.
And the root of such bondage is always within the mind.
Where then, I ask again, is the argument, that in our

country Swaraj can be brought about by everyone engaging for a time in spinning? A mere statement, in lieu of argument, will surely never do. If once we consent to receive fate's oracle from human lips, that will add one more to the torments of our slavery, and not the least one either. If nothing but oracles will serve to move us, oracles will have to be manufactured, morning, noon and night, for the sake of urgent needs, and all other voices would be defeated. Those for whom authority is needed in place of reason, will invariably accept despotism in place of freedom. It is like cutting at the root of a tree while pouring water on the top. This is not a new thing, I know. We have enough of magic in the country,—magical revelation, magical healing, and all kinds of divine intervention in mundane affairs. That is exactly why I am so anxious to re-instate reason on its throne. As I have said before, God himself has given the mind sovereignty in the material world. And I say to-day, that only those will be able to get and keep Swaraj in the material world who have realized the dignity of self-reliance and self-mastery in the spiritual world, those whom no temptation, no delusion, can induce to surrender the dignity of intellect into the keeping of others.

Consider the burning of cloth, heaped up before the very eyes of our motherland shivering and ashamed in her nakedness. What is the nature of the call to do this? Is it not another instance of a magical formula? The question of using or refusing cloth of a particular manufacture belongs mainly to economic science. The discussion of the matter by our countrymen should have been in the language of economics. If the country has really come to such a habit of mind that precise thinking has become impossible for it, then our very first fight should be against such a fatal habit, to the temporary exclusion of all else if need be. Such a habit would clearly be the original sin from which all our ills are flowing. But far from this, we take the course of confirming ourselves in it by relying on the magical formula that foreign cloth is 'impure'. Thus economics is bundled out and a fictitious moral dictum dragged into its place.

Untruth is impure in any circumstances, not merely because it may cause us material loss, but even when it does not; for it makes our inner nature unclean. This is a moral law and belongs to a higher plane. But if there be anything wrong in wearing a particular kind of cloth, that would be an offence against economics, or hygiene, or aesthetics, but certainly not against morality. Some urge that any mistake which brings sorrow to body or mind is a moral wrong. To which I reply that sorrow follows in the train of every mistake. A mistake in geometry may make a road too long, or a foundation weak, or a bridge dangerous. But mathematical mistakes cannot be cured by moral maxims. If a student makes a mistake in his geometry problem and his exercise book is torn up in consequence, the problem will nevertheless remain unsolved until attacked by geometrical methods. But what if the schoolmaster comes to the conclusion that unless the exercise books are condemned and destroyed, his boys will never realize the folly of their mistakes? If such conclusion be well-founded, then I can only repeat that the reformation of such moral weakness of these particular boys should take precedence over all other lessons, otherwise there is no hope of their becoming men in the future.

The command to burn our foreign clothes has been laid on us. I, for one, am unable to obey it. Firstly, because I conceive it to be my very first duty to put up a valiant fight against this terrible habit of blindly obeying orders, and this fight can never be carried on by our people being driven from one injunction to another. Secondly, I feel that the clothes to be burnt are not mine, but belong to those who most sorely need them. If those who are going naked should have given us the mandate to burn, it would, at least, have been a case of self-immolation and the crime of incendiarism would not lie at our door. But how can we expiate the sin of the forcible destruction of clothes which might have gone to women whose nakedness is actually keeping them prisoners, unable to stir out of the privacy of their homes?

I have said repeatedly and must repeat once more that we cannot afford to lose our mind for the sake of any external gain. Where Mahatma Gandhi has declared war against the tyranny of the machine which is oppressing the whole world, we are all enrolled under his banner. But we must refuse to accept as our ally the illusion-haunted magic-ridden slave-mentality that is at the root of all the poverty and insult under which our country groans. Here is the enemy itself, on whose defeat alone Swaraj within and without can come to us.

The time, moreover, has arrived when we must think of one thing more, and that is this. The awakening of India is part of the awakening of the world. The door of the New Age has been flung open at the trumpet blast of a great war. We have read in the Mahabharata how the day of self-revelation had to be preceded by a year of retirement. The same has happened in the world to-day. Nations had attained nearness to each other without being aware of it, that is to say, the outside fact was there, but it had not penetrated into the mind. At the shock of the war, the truth of it stood revealed to mankind. The foundation of modern, that is Western, civilization was shaken; and it has become evident that the convulsion is neither local nor temporary, but has traversed the whole earth and will last until the shocks between man and man, which have extended from continent to continent, can be brought to rest, and a harmony be established.

From now onward, any nation which takes an isolated view of its own country will run counter to the spirit of the New Age, and know no peace. From now onward, the anxiety that each country has for its own safety must embrace the welfare of the world. For some time the working of the new spirit has occasionally shown itself even in the Government of India, which has had to make attempts to deal with its own problems in the light of the world problem. The war has torn away a veil from before our minds. What is harmful to the world, is harmful to each one of us. This was a maxim which we used to read in books. Now mankind has seen it at work and has understood that wherever there is injustice, even if the external right of possession is there, the true right is wanting. So that it is worth while even to sacrifice some outward right in order to gain the reality. This immense change, which is coming over the spirit of man raising it from the petty to the great, is already at work even in Indian politics. There will doubtless be imperfections and obstacles without number. Self-interest is sure to attack enlightened interest at every step. Nevertheless it would be wrong to come to the decision that the working of self-interest alone is honest, and the larger-hearted striving is hypocritical.

After sixty years of self-experience, I have found that

out and out hypocrisy is an almost impossible achievement, so that the pure hypocrite is a rarity indeed. The fact is, that the character of man has always more or less of duality in it. But our logical faculty, the trap-door of our mind, is unable to admit opposites together. So when we find the good with the bad, the former is promptly rejected as spurious. In the universal movement, as it becomes manifest in different parts of the world, this duality of man's character cannot but show itself. And whenever it does, if we pass judgment from past experience, we are sure to pronounce the selfish part of it to be the real thing; for the spirit of division and exclusion did in fact belong to the past age. But if we come to our judgment in the light of future promise, then shall we understand the enlightened large-heartedness to be the reality, and the counsel which will unite each to each to be the true wisdom.

I have condemned, in unsparing terms, the present form and scope of the League of Nations and the Indian Reform Councils. I therefore feel certain that there will be no misunderstanding when I state that, even in these, I find signs of the Time Spirit, which is moving the heart of the West. Although the present form is unacceptable, yet there is revealed an aspiration, which is towards the truth, and this aspiration must not be condemned. In this morning of the world's awakening, if in only our own national striving there is no response to its universal aspiration, that will betoken the poverty of our spirit. I do not say for a moment that we should belittle the work immediately to hand. But when the bird is roused by the dawn, all its awakening is not absorbed in its search for food. Its wings respond unweariedly to the call of the sky, its throat pours forth songs for joy of the new light. Universal humanity has sent us its call to-day. Let our mind respond in its own language; for response is the only true sign of life. When of old we were immersed in the politics of dependence on others, our chief business was the compilation of others' shortcomings. Now that we have decided to dissociate our politics from dependence, are we still to establish and maintain it on the same recital of others' sins? The state of mind so engendered will only raise the dust of angry passion, obscuring the greater world from our vision, and urge us more and more to take futile short cuts for the satisfaction of our passions. It is a sorry picture of India, which we shall display if we fail to realize for ourselves the greater India. This picture will have no light. It will have in the foreground only the business side of our aspiration. Mere business talent, however, has never created anything.

In the West, a real anxiety and effort of their higher mind to rise superior to business considerations, is beginning to be seen. I have come across many there whom this desire has imbued with the true spirit of the *sannyasin*, making them renounce their home-world in order to achieve the unity of man, by destroying the bondage of nationalism; men who have within their own soul realized the *Advaita* of humanity. Many such have I seen in England who have accepted persecution and contumely from their fellow-countrymen in their struggles to free other peoples from the oppression of their own country's pride of power. Some of them are amongst us here in India. I have seen *sannyasins* too in France—Romain Rolland for one, who is an outcast from his own people. I have also seen them in the minor countries of Europe. I have watched the faces of European students all aglow with the hope of a united mankind, prepared manfully to bear all the blows, cheerfully to submit to all the insults, of the present age for the glory of the age to come. And are we alone to be content with proceeding with the erection of Swaraj on a foundation of telling the beads of negation, harping on others' faults and quarrelsomeness? Shall it not be our first duty in the dawn to remember Him, who is One, who is without distinction of class or colour, and who with his varied *shakti* makes true provision for the inherent need of each and every class; and to pray to the Giver of Wisdom to unite us all in right understanding—

> *Yo ekōvarno vahudhā shakti yōgāt*
> *Varnānanekān nihitārthodadhāti*
> *Vichaiti chānte vishwamādau*
> *Sa no buddhyā subhayā samyunaktu!*

A REPLY TO TAGORE

The Poet of Asia, as Lord Hardinge called Dr Tagore, is fast becoming, if he has not already become, the Poet of the world. Increasing prestige has brought to him increasing responsibility. His greatest service to India must be his poetic interpretation of India's message to the world. The Poet is therefore sincerely anxious that India should deliver no false or feeble message in her name. He is naturally jealous of his country's reputation. He says he has striven hard to find himself in tune with the present movement. He confesses that he is baffled. He can find nothing for his lyre in the din and the bustle of non-co-operation. In three forceful letters, he has endeavoured to give expression to his misgivings, and he has come to the conclusion that non-co-operation is not dignified enough for the India of his vision, that it is a doctrine of negation and despair. He fears that it is a doctrine of separation, exclusiveness, narrowness and negation.

No Indian can feel anything but pride in the Poet's exquisite jealousy of India's honour. It is good that he should have sent to us his misgivings in language at once beautiful and clear.

In all humility, I shall endeavour to answer the Poet's doubts. I may fail to convince him or the reader who may have been touched by his eloquence, but I would like to assure him and India that non-co-operation in conception is not any of the things he fears, and he need have no cause to be ashamed of his country for having adopted non-co-operation. If, in actual application, it appears in the end to have failed, it will be no more the fault of the doctrine, than it would be of Truth, if those who claim to apply it in practice do not appear to succeed. Non-co-operation may have come in advance of its time. India and the world must then wait, but there is no choice for India save between violence and non-co-operation.

Nor need the Poet fear that non-co-operation is intended to erect a Chinese wall between India and the West. On the contrary, non-co-operation is intended to pave the way to real, honourable and voluntary co-operation based on mutual respect and trust. The present struggle is being waged against compulsory co-operation, against one-sided combination, against the armed imposition of modern methods of exploitation masquerading under the name of civilization.

Non-co-operation is a protest against an unwitting and unwilling participation in evil.

The Poet's concern is largely about the students. He is of

opinion that they should not have been called upon to give up Government schools before they had other schools to go to. Here I must differ from him. I have never been able to make a fetish of literary training. My experience has proved to my satisfaction that literary training by itself adds not an inch to one's moral height and that character-building is independent of literary training. I am firmly of opinion that the Government schools have unmanned us, rendered us helpless and Godless. They have filled us with discontent, and providing no remedy for the discontent, have made us despondent. They have made us what we were intended to become—clerks and interpreters. A government builds its prestige upon the apparently voluntary association of the governed. And if it was wrong to co-operate with the Government in keeping us slaves, we were bound to begin with those institutions in which our association appeared to be most voluntary. The youth of a nation are its hope. I hold that, as soon as we discovered that the system of government was wholly, or mainly evil, it became sinful for us to associate our children with it.

It is no argument against the soundness of the proposition laid down by me that the vast majority of the students went back after the first flush of enthusiasm. Their recantation is proof rather of the extent of our degradation than of the wrongness of the step. Experience has shown that the establishment of national schools has not resulted in drawing many more students. The strongest and the truest of them came out without any national schools to fall back upon, and I am convinced that these first withdrawals are rendering service of the highest order.

But the Poet's protest against the calling out of the boys is really a corollary to his objection to the very doctrine of non-co-operation. He has a horror of everything negative. His whole soul seems to rebel against the negative commandments of religion. I must give his objection in his own inimitable language. 'R. in support of the present movement has often said to me that passion for rejection is a stronger power in the beginning than the acceptance of an ideal. Though I know it to be a fact, I cannot take it as a truth. . . . Brahmavidya in India has for its object *mukti* (emancipation), while Buddhism has *nirvana* (extinction). *Mukti* draws our attention to the positive and *nirvana* to the negative side of truth. Therefore, he emphasized the fact of *duhkha* (misery) which has to be avoided and the Brahmavidya emphasized the fact of *ananda* (joy) which had to be attained.' In these and kindred passages, the reader will find the key to the Poet's mentality. In my humble opinion, rejection is as much an ideal as the acceptance of a thing. It is as necessary to reject untruth as it is to accept truth. All religions teach that two opposite forces act upon us and that the human endeavour consists in a series of eternal rejections and acceptances. Non-co-operation with evil is as much a duty as co-operation with good. I venture to suggest that the Poet has done an unconscious injustice to Buddhism in describing *nirvana* as merely a negative state. I make bold to say that *mukti* (emancipation) is as much a negative state as *nirvana*. Emancipation from or extinction of the bondage of the flesh leads to *ananda* (eternal bliss). Let me close this part of my argument by drawing attention to the fact that the final word of the Upanishads (Brahmavidya) is Not. Neti[2] was the best description the authors of the Upanishads were able to find for Brahman.

Correspondents have written to me in pathetic language asking me not to commit suicide in January, should Swaraj be not attained by then, and should I find myself outside the prison walls. I find that language but inadequately expresses one's thought, especially when the thought itself is confused or incomplete. My writing in the Navajivan was, I fancied, clear enough. But I observe that its translation has been misunderstood by many. The original too has not escaped the tragedy that has overtaken the translation.

One great reason for the misunderstanding lies in my being considered almost a perfect man. Friends who know my partiality for the Bhagavad Gita have thrown relevant verses at me, and show how my threat to commit suicide contradicts the teachings which I am attempting to live. All these mentors of mine seem to forget that I am but a seeker after Truth. I claim to have found the way to it. I claim to be making a ceaseless effort to find it. But I admit that I have not yet found it. To find Truth completely is to realize oneself and one's destiny, i.e. to become perfect. I am painfully conscious of my imperfections, and therein lies all the strength I possess, because it is a rare thing for

2. Meaning : 'Not This.'

a man to know his own limitations.

If I was a perfect man, I own I should not feel the miseries of my neighbours as I do. As a perfect man, I should take note of them, prescribe a remedy and compel adoption by the force of unchallengeable Truth in me. But as yet, I only see as through a glass darkly and, therefore, have to carry conviction by slow and laborious processes, and then too, not always with success. That being so, I would be less than human if, with all my knowledge of avoidable misery pervading the land and of the sight of mere skeletons under the very shadow of the Lord of the Universe, I did not feel with and for all the suffering but dumb millions of India. The hope of a steady decline in that misery sustains me; but suppose that, with all my sensitiveness to sufferings, to pleasure and pain, cold and heat, and with all my endeavour to carry the healing message of the spinning wheel to the heart, I have reached only the ear and never pierced the heart, suppose further that at the end of the year I find that the people are as sceptical as they are to-day about the present possibility of attainment of Swaraj by means of the peaceful revolution of the wheel. Suppose further, that I find that the excitement during the past twelve months and more has been only an excitement and a stimulation, but no settled belief in the programme, and lastly suppose that the message of peace has not penetrated the hearts of Englishmen, should I not doubt my tapasya and feel my unworthiness for leading the struggle? As a true man, what should I do? Should I not kneel down in all humility before my Maker, and ask Him to take away this useless body and make me a fitter instrument of service?

Swaraj does consist in the change of government and its real control by the people, but that would be merely the form. The substance that I am hankering after is a definite acceptance of the means and, therefore, a real change of heart on the part of the people. I am certain that it does not require ages for Hindus to discard the error of untouchability, for Hindus and Mussulmans to shed enmity and accept heart friendship as an eternal factor of national life, for all to adopt the *charkha* as the only universal means of attaining India's economic salvation and finally for all to believe that India's freedom lies only through non-violence, and no other method. Definite, intelligent and free adoption by the nation of this programme, I hold, as the attainment of the substance. The symbol, the transfer of power, is sure to follow, even as the seed truly laid must develop into a tree.

The reader will thus perceive that, what I accidentally stated to friends for the first time in Poona and then repeated to others, was but a confession of my imperfections and an expression of my feeling of unworthiness for the great cause which, for the time being, I seem to be leading. I have enunciated no doctrine of despair. On the contrary, I have never felt so sanguine, as I do at the time of writing, that we shall gain the substance during this year. I have stated at the same time as a practical idealist that I should no more feel worthy to lead a cause which I might feel myself diffident of handling. The doctrine of labouring without attachment means as much a relentless pursuit of truth as a retracing after discovery of error and a renunciation of leadership without a pang after discovery of unworthiness. I have but shadowed forth my intense longing to lose myself in the Eternal and become merely a lump of clay in the Potter's divine hands, so that my service may become more certain, because uninterrupted by the baser self in me.

POLITICS AND RELIGION

The politician in me has never dominated a single decision of mine, and if I seem to take part in politics, it is only because politics encircle us to-day like the coil of a snake from which one cannot get out, no matter how much one tries. I wish therefore to wrestle with the snake, as I have been doing with more or less success consciously since 1894, unconsciously, as I have now discovered, ever since reaching years of discretion. Quite selfishly, as I wish to live in peace in the midst of a bellowing storm howling round me, I have been experimenting with myself and my friends by introducing religion into politics. Let me explain what I mean by religion. It is not the Hindu religion which I certainly prize above all other religions, but the religion which transcends Hinduism, which changes one's very nature, which binds one indissolubly to the truth within and which ever purifies. It is the permanent element in human nature which counts no cost too great in order to find full expression and which leaves the soul utterly restless until it has found itself, known its Maker and appreciated the true correspondence between the Maker and itself.[8]

What was the larger 'symbiosis' that Buddha and Christ preached? Buddha fearlessly carried the war into the enemy's camp and brought down on its knees an arrogant priesthood. Christ drove out the money-changers from the temple of Jerusalem and drew down curses from Heaven upon the hypocrites and the pharisees. Both were for intensely direct action. But even as Buddha and Christ chastised, they showed unmistakable gentleness and love behind every act of theirs. They would not raise a finger against their enemies, but would gladly surrender themselves rather than the truth for which they lived. Buddha would have died resisting the priesthood, if the majesty of his love had not proved to be equal to the task of bending the priesthood. Christ died on the cross with a crown of thorns on his head defying the might of a whole empire. And if I raise resistances of a non-violent character, I simply and humbly follow in the footsteps of the great teachers.

Lastly, the writer of the paragraph quarrels with my 'grouping unities' and would have me to take up 'the larger mission of uniting the world'. I once told him under a common roof that I was probably more cosmopolitan than he. I abide by that expression. Unless I group unities, I shall never be able to unite the whole world. Tolstoy once said that, if we would but get off the backs of our neighbours, the world would be quite all right without any further help from us. And if we can only serve our immediate neighbours by ceasing to prey upon them, the circle of unities thus grouped in the right fashion will ever grow in circumference till at last it is conterminous with that of the whole world. More than that it is not given to any man to try or achieve. *Yatthaa pindé thatthaa brahmandé* is as true to-day as ages ago when it was first uttered by an unknown Rishi.

3. Extract from *Young India*, Vol. II.

ADVICE TO SATYAGRAHIS IN AN INDUSTRIAL STRIKE

I do not propose to examine the duty of the capitalist. If the labourer alone were to understand his rights and responsibilities and confine himself to the purest means, both must gain. But two things are needful—both the demands and the means adopted to enforce them must be just and clear. It is an unlawful demand which seeks merely to take advantage of the capitalists' position. But it is an altogether lawful demand when the labourer asks for enough wages to enable him to maintain himself and to educate his children decently. To seek justice without resorting to violence and by an appeal to the good sense of the capitalist by arbitration is lawful means.

In order to achieve the end, you must have Unions. A beginning has already been made. I trust that the mill-hands in every department will form their unions and every one should scrupulously observe the rules that may be formed for them. You will then approach the mill-owners through your unions, and if the decisions of the former do not satisfy you, you will appeal to arbitration. It is a matter of satisfaction that both parties have accepted the principle of arbitration. I hope that that principle will be fully developed and that strikes will for ever become an impossibility. I know that strikes are an inherent right of the working men for the purpose of securing justice, but they must be considered a crime immediately the capitalists accept the principle of arbitration. Ways are improving and there is every possibility of a continuous improvement. But there is equal need for reducing hours of labour. The mill-hands seem to be working twelve hours or more.

The mill-owners tell me that the mill-hands are lazy, they do not give full time to their work and they are inattentive. I for one cannot expect attention and application from those who are called upon to work twelve hours per day. But I would certainly hope that when the hours are reduced to ten the labourers will put in better and almost the same amount of work as in twelve hours. Reduction in hours of labour has brought about happy results in England. When mill-hands learn to identify themselves with the interest of the mill-owners, they will rise and with them will rise the industries of our country. I would therefore urge the mill-owners to reduce the hours of labour to ten and urge the mill-hands to give as much work in ten, as they have been doing in twelve.

It is now time to examine the use we should make of the increasing wages and the hours saved. It would be like going into the frying-pan out of the fire to use the increase in wages in the grog-shop and the hours saved from the gambling den. The money received, it is clear, should be devoted to education of our children, and the time saved to our education. In both these matters the mill-owners can render much assistance. They can open cheap restaurants for the working men where they can get pure milk and wholesome refreshments. They can open reading-rooms and provide harmless amusements and games for them. Provided such healthy surroundings, the cravings for drink and gambling will leave them. The unions also should attempt similar things. They will be better employed in devising means of improvement from within than in fighting the capitalists.

It is a sign of national degradation when little children are removed from schools and are employed in earning wages. No nation worthy of the name can possibly afford so to misuse her children. At least up to the age of sixteen they must be kept in schools. Similarly women also must be gradually weaned from mill labour. If man and woman are partners in life and complementary each of the other, they become good householders only by dividing their labour, and a wise mother finds her time fully occupied in looking after her household and children. But where both husband and wife have to labour for mere maintenance, the nation must become degraded. It is like a bankrupt living on his capital.

And just as it is necessary for the labourers to develop their minds by receiving education and to educate their children, so it is necessary to develop the moral faculty in them. Development of the moral faculty means that of the religious sense. The world does not quarrel with those who have a true faith in God and who understand the true nature of religion. And if it does, such men turn away the wrath of their adversaries by their gentleness. Religion here does not mean merely offering one's *namaz* or going to the temple. But it means knowledge of one's self and knowledge of God, and just as a person does not become a weaver unless he knows the art of weaving so does he fail to know himself unless he complies with certain rules. Chief among these are three that are of universal observance. The first is observance of Truth. He who does not know what it is to speak the truth is like a false coin, valueless. The second is not to injure others. He who injures others, is jealous of others, is not fit to live in the world. For the world is at war with him, and he has to live in perpetual fear of the world. We all are bound by the tie of love. There is in everything a centripetal force without which nothing could have existed. Scientists tell us that without the presence of the cohesive force amongst the atoms that comprise this globe of ours, it would crumble to pieces and we would cease to exist, and even as there is cohesive force in blind matter, so much must there be in all things animate and the name for that cohesive force among animate beings is Love. We notice it between father and son, between brother and sister, friend and friend. But we have to learn to use that force among all that lives, and in the use of it consists our knowledge of God. Where there is love there is life; hatred leads to destruction.

SELF-RESTRAINT AND SELF-INDULGENCE

The third rule is that we have to conquer our passions. It is called Brahmacharya in Sanskrit. I do not use it here merely in its accepted narrow sense. He is not a Brahmachari, who, although he may be a celibate or may be living a chaste life as a married man, otherwise gives himself up to a variety of indulgences. He alone is capable of knowing himself who brings under complete subjection all his passions. He who exercises self-restraint in its widest sense is also a Brahmachari—a man of faith, a true Hindu or a true Mohammedan.

It is a breach of Brahmacharya to hear questionable language or obscene songs. It is licentiousness of the tongue to utter foul abuse, instead of reciting the name of God, and so with the other senses. He alone can be considered the true man who having subjected his passions becomes perfectly self-restrained. We are like a rider who cannot keep his horse under control and is quickly brought down. But one who, drawing in the reins keeps the animal under subjection, stands a fair chance of reaching his destination. Even so does a man who can control his passions make for the goal. He alone is fit for swarajya. He alone is a seeker after truth. He alone becomes capable of knowing God. It is my earnest wish that you will not reject these remarks as if they were copybook maxims. I ask you to believe that we shall never go forward until we have learnt the value of observing these truths. What I have told you is a fragment of my own experiences. My service of you is due simply to my love for you and I partake of your sorrows, because I hope thereby to justify myself before my Maker. What though your wages were quadrupled and you had to work only a quarter of the time you are doing now, if notwithstanding, you did not know the value of true speech, if Rakshasa in you injured others and gave the reins to your passions. We must have more wages, we must have less work, because we want clean houses, clean bodies, clean minds and a clean soul, and we strive for better wages and less work in the belief that both are essential for this fourfold cleanliness. But if that be not the object to be achieved, it would be a sin to attempt to get better wages and reduce the hours of labour.

A LETTER TO THE VICEROY,
INAUGURATING THE
NON-CO-OPERATION MOVEMENT

It is not without a pang that I return the Kaisar-i-Hind gold medal granted to me by your predecessor for my humanitarian work in South Africa, the Zulu War medal granted in South Africa for my services as officer in charge of the Indian Volunteer Ambulance Corps in 1906 and the Boer War medal for my services as assistant superintendent of the Indian Volunteer Stretcher-bearer Corps during the Boer War of 1899-1902. I venture to return these medals in pursuance of the scheme of non-co-operation inaugurated to-day in connection with the Khilafat movement. Valuable as these honours have been to me, I cannot wear them with an easy conscience so long as my Mussulman countrymen have to labour under a wrong done to their religious sentiment. Events that have happened during the past month have confirmed me in the opinion that the Imperial Government have acted in the Khilafat matter in an unscrupulous, immoral and unjust manner and have been moving from wrong to wrong in order to defend their immorality. I can retain neither respect nor affection for such a government.

The attitude of the Imperial and Your Excellency's Governments on the Punjab question has given me additional cause for grave dissatisfaction. I had the honour, as Your Excellency is aware, as one of the congress commissioners, to investigate the causes of the disorders in the Punjab during the April of 1919. And it is my deliberate conviction that Sir Michael O'Dwyer was totally unfit to hold the office of Lieutenant-Governor of Punjab and that his policy was primarily responsible for infuriating the mob at Amritsar. No doubt the mob excesses were unpardonable; incendiarism, murder of five innocent Englishmen and the cowardly assault on Miss Sherwood were most deplorable and uncalled for. But the punitive measures taken by General Dyer, Colonel Frank Johnson, Colonel O'Brien, Mr Bosworth Smith, Rai Shri Ram Sud, Mr Mallik Khan and other officers were out of all proportion to the crime of the people and amounted to wanton cruelty and inhumanity almost unparalleled in modern times. Your Excellency's light-hearted treatment of the official crime, your exoneration of Sir Michael O'Dwyer, Mr Montagu's dispatch and above all the shameful ignorance of the Punjab events and callous disregard of the feelings of Indians betrayed by the House of Lords, have filled me with the gravest misgivings regarding the future of the Empire, have estranged me completely from the present Government and have disabled me from tendering, as I have hitherto whole-heartedly tendered, my loyal co-operation.

In my humble opinion the ordinary method of agitating by way of petitions, deputations and the like is no remedy for moving to repentance a government so hopelessly indifferent to the welfare of its charge as the Government of India has proved to be. In European countries, condonation of such grievous wrongs as the Khilafat and the Punjab would have resulted in a bloody revolution by the people. They would have resisted at all cost national emasculation such as the said wrongs imply. But half of India is too weak to offer violent resistance and the other half is unwilling to do so. I have therefore ventured to suggest the remedy of non-co-operation which enables those who wish, to dissociate themselves from the Government and which, if it is unattended by violence and undertaken in an ordered manner, must compel it to retrace its steps and undo the wrongs committed. But while I shall pursue the policy of non-co-operation in so far as I can carry the people with me, I shall not lose hope that you will yet see your way to do justice. I therefore respectfully ask Your Excellency to summon a conference of the recognized leaders of the people and in consultation with them find a way that would placate the Mussulmans and do reparation to the unhappy Punjab.

AN APPEAL TO HIS FOLLOWERS

No country has ever risen without being purified through the fire of suffering. Mother suffers so that her child may live. The condition of wheat-growing is that the seed grain should perish. Life comes out of death. Will India rise out of her slavery without fulfilling this eternal law of purification through suffering?

If my advisers are right, evidently India will realize her destiny without travail. For their chief concern is that the events of April 1919 should not be repeated. They fear non-co-operation, because it would involve the sufferings of many. If Hampden had argued thus, he would not have withheld payment of ship-money, nor would Wat Tyler have raised the standard of revolt. English and French histories are replete with instances of men continuing their pursuit of the right, irrespective of the amount of suffering involved. The actors did not stop to think whether ignorant people would not have involuntarily to suffer. Why should we expect to write our history differently? It is possible for us, if we would, to learn from the mistakes of our predecessors to do better, but it is impossible to do away with the law of suffering which is the one indispensable condition of our being. The way to do better is to avoid, if we can, violence from our side and thus quicken the rate of progress and to introduce greater purity in the methods of suffering. We can, if we will, refrain, in our impatience, from bending the wrong-doer to our will by physical force as Sinn Feiners are doing to-day, or from coercing our neighbours to follow our methods, as was done last year by some of us in bringing about hartal. Progress is to be measured by the amount of suffering undergone by the sufferer. The purer the suffering, the greater is the progress. Hence did the sacrifice of Jesus suffice to free a sorrowing world. In his onward march, he did not count the cost of suffering, entailed upon his neighbours, whether it was undergone by them voluntarily or otherwise. Thus did the sufferings of a Harischandra suffice to re-establish the kingdom of truth. He must have known that his subjects would suffer involuntarily by his abdication. He did not mind, because he could not do otherwise than follow truth.

I have already stated that I do not deplore the massacre of Jallianwala Bagh so much as I deplore the murders of Englishmen and destruction of property by ourselves. The frightfulness at Amritsar drew away public attention from greater, though slower, frightfulness at Lahore where attempt was made to emasculate the inhabitants by slow processes. But before we rise higher, we shall have to undergo such processes many more times, till they teach us to take up suffering voluntarily and to find joy in it. I am convinced that the Lahorians never deserved the cruel insults that they were subjected to; they never hurt a single Englishman; they never destroyed any property. But a wilful ruler was determined to crush the spirit of a people just trying to throw off his chafing yoke. And if I am told that all this was due to my preaching *satyagraha*, my answer is that I would preach *satyagraha* all the more forcibly for that, so long as I have breath left in me, and tell the people that next time they would answer O'Dwyerean insolence, not by opening shops by reason of threats of forcible sales, but by allowing the tyrant to do his worst and let him sell their all but their unconquerable souls. Sages of old mortified the flesh, so that the spirit within might be set free, so that their trained bodies might be proof against any injury that might be inflicted on them by tyrants seeking to impose their will on them. And if India wishes to revise her ancient wisdom and to avoid the errors of Europe, if India wishes to see the Kingdom of God established on earth, instead of that of Satan which has enveloped Europe, then I would urge her sons and daughters not to be deceived by fine phrases, the terrible subtleties that hedge us in, the fears of suffering that India may have to undergo, but to see what is happening to-day in Europe, and from it understand that we must go through the suffering even as Europe has gone through, but not the process of making others suffer. Germany wanted to dominate Europe and the Allies wanted to do likewise by crushing Germany. Europe is no better for Germany's fall. The Allies have proved themselves to be just as deceitful, cruel, greedy and selfish as Germany was or would have been. Germany would have avoided the sanctimonious humbug that one sees associated with the many dealings of the Allies.

The miscalculation that I deplored last year was not in connection with the sufferings imposed upon the people, but about the mistakes made by them and violence done by them, owing to their not having sufficiently understood the message of *satyagraha*. What, then, is the meaning of non-co-operation in terms of the Law of Suffering? We must voluntarily put up with the losses and inconveniences that arise from having to withdraw our support from a government that is ruling against our will. Possession of power and riches is a crime under an unjust government, poverty in that case is a virtue, says Thoreau. It may be that, in the transition state, we may make mistakes; there may be avoidable suffering. These things are preferable to national emasculation.

We must refuse to wait for the wrong to be righted till the wrong-doer has been roused to a sense of his iniquity. We must not, for fear of ourselves or others having to suffer, remain participators in it. But we must combat the wrong by ceasing to assist the wrong-doer directly or indirectly.

If a father does an injustice, it is the duty of his children to leave the parental roof. If the headmaster of a school conducts his institution on an immoral basis, the pupils must leave the school. If the chairman of a corporation is corrupt, the members thereof must wash their hands clean of his corruption by withdrawing from it; even so, if a government does a grave injustice, the subject must withdraw co-operation wholly or partially, sufficiently to wean the ruler from his wickedness. In each of the cases conceived by me, there is an element of suffering whether mental or physical. Without such suffering it is not possible to attain freedom.[4]

I still believe that man not having been given the power of creation does not possess the right of destroying the meanest creature that lives. The prerogative of destruction belongs solely to the creator of all that lives. I accept the interpretation of *ahimsa*, namely, that it is not merely a negative state of harmlessness but it is a positive state of love, of doing good even to the evil-doer. But it does not mean helping the evil-doer to continue the wrong or tolerating it by passive acquiescence. On the contrary, love, the active state of *ahimsa*, requires you to resist the wrong-doer by dissociating yourself from him even though it may offend him or injure him physically. Thus if my son lives a life of shame, I may not help him to do so by continuing to support him; on the contrary, my love for him requires me to withdraw all support from him although it may mean even his death. And the same love imposes on me the obligation of welcoming him to my bosom when he repents. But I may not by physical force compel my son to become good. That, in my opinion, is the moral of the story of the Prodigal Son.

Non-co-operation is not a passive state, it is an intensely active state—more active than physical resistance or violence. Passive resistance is a misnomer. Non-co-operation in the sense used by me must be non-violent and therefore neither punitive nor vindictive nor based on malice, ill-will or hatred. It follows therefore that it would be sin for me to serve General Dyer and co-operate with him to shoot innocent men. But it would be an exercise of forgiveness or love for me to nurse him back to life, if he was suffering from a physical malady. I would co-operate a thousand times with this Government to wean it from its career of crime, but I will not for a single moment co-operate with it to continue that career. And I would be guilty of wrong-doing if I retained a title from it or 'a service under it or supported its law courts or schools'. Better for me a beggar's bowl than the richest possession from hands stained with the blood of the innocents of Jallianwala. Better by far a warrant or imprisonment than honeyed words from

4. *Young India*, Vol. II.

those who have wantonly wounded the religious sentiment of my seventy million brothers.

I do not believe that the Gita teaches violence for doing good. It is pre-eminently a description of the duel that goes on in our own hearts. The divine author has used a historical incident for inculcating the lesson of doing one's duty even at the peril of one's life. It inculcates performance of duty irrespective of the consequences, for, we mortals, limited by our physical frames, are incapable of controlling actions save our own. The Gita distinguishes between the powers of light and darkness and demonstrates their incompatibility.

Jesus, in my humble opinion, was a prince among politicians. He did render unto Caesar that which was Caesar's. He gave the devil his due. He ever shunned him and is reported never once to have yielded to his incantations. The politics of his time consisted in securing the welfare of the people by teaching them not to be seduced by the trinkets of the priests and the Pharisees. The latter then controlled and moulded the life of the people. To-day the system of government is so devised as to affect every department of our life. It threatens our very existence. If therefore we want to conserve the welfare of the nation, we must religiously interest ourselves in the doings of the governors and exert a moral influence on them by insisting on their obeying the laws of morality. General Dyer did produce a 'moral effect' by an act of butchery. Those who are engaged in forwarding the movement of non-co-operation, hope to produce a moral effect by a process of self-denial, self-sacrifice and self-purification.[5]

THE SWADESHI MOVEMENT

After much thinking, I have arrived at a definition of Swadeshi that perhaps best illustrates my meaning. Swadeshi is that spirit in us which restricts us to the use and service of our immediate surroundings to the exclusion of the more remote. Thus, as for religion, in order to satisfy the requirements of the definition, I must restrict myself to my ancestral religion. That is the use of my immediate religious surrounding. If I find it defective, I should serve it by purging it of its defects. In the domain of politics I should

5. *Idem.*

make use of the indigenous institutions and serve them by curing them of their proved defects. In that of economics I should use only things that are produced by my immediate neighbours and serve those industries by making them efficient and complete where they might be found wanting. It is suggested that such Swadeshi, if reduced to practice, will lead to the millennium. And as we do not abandon our pursuits after the millennium, because we do not expect quite to reach it within our times, so may we not abandon Swadeshi, even though it may not be fully attained for generations to come.

Let us briefly examine the three branches of Swadeshi as sketched above. Hinduism has become a conservative religion and therefore a mighty force, because of the Swadeshi spirit underlying it. It is the most tolerant because it is non-proselytizing, and it is as capable of expansion to-day as it has been found to be in the past. It has succeeded, not in driving out, as I think it has been erroneously held, but in absorbing Buddhism. By reason of the Swadeshi spirit, a Hindu refuses to change his religion, not necessarily because he considers it to be the best, but because he knows that he can complement it by introducing reforms. And what I have said about Hinduism is, I suppose, true of other great faiths of the world, only it is held that it is specially so in the case of Hinduism. But here comes the point I am labouring to reach. If there is any substance in what I have said, will not the great missionary bodies of India, to whom we owe a deep debt of gratitude for what they have done and are doing, do still better and serve the spirit of Christianity better by dropping the goal of proselytizing, while continuing their philanthropic work? I hope you will not consider this to be an impertinence on my part. I make the suggestion in all sincerity and with due humility. Moreover I have some claim upon your attention. I have endeavoured to study the Bible. I consider it as part of my scriptures. The spirit of the Sermon on the Mount competes almost on equal terms with the Bhagavad Gita for the domination of my heart. I yield to no Christian in the strength of devotion with which I sing 'Lead kindly Light' and several other inspired hymns of a similar nature. I have come under the influence of noted Christian missionaries belonging to different denominations, and I enjoy to this day the privilege of friendship with some of them.

You will perhaps, therefore, allow that I have offered the above suggestion not as a biased Hindu, but as a humble and impartial student of religion with great leanings towards Christianity. May it not be that the 'Go ye unto all the world' message has been somewhat narrowly interpreted and the spirit of it missed? It will not be denied, I speak from experience, that many of the conversions are only so-called. In some cases the appeal has gone not to the heart but to the stomach. And in every case a conversion leaves a sore behind it which, I venture to think, is avoidable. Quoting again from experience, a new birth, a change of heart, is perfectly possible in every one of the great faiths. I know I am now treading upon thin ice. But I do not apologize, in closing this part of my subject, for saying that the frightful outrage that is just going on in Europe, perhaps shows that the message of Jesus of Nazareth the Son of Peace, has been little understood in Europe and that light upon it may have to be thrown from the East.

I have sought your help in religious matters, which it is yours to give in a special sense. But I make bold to seek it even in political matters. I do not believe that religion has nothing to do with politics. The latter divorced from religion is like a corpse only fit to be buried. As a matter of fact, in your own silent manner you influence politics not a little. And I feel that if the attempt to separate politics from religon had not been made as it is even now made, they would not have degenerated as they often appear to have done. No one considers that the political life of the country is in a happy state. Following out the Swadeshi spirit, I observe the indigenous institutions and the village panchayat hold me. India is really a republican country, and it is because it is that that it has survived every shock hitherto delivered. Princes and potentates whether they were Indian born or foreigners have hardly touched the vast masses except for collecting revenue. The latter in their turn seem to have rendered unto Caesar what was Caesar's, and for the rest have done much as they have liked. The vast organization of caste answered not only the religious wants of the community, but it answered to its political needs. The villagers managed their internal affairs through the caste system, and through it they dealt with any oppression from the ruling power or powers. It is not possible to deny of a nation that was capable of producing the caste system its wonderful power of organization. One had but to attend the great Kumbha Mela at Hardwar last year to know how skilful that organization must have been, which without any seeming effort was able effectively to cater for more than a million pilgrims. Yet it is the fashion to say that we lack organizing ability. This is true, I fear, to a certain extent, of those who have been nurtured in the new traditions. We have laboured under a terrible handicap owing to an almost fatal departure from the Swadeshi spirit. We, the educated classes have received our education through a foreign tongue. We have therefore not reacted upon the masses. We want to represent the masses, but we fail. They recognize us not much more than they recognize the English officers. Their hearts are an open book to neither. Their aspirations are not ours. Hence there is a break. And you witness, not in reality, failure to organize but want of correspondence between the representatives and represented. If during the last fifty years had we been educated through the vernaculars, our elders and our servants and our neighbours would have partaken of our knowledge; the discoveries of a Bose or a Ray would have been household treasures as are the Ramayan and Mahabharat. As it is, so far as the masses are concerned, those great discoveries might as well have been made by foreigners. Had instruction in all the branches of learning been given through the vernaculars, I make bold to say that they would have been enriched wonderfully. The question of village sanitation, etc., would have been solved long ago. The village panchayats would be now a living force in a special way, and India would almost be enjoying self-government suited to its requirements and would have been spared the humiliating spectacle of organized assassination on its sacred soil. It is not too late to mend. And you can help if you will, as no other body or bodies can.

And now for the last division of Swadeshi. Much of the deep poverty of the masses is due to the ruinous departure from Swadeshi in the economic and industrial life. If not an article of commerce had been brought from outside India, she would be to-day a land flowing with milk and honey. But that was not to be. We were greedy and so was England. The connection between England and India was based clearly upon an error. But she (England) does not remain in India in error. It is her declared policy that India is to be held in trust for her people. If this be true, Lancashire must stand aside. And if the Swadeshi doctrine is a sound doctrine, Lancashire can stand aside without hurt, though it may sustain a shock for the time being. I think of Swadeshi not as a boycott movement undertaken by way of revenge. I conceive it as a religious principle to be followed by all. I am no economist, but I have read some treatises which show that England could easily become a self-sustained country, growing all the produce she needs. This may be an utterly ridiculous proposition, and perhaps the best proof that it cannot be true is that England is one of the largest importers in the world. But India cannot live for Lancashire or any other country before she is able to live for herself. And she can live for herself only if she produces and is helped to produce everything for her requirements, within her own borders. She need not be, she ought not to be drawn into the vortex of mad and ruinous competition which breeds fratricide, jealousy and many other evils. But who is to stop her great millionaires from entering on to the world competition? Certainly not legislation. Force of public opinion, proper education, however, can do a great deal in the desired direction. The hand-loom industry is in a dying condition. I took special care during my wanderings last year to see as many weavers as possible, and my heart ached to find how much they had lost, how families had retired from this once flourishing and honourable occupation. If we follow the Swadeshi doctrine, it would be your duty and mine to find out neighbours who can supply our wants and teach them to supply them where they do not know how to proceed, assuming that there are neighbours who are in want of healthy occupation. Then every village of India will almost be a self-supporting and self-contained unit, exchanging only such necessary commodities with other villages where they are not locally producible. This may all sound nonsensical. Well, India is a country of nonsense. It is nonsensical to parch one's throat with thirst when a kindly Mohammedan is ready to offer pure water to drink. And yet thousands of Hindus would rather die of thirst than drink water from a Mohammedan household. These nonsensical men can also, once they are convinced that their religion demands that they should wear garments manufactured in India only and eat food only grown in India, decline to wear any other clothing or eat any other food. Lord Curzon set the fashion of tea-drinking. And that pernicious drug now bids fair to overwhelm the nation. It has already undermined the digestive apparatus of hundreds of thousands of men and women and constitutes an additional tax upon their slender purses. Lord Hardinge can set the fashion for Swadeshi, and almost the whole of India will forswear foreign goods. There is a verse in the Bhagavad Gita which, freely rendered, means masses follow the classes. It is easy to undo the evil of the thinking portion if the community were to take the Swadeshi vow, even though it may for a time cause considerable inconvenience. I hate legislative interference in any department of life. At best, it is the lesser evil. But I would tolerate, welcome, indeed plead for a stiff protective duty upon foreign goods. Natal, a British Colony, protected its sugar by taking the sugar that came from another British colony, Mauritius. England has sinned against India by forcing free trade upon her. It may have been food for her, but it has been poison for this country.

It has often been urged that India cannot adopt Swadeshi in the economic life at any rate. Those who advance this objection do not look upon Swadeshi as a rule of life. With them it is a mere patriotic effort, not to be made if it involved any self-denial. Swadeshi, as defined here, is a religious discipline to be undergone in utter disregard of the physical discomfort it may cause to individuals. Under its spell the deprivation of a pin or a needle, because these are not manufactured in India, need cause no terror. A Swadeshist will learn to do without hundreds of things which to-day he considers necessary. Moreover, those who dismiss Swadeshi from their minds by arguing the impossible forget that Swadeshi after all is a goal to be reached by steady effort. And we would be making for the goal, even if we confined Swadeshi to a given set of articles; allowing ourselves as a temporary measure to use such things as might not be procurable in the country.

There now remains for me to consider one more objection that has been raised against Swadeshi. The objectors consider it to be a most selfish doctrine without any warrant in the civilized code of morality. With them, to practise

Swadeshi is to revert to barbarism. I cannot enter into a detailed analysis of the proposition. But I would urge that Swadeshi is the only doctrine consistent with the law of humility and love. It is arrogance to think of launching out to serve the whole of India, when I am hardly able to serve even my own family. It were better to concentrate my effort upon the family, and consider that through them I was serving the whole nation, and if you will, the whole of humanity. This is humility and it is love. The motive will determine the quality of the act. I may serve my family, regardless of the sufferings I may cause to others, as if for instance, I may accept an employment which enables me to extort the money from people; I enrich myself thereby and then satisfy many unlawful demands of the family. Here I am neither serving the family nor the state. Or I may recognize that God has given me hands and feet only to work with for my sustenance and for that of those who may be dependent upon me. I would then at once simplify my life and that of those whom I can directly reach. In this instance I would have served the family without causing injury to anyone else. Supposing that everyone followed this mode of life, we should have at once an ideal state. All will not reach that state at the same time. But those of us who, realizing its truth, enforce it in practice will clearly anticipate and accelerate the coming of that happy day. Under this plan of life, in seeming to serve India to the exclusion of every other country, I do not harm any other country. My patriotism is both exclusive and inclusive. It is exclusive in the sense that in all humility I confine my attention to the land of my birth. But it is inclusive in the sense that my service is not of a competitive or antagonistic nature. *Sic utere tuo ut alienum non laedas*. It is not merely a legal maxim, but it is a grand doctrine of life. It is the way to a proper practice of *ahimsa* or love. It is for you, the custodians of a great faith, to set the fashion and show by your preaching, sanctified by practice, that patriotism based on hatred 'killeth', and that patriotism based on love 'giveth life'.

PART V

Report of the Trial of Mahatma Gandhi; a Letter to Gandhi from Prison

---

REPORT OF THE TRIAL OF MAHATMA GANDHI

At the Circuit House at Shahi Bag, the trial of Mr Gandhi and Mr Banker commenced on Saturday noon, 18th March 1922, before Mr C. N. Broomsfield, I.C.S., District and Sessions Judge of Ahmedabad.

Sir J. T. Strangman with Rao Bahadur Girdharlal conducted the prosecution, while the accused were undefended. The Judge took his seat at 12 noon, and said there was a slight mistake in the charges framed, which he corrected. The charges were then read out by the Registrar, the offence being in three articles[1] published in the *Young India* of 29th September, 15th December, of 1921 and 23rd February, 1922. The offending articles were then read out : first of them was 'Tampering with Loyalty'; the second, 'The Puzzle and Its Solution'; and the last was 'Shaking the Manes'.

The Judge said the law required that the charge should not only be read out, but explained. In this case, it would not be necessary for him to say much by way of explanation. The charge in each case was that of bringing or attempting to bring into hatred or contempt or exciting or attempting to excite disaffection towards His Majesty's Government, established by law in British India. Both the accused were charged with the three offences under Section 124A, contained in the articles read out, written by Mr Gandhi and printed by Mr Banker. The words 'hatred and contempt' were words the meaning of which was sufficiently obvious. The word 'disaffection' was defined under the section, where they were told that disaffection included

1. The complaint in respect of the earlier article, 'Disaffection, a Virtue', seems to have been dropped subsequently after inquiry by the magistrate.

disloyalty and feelings of enmity, and the word used in the section had also been interpreted by the High Court of Bombay in a reported case as meaning political alienation or discontent, a spirit of disloyalty to government or existing authority. The charges having been read out, the Judge called upon the accused to plead to the charges. He asked Mr Gandhi whether he pleaded guilty or claimed to be tried.

Mr Gandhi: I plead guilty to all the charges. I observe that the King's name has been omitted from the charge, and it has been properly omitted.

The Judge: Mr Banker, do you plead guilty, or do you claim to be tried?

Mr Banker: I plead guilty.

Sir J. T. Strangman then wanted the Judge to proceed with the trial fully, but the Judge said that from the time he knew he was going to try the case, he had thought over the question of sentence, and he was prepared to hear anything that the Counsel might have to say, or Mr Gandhi wished to say, on the sentence. He honestly did not believe that the mere recording of evidence in the trial which Counsel had called for would make no [sic] difference to them, one way or the other. He, therefore, proposed to accept the pleas.

Mr Gandhi smiled at this decision.

The Judge said nothing further remained but to pass sentence, and before doing so, he liked to hear Sir J. T. Strangman. He was entitled to base his general remarks on the charges against the accused and on their pleas.

Sir J. T. Strangman: It will be difficult to do so. I ask the court that the whole matter may be properly considered. If I stated what has happened before the committing magistrate, then I can show that there are many things which are material to the question of the sentence.

The first point, he said, he wanted to make out, was that the matter which formed the subject of the present charges formed a part of the campaign to spread disaffection openly and systematically to render government impossible and to overthrow it. The earliest article that was put in from *Young India* was dated 25th May 1921, which said that it was the duty of a non-co-operator to create disaffection towards the Government. The Counsel then read out portions of articles written by Mr Gandhi in the *Young India*.

Court said, nevertheless, it seemed to it that the court could accept plea on the materials on which the sentence had to be based.

Sir J. T. Strangman said the question of sentence was entirely for the court to decide. The court was always entitled to deal in a more general manner in regard to the question of the sentence, than the particular matter resulting in the conviction. He asked leave to refer to articles before the court, and what result might have been produced, if the trial had proceeded in order to ascertain what the facts were. He was not going into any matter which involved dispute.

The Judge said there was not the least objection.

Sir J. Strangman said he wanted to show that these articles were not isolated. They formed part of an organized campaign, but so far as *Young India* was concerned, they would show that from the year 1921. The Counsel then read out extracts from the paper, dated 8th June, on the duty of a non-co-operator, which was to preach disaffection towards the existing Government and preparing the country for civil disobedience. Then in the same number, there was an article on disobedience. Then in the same number there was an article on 'Disaffection—a virtue' or something to that effect. Then there was an article on 28th July 1921, in which it was stated that 'we have to destroy the system'. Again, on 30th September 1921, there was an article headed 'Punjab Prosecutions', where it was stated that a non-co-operator worth his name should preach disaffection. That was all so far as *Young India* was concerned. They were earlier in date than the article, 'Tampering with Loyalty', and it was referred to the Government of Bombay. Continuing, he said the accused was a man of high educational qualifications and evidently from his writings a recognized leader. The harm that was likely to be caused was considerable. They were the writings of an educated man, and not the writings of an obscure man, and the court must consider to what the results of a campaign of the nature disclosed in the writings must inevitably lead. They had examples before them in the last few months. He referred to the occurrences in Bombay last November and Chauri Chaura, leading to murder and destruction of property, involving many people in misery and misfortune. It was true that in the course of those articles they would find

REPORT OF THE TRIAL OF GANDHI

non-violence was insisted upon as an item of the campaign and as an item of the creed. But what was the use of preaching non-violence when he preached disaffection towards government or openly instigated others to overthrow it? The answer to that question appeared to him to come from Chauri Chaura, Madras and Bombay. These were circumstances which he asked the court to take into account in sentencing the accused, and it would be for the court to consider those circumstances which involve sentences of severity.

As regards the second accused, his offence was lesser. He did the publication and he did not write. His offence nevertheless was a serious one. His instructions were that he was a man of means and he asked the court to impose a substantial fine in addition to such term of imprisonment as might be inflicted. He quoted Section 10 of the Press Act as bearing on the question of fine. When making a fresh declaration, he said a deposit of Rs 1,000 to Rs 10,000 was asked in many cases.

Court: Mr Gandhi, do you wish to make a statement on the question of sentence?

Mr Gandhi: I would like to make a statement.

Court: Could you give me it in writing to put it on record?

Mr Gandhi: I shall give it as soon as I finish reading it.

Before reading his written statement, Mr Gandhi spoke a few words as introductory remarks to the whole statement. He said:

Before I read this statement, I would like to state that I entirely endorse the learned Advocate-General's remarks in connection with my humble self. I think that he was entirely fair to me in all the statements that he has made, because it is very true and I have no desire whatsoever to conceal from this court the fact that to preach disaffection towards the existing system of government has become almost a passion with me, and the learned Advocate-General is also entirely in the right when he says that my preaching of disaffection did not commence with my connection with *Young India*, but that it commenced much earlier; and in the statement that I am about to read, it will be my painful duty to admit before this court that it commenced much earlier than the period stated by the Advocate-General. It is the most painful duty with me, but I have to discharge that duty knowing the responsibility that rests upon my shoulders, and I wish to endorse all the blame that the learned Advocate-General has thrown on my shoulders in connection with the Bombay occurrences, Madras occurrences and the Chauri Chaura occurrences. Thinking over these deeply and sleeping over them night after night, it is impossible for me to dissociate myself from the diabolical crimes of Chauri Chaura or the mad outrages of Bombay. He is quite right when he says that as a man of responsibility, a man having received a fair share of education, having had a fair share of experience of this world, I should have known the consequences of every one of my acts. I knew that I was playing with fire. I ran the risk, and if I was set free, I would still do the same. I have felt it this morning that I would have failed in my duty, if I did not say what I said here just now.

I wanted to avoid violence. Non-violence is the first article of my faith. It is also the last article of my creed. But I had to make my choice. I had either to submit to a system which I considered had done an irreparable harm to my country, or incur the risk of the mad fury of my people bursting forth, when they understood the truth from my lips. I know that my people have sometimes gone mad. I am deeply sorry for it and I am therefore here to submit not to a light penalty but to the highest penalty. I do not ask for mercy. I do not plead any extenuating act. I am here, therefore, to invite and cheerfully submit to the highest penalty that can be inflicted upon me for what in law is a deliberate crime and what appears to me to be the highest duty of a citizen. The only course open to you, the Judge, is, as I am just going to say in my statement, either to resign your post, or inflict on me the severest penalty, if you believe that the system and law you are assisting to administer are good for the people. I do not expect that kind of conversion, but by the time I have finished with my statement, you will perhaps have a glimpse of what is raging within my breast to run this maddest risk which a sane man can run.

The statement was then read out.

STATEMENT

'I owe it perhaps to the Indian public and to the public in England to placate which this prosecution is mainly taken up that I should explain why from a staunch loyalist and co-operator I have become an uncompromising disaffectionist and non-co-operator. To the court too I should say why I plead guilty to the charge of promoting disaffection towards the Government established by law in India.

'My public life began in 1893 in South Africa, in troubled weather. My first contact with British authority in that country was not of a happy character. I discovered that as a man and an Indian I had no rights. More correctly, I discovered that I had no rights as a man, because I was an Indian.

'But I was not baffled. I thought that this treatment of Indians was an excrescence upon a system that was intrinsically and mainly good. I gave the Government my voluntary and hearty co-operation, criticizing it freely where I felt it was faulty but never wishing its destruction.

'Consequently when the existence of the Empire was threatened in 1899 by the Boer challenge, I offered my services to it, raised a volunteer ambulance corps and served at several actions that took place for the relief of Ladysmith. Similarly in 1906, at the time of the Zulu revolt, I raised a stretcher-bearer party and served till the end of the "rebellion". On both these occasions I received medals and was even mentioned in dispatches. For my work in South Africa I was given by Lord Hardinge a Kaisar-i-Hind gold medal. When the war broke out in 1914 between England and Germany, I raised a volunteer ambulance corps in London consisting of the then resident Indians in London, chiefly students. Its work was acknowledged by the authorities to be valuable. Lastly, in India, when a special appeal was made at the War Conference in Delhi in 1918 by Lord Chelmsford for recruits, I struggled at the cost of my health to raise a corps in Kheda and the response was being made when the hostilities ceased and orders were received that no more recruits were wanted. In all these efforts at service I was actuated by the belief that it was possible by such services to gain a status of full equality in the Empire for my countrymen.

'The first shock came in the shape of the Rowlatt Act, a law designed to rob the people of all real freedom. I felt called upon to lead an intensive agitation against it. Then followed the Punjab horrors beginning with the massacre at Jallianwala Bagh and culminating in crawling orders, public floggings and other indescribable humiliations. I discovered too that the plighted word of the Prime Minister to the Mussulmans of India regarding the integrity of Turkey and the holy places of Islam was not likely to be fulfilled. But in spite of the forebodings and the grave warnings of friends, at the Amritsar Congress in 1919, I fought for co-operation in working the Montagu-Chelmsford reforms, hoping that the Prime Minister would redeem his promise to the Indian Mussulmans, that the Punjab wound would be healed and that the reforms, inadequate and unsatisfactory though they were, marked a new era of hope in the life of India.

'But all that hope was shattered. The Khilafat promise was not to be redeemed. The Punjab crime was white-washed and most culprits went not only unpunished but remained in service and in some cases continued to draw pensions from the Indian revenue, and in some cases were even rewarded. I saw too that not only did the reforms not mark a change of heart, but they were only a method of further draining India of her wealth and of prolonging her servitude.

'I came reluctantly to the conclusion that the British connection had made India more helpless than she ever was before, politically and economically. A disarmed India has no power of resistance against any aggressor if she wanted to engage in armed conflict with him. So much is this the case that some of our best men consider that India must take generations before she can achieve Dominion status. She has become so poor that she has little power of resisting famines. Before the British advent, India spun and wove in her millions of cottages just the supplement she needed for adding to her meagre agricultural resources. This cottage industry, so vital for India's existence, has been ruined by incredibly heartless and inhuman processes as described by English witnesses. Little do town dwellers know how the semi-starved masses of India are slowly sinking to lifelessness. Little do they know that their miserable comfort represents the brokerage they get for the work they do for the foreign exploiter, that the profits and the broker-age are sucked from the masses. Little do they realize that the Government established by law in British India is carried on for this exploitation of the masses. No sophistry, no jugglery in figures can explain away the evidence that the skeletons in many villages present to the naked eye. I have no doubt whatsoever that both England and the town dwellers of India will have to answer, if there is a God above, for this crime against humanity which is perhaps unequalled in history. The law itself in this country has been used to serve the foreign exploiter. My unbiased examination of the Punjab Martial Law cases has led me to believe that at least ninety-five per cent of convictions were wholly bad. My experience of political cases in India leads me to the conclusion that in nine out of ten the condemned men were totally innocent. Their crime consisted in love of their country. In ninety-nine cases out of a hundred justice has been denied to Indians as against Europeans in the courts of India. This is not an exaggerated picture. It is the experience of almost every Indian who has had anything to do with such cases. In my opinion, the administration of the law is thus prostituted consciously or unconsciously for the benefit of the exploiter.

'The greatest misfortune is that Englishmen and their Indian associates in the administration of the country do not know that they are engaged in the crime I have attempted to describe. I am satisfied that many Englishmen and Indian officials honestly believe that they are administering one of the best systems devised in the world and that India is making steady though slow progress. They do not know that a subtle but effective system of terrorism and an organized display of force on the one hand, and the deprivation of all powers of retaliation or self-defence on the other, have emasculated the people and induced in them the habit of simulation. This awful habit has added to the ignorance and the self-deception of the administrators. Section 124A under which I am happily charged is perhaps the prince among the political sections of the Indian Penal Code designed to suppress the liberty of the citizen. Affection cannot be manufactured or regulated by law. If one has no affection for a person or system, one should be free to give the fullest expression to his disaffection, so long as he does not contemplate, promote or incite to violence. But the section under which Mr Banker and I are charged is one under which mere promotion of disaffection is a crime. I have studied some of the cases tried under it, and I know that some of the most loved of India's patriots have been convicted under it. I consider it a privilege, therefore, to be charged under that section. I have endeavoured to give in their briefest outline the reasons for my disaffection. I have no personal ill-will against any single administrator, much less can I have any disaffection towards the King's person. But I hold it to be a virtue to be disaffected towards a government which in its totality has done more harm to India than any previous system. India is less manly under the British rule than she ever was before. Holding such a belief, I consider it to be a sin to have affection for the system. And it has been a precious privilege for me to be able to write what I have in the various articles, tendered in evidence against me.

'In fact, I believe that I have rendered a service to India and England by showing in non-co-operation the way out of the unnatural state in which both are living. In my humble opinion, non-co-operation with evil is as much a duty as is co-operation with good. But in the past, non-co-operation has been deliberately expressed in violence to the evil doer. I am endeavouring to show to my country-men that violent non-co-operation only multiplies evil and that as evil can only be sustained by violence, withdrawal of support of evil requires complete abstention from vio-lence. Non-violence implies voluntary submission to the penalty for non-co-operation with evil. I am here, therefore, to invite and submit cheerfully to the highest penalty that can be inflicted upon me for what in law is a deliberate crime and what appears to me to be the highest duty of a citizen. The only course open to you, the Judge, is either to resign your post and thus dissociate yourself from evil, if you feel that the law you are called upon to administer is an evil and that in reality I am innocent; or to inflict on me the severest penalty if you believe that the system and the law you are assisting to administer are good for the people of this country and that my activity is therefore injurious to the public weal.'

Mr Banker: I only want to say that I had the privilege of printing these articles and I plead guilty to the charge. I have got nothing to say as regards the sentence.

THE JUDGMENT

The following is the full text of the judgment:

Mr Gandhi, you have made my task easy in one way by pleading guilty to the charge. Nevertheless, what remains, namely, the determination of a just sentence, is perhaps as difficult a proposition as a judge in this country could have to face. The law is no respecter of persons. Nevertheless, it will be impossible to ignore the fact that you are in a different category from any person I have ever tried or am likely to have to try. It would be impossible to ignore the fact that, in the eyes of millions of your countrymen, you are a great patriot and a great leader. Even those who differ from you in politics look upon you as a man of high ideals and of noble and of even saintly life. I have to deal with you in one character only. It is not my duty and I do not presume to judge or criticize you in any other character. It is my duty to judge you as a man subject to the law, who by his own admission has broken the law and committed what to an ordinary man must appear to be grave offence against the State. I do not forget that you have consistently preached against violence and that you have on many occasions, as I am willing to believe, done much to prevent violence. But having regard to the nature of your political teaching and the nature of many of those to whom it was addressed, how you could have continued to believe that violence would not be the inevitable consequence it passes my capacity to understand.

There are probably few people in India who do not sincerely regret that you should have made it impossible for any government to leave you at liberty. But it is so. I am trying to balance what is due to you against what appears to me to be necessary in the interest of the public, and I propose in passing sentence to follow the precedent of a case in many respects similar to this case that was decided some twelve years ago, I mean the case against Bal Gangadhar Tilak under the same section. The sentence that was passed upon him as it finally stood was a sentence of simple imprisonment for six years. You will not consider it unreasonable, I think, that you should be classed with Mr Tilak, i.e. a sentence of two years' simple imprisonment on each count of the charge; six years in all, which I feel it my duty to pass upon you, and I should like to say in doing so that, if the course of events in India should make it possible for the Government to reduce the period and release you, no one will be better pleased than I.

The Judge to Mr Banker: I assume you have been to a large extent under the influence of your chief. The sentence that I propose to pass upon you is simple imprisonment for six months on each of the first two counts, that is to say, simple imprisonment for one year and a fine of a thousand rupees on the third count, with six months' simple imprisonment in default.

MR GANDHI ON THE JUDGMENT

Mr Gandhi said: I would say one word. Since you have done me the honour of recalling the trial of the late Loka-manya Bal Gangadhar Tilak, I just want to say that I consider it to be the proudest privilege and honour to be associated with his name. So far as the sentence itself is concerned, I certainly consider that it is as light as any judge would inflict on me, and so far as the whole proceedings are concerned, I must say that I could not have expected greater courtesy.

Then the friends of Mr Gandhi crowded round him as the Judge left the court and fell at his feet. There was much sobbing on the part of both men and women. But all the while, Mr Gandhi was smiling and cool and giving encouragement to everybody who came to him. Mr Banker also was smiling and taking this in a light-hearted way. After all his friends had taken leave of him, Mr Gandhi was taken out of the court to the Sabarmati Jail.

A LETTER TO MAHATMA GANDHI
FROM PRISON

Near Etawa
En route to Agra
Dated 10th morning

I feel like one who has long been pent up in a dark and ill-ventilated cell and who all at once finds himself inhaling deep draughts of the fresh air of heaven. You can easily imagine what longing I must have had to write to you, I who was in the habit of writing to you almost daily and of thus easing the many troubles of my mind. We are permitted to write one letter a fortnight; the letter again must be in English and must be forwarded through the Superintendent. How, then, could I hope to tell you everything that was happening behind the prison walls? But yesternight we were set free, at least till we reached

Agra. And this morning we are on our way thereto.

Yesternight, thirty-nine of us started from Naini in a prison van comprising four barred compartments, each being three cubits long and five broad. The bars were apparently not considered to be an adequate safeguard; for the prison van has no doors and no windows. Only there are crooked holes, one inch broad by the side of the carriage for the passage of air. I asked the Sergeant who escorts us whether there was any intention of repeating the Moplah tragedy. The poor fellow naïvely replied that there was no fear, as it was winter and that it would have been intolerable, had it been summer. Besides the four prisoners' compartments, there was a fifth which was like ordinary third class and was meant for our friends, the guard. Should they not have sufficient light and air to be able to keep us in a suffocated condition?

Devdas and Durga (Mrs Desai) were at Allahabad Station to see us. They could not have a view of our faces, but they stood outside, near the place where I was, and we could have a hearty talk. From this prison van I could inform Devdas of the many horrors about which I had been unable to tell him anything in the jail; for the police who escort us do not act as jailers. So some of the things in this letter will have already appeared in Devdas' *Independent* before this reaches you.

We had had hardly a wink of sleep from about one or two o'clock, when at four we were roused at Cawnpore. The Sergeant said, 'Desai, Govind and Krishnakant Malaviya, Shahsaheb, and two others, follow me. We shall seat you elsewhere, so that there might be more room here.' I could not understand how this selection was made, but it looked like segregation, and so I said that any seven of us would come, but not the seven that were named. The Sergeant replied that only those whom he named must come as he did not know the rest and therefore could not take the risk of seating any of them in an ordinary compartment. As 'political' prisoners, some of us had our own clothes on; with the exception of these three or four, the rest were in jail dress and in irons, so that our shame (even as it was) was boundless. To it was now added the insult of being considered more 'trustworthy' than the rest. I thought the three out of the seven would be ordinary prisoners, and that with the aid of light, I would have an opportunity of writing to you, an opportunity not lightly to be allowed to slip as I could not hope to have it anywhere else; and so we came out. I am writing this in an ordinary third-class compartment. Seven policemen are mounting guard over us seven!

But I must cut this story short, as there is little time and much to write. How can I give you an idea of the perplexities we have suffered on account of your injunction that we should obey all orders in jail? Every moment we are troubled by doubts as to what to obey and what not to obey, as always the sun sets on novel experiences and on various oppressions. So I am not at all certain as to the propriety of my conduct on every occasion when I have been anxious to obey.

I am not going to detail here all the experiences in jail. That would take many letters like this, and this is hardly the time for it. I am going to give such select information as I think ought to be placed before the public.

I was taken to Naini Jail on the 24th and was at once taken in the presence of the Superintendent, who said angrily, 'Look here, you may be a non-co-operator or anything you please, but here you are a prisoner like all the others and will be treated accordingly. You will tire of your life out here, but I can't help it. We will not trouble you so long as you do not trouble us.'

This homily over, I was soon taken to my own cell. I had previously resolved that I should accept everything cheerfully including jail dress and irons. So I put on jail dress as soon as it was given to me. Fifteen members of the Provincial Committee had arrived here a week before me, and their cell was adjoining mine. I got the news, after I had changed my dress, that one of them had refused to put on jail dress and had consequently received a flogging. The jail authorities were somewhat surprised to find that I had accepted the change in dress without demur. I was given a rough woollen coat, worn almost threadbare by long use, a shirt worn out by some prisoner of twice my size and emitting horrible stink, an equally dirty pair of shorts and loincloth, along with two blankets as bedding. In a few minutes I felt an itching sensation, and an inspection at one or two places resulted in the find of a pretty big louse. It was difficult to say whether the vermin lived in the blanket or the shirt, but as there was fairly bitter cold, I had

to choose between lice and offensive smell, I elected against
the smell, placed the coat as a pillow, put away the shirt,
and decided to pass the night under the sole protection of
the blanket. I had thought that as I was dead tired, I
would sleep soundly. But the lice in the blanket never ceased
troubling me. My friends in the adjoining cell gave me
from their place an account of the misbehaviour of the jailer
and the Superintendent. One of them was flogged for the
grave offence of not standing up and pushing his hand
out through the bars, when the jailer arrived! Another
suffered the same punishment for refusing to wear dirty
clothes! Add to the stings of lice, the noisy cries, rending
the heavens, with which prisoners were counted every
quarter of an hour from 6 p.m. to 6 a.m. and you can
understand that I got hardly any sleep. But I knew that
sheer physical necessity would induce sleep on the following days, no matter if I was unable to sleep on the first.

I took no food in the evening, as I did not feel inclined.
I was given a large iron bowl for eating and drinking. In
spite of all the scrubbing I could give it, I found in the
morning that the water in it had turned blood-red with
rust. We were taken out thrice in the day for drinking
water and for natural purposes. There was a paved reservoir
from which all of us were to have our water by putting
our bowls into it. Filtering the water was out of the
question, as we were not provided with any extra piece of
cloth.

(At this point the Sergeant sees me writing and gives me
notice that I should not pass any of my writing to my
friends. So I must be brief.)

For bathing purposes, there was a long paved channel
joining with the reservoir mentioned above. We were all
to sit in it and bathe. As for food, we were given *dalia* (a
porridge of pounded wheat) in the morning, wheat bread and
dal at noon, and the same bread and a vegetable in the
evening. What shall I say as to how I liked this appetizing
menu? The other prisoners were taking it all right, and
so I can hardly describe it as falling within your definition
of food unfit for human consumption.

But let me now come to other matters. There is a rule
that a newly arrived prisoner is only confined and not
given any work for first ten days of his term. So my friends
of the Provincial Committee and myself, having no work,

were given books which we read, heard the bitter language of the jailer and the Superintendent in the mornings and saw prisoners striking and abusing one another. The second day, I requested the Superintendent to give us spinning wheels or let us have them from our homes. He replied that wheels were given to women and that the Government who spent ten rupees on each prisoner had somehow to manage to raise a like amount out of his labour and that therefore grinding was given to him. I said that, if the Government had common sense, they could earn 500 rupees out of our work. He angrily asked if he was to get us to write articles.

In answer to my companions, the Superintendent said, 'Owing to you disloyal people having arrived, I could not get my leave for ten days sanctioned. We have to suffer much on account of you. You must behave properly. Do not think I am alone. I have fifty millions of people behind me (referring to the population of England).'

This went on for a few days. The ten days period of the Provincial Committee people was soon over, and they were made to wear an iron neckring and a wooden tablet, showing the section against which they had offended and the term of the sentence of imprisonment. They already had irons on their feet. The same day they lost their lousy clothes and got new ones. My clothes were still the same, but I had remained bare-bodied for two days, and washed them thoroughly with earth. Thus the stink had disappeared and my friends had combined for one or two days to pick out the lice from my blankets in the sunshine.

When the friends left, I felt somewhat lonely and so gradually grew very friendly with the other prisoners, some of them dacoits. An old man with a term of seven years' imprisonment came near my cell and sat near the door. I read the Ramayana to him and he expounded it. He was a man of much common sense and knowledge. He had the Ramayana by heart. Then we recited *bhajans* and many prisoners began to sit near my cell. Prisoners here are finely divided into two classes, national and Government prisoners, i.e. ordinary prisoners and politicals. The politicals are gratefully admired and served by the others.

While my new friendships were thus flourishing, I had heard that the provincial friends had been given hard labour. Eleven had to grind fifteen seers of corn every day, and the deputy jailer had ordered the convict warder to harass them in all possible ways, in order that they might weaken and apologize. One or two of these poor men fell ill in two days. All had warts on their palms, but had in three or four days progressed up to about nine seers, when I received the news that the Government had directed that I should be treated as a political prisoner. I was sorry for this. While my friends were given hard labour, I was denied the privilege of spiritual elevation through physical suffering. My own clothes in which I had arrived in jail and in which I was furbished up for the day when Devdas and Durga were to see me in order that she might not take fright at the convict's dress, were returned to me, but the 'Gandhi cap' was withheld. I asked the Superintendent what it was. He could not explain anything beyond saying that it was like the one I wore and that I would not be allowed to wear it. I might change the shape, he said, or wear a fez like Sherwani's. I laughed and said that I would do neither. 'Then you must go bareheaded,' he said. I agreed. I had thought of refusing to take the other ordinary clothes, but then I remembered your 'Model Prisoner' and quietly submitted.

I passed my first day as a political prisoner in great trouble. But the next day I was at ease, as I realized that even so there was an opportunity of suffering. Some of my friends described their personal experience. There is a young man, named Kailasnath, still in his teens, the son of a well-known pleader of Cawnpore, and a political prisoner. Being religiously minded, he takes food after bath, worship, and the application of sandal paint, etc., to the forehead. The jailer had admitted sandal and other things for him, but when one day he saw the sandal mark, he ordered Kailasnath to rub it out. The young man obeyed but refused to take food. And so the jailer arrived on the scene and threatened punishment, but Kailasnath persisted in his refusal all the same. For this, he received filthy abuse, was severely flogged with a wooden cudgel and kicked with boots. His utensils were dashed to the ground. The hero responsible for this is Hamilton, an Englishman who has been promoted to jailership for his services during the war. This incident got into the newspapers, though not in detail, and there was an inquiry. The Inspector-General visited the prison and told Kailasnath that he must obey all orders.

Apparently he took the jailer also to task, as the latter came to Kailasnath and abused the Inspector-General before him!

On hearing this, I could see that life even as a political prisoner need not be uneventful. Meanwhile the attitude of the jailer and the Superintendent towards me had changed and I had friendly conversations with them about non-co-operation and other topics. I did not quite relish this development, as I was afraid that these officers might be trying to win me over as a prelude to oppressing the rest.

The same evening I heard successive cries of 'Gandhijiki Jai'. In the morning, I had read your observations in *Young India* and wished I could communicate them to the friends who had been given hard labour. Here was no means of doing so. The cry started from one block and received a response from other blocks, one after another. To the Super-intendent and the jailer it looked like a mutiny. They ran up. One of those fifteen friends was seized and the warder fell upon him like a wolf. The poor man was greeted with foul abuse and flogged with *lathis* along with an ironical order to repeat 'Gandhijiki Jai'. After he had received ten blows of a *lathi*, one inch and a half in diameter, his magnificent frame tottered to the ground and then he was beaten with fists, etc.

The friend who thus suffered is Lakshminarayan Sharma, a pious and inoffensive young man of twenty-two, who used to be secretary, Aligarh Congress Committee. The other prisoners could not bear the sight of this suffering, and offered to retaliate upon the warder. But Lakshminarayan prevented them all and said it was their duty to suffer. The others, however, were greatly enraged and continued the cries of 'Gandhijiki Jai' for which about fifty or sixty of them were cruelly flogged. As if this were not enough, the next morning all the prisoners were taken outside, including the Provincial Committee men, and in the presence of all of them, two prisoners who were suspects had their hands fastened with a stick and then caned. The caning was so severe that the cries of the sufferers could be heard in my cell at a distance of two or three furlongs. When a prisoner swooned after some blows, he was given rest; and as he revived, the caning was continued. In this way, two of them received twenty-three cuts. It is worthy of remark that at each cut the sufferer and his fellow prisoners set up a joint cry of 'Gandhijiki Jai' in spite of the jailer and the Superintendent, and these cries stopped only when the authorities were tired of inflicting any more punishment. After this, three or four were flogged with sticks and fists. One of them suffered so severely that there was an involuntary discharge of excreta and urine. Two or three are in hospital. I was told that prisoners had died in this jail before, in consequence of such oppression.

Having performed his 'dirty job' (Dyer's phrase) in this way, the jailer came to see me. I asked him for an explanation of the trouble. He replied that there might have been a big mutiny and that severe punishment was necessary to prevent it. I told him that, be that as it might, I would fast and pray for the day. He asked me why. I said I would pray not only for my brethren who were no doubt in error, but for those who despitefully used them. The jailer asked me what was the value of prayer. The talk then turned upon the Bible. I explained to him that Jesus and the Bible were not the sole property of Christians like himself, but the joint estate of humanity at large. He then appeared to melt somewhat. I said how good it would be, if I was permitted to read to the prisoners Mr Gandhi's observations pertinent to their case, and I offered to meet all of them and talk to them about our duty. But this was not at all acceptable to the jailer. Only last evening, he was saying to the prisoners, 'There is no victory to Gandhi here, the victory is to Government. So you must cry victory to Government.' He was however abashed a little, said it was no use crying over spilt milk and then left me.

After the jailer came the Superintendent. He also tried to tease me, saying ironically how obedient my non-co-operator friends were. I was quiet and only said that he at least was amused by the whole affair. Then he told me I did not know the utility of punishment. I replied I did not care to, as there was a world of difference between his mentality and mine, and that he on his part had no appreciation of our methods. He then expatiated upon the value of 'force' and said, 'You Indians are unpractical visionaries. We are practical. You only talk big.' I was listening quietly and contented myself with asking whether it was I or he that was talking big. He said nothing more and left me. Meanwhile I had obtained permission to see Lakshminarayan, that friend who had been so cruelly dealt with. I saw him. He showed me terrible marks of the flogging upon his body. I told him we were forbidden to cry 'Gandhijiki Jai' and that I read about it in the papers only the other day. On hearing this the young man burst into tears and said at once he must then tell the Superintendent that he had done wrong. Thus he evidenced the incomparable tenderness of his soul. But what does the enemy know or care about our tenderness? So that we can only learn to send forth like sandalwood greater fragrance, the more roughly we are handled. I assure you, after the experiences that I have had, that our people are mastering this lesson in some miraculous manner.

But now I must close. There is much to say, but I shall rest content if this much reaches you by post for the present. We are not permitted to post letters, but how long should these facts be kept from the public? It is also a question to be considered how far we should obey the order not to give out anything.

I have had no sleep last night, am thoroughly fatigued and must seize an early opportunity of posting this. I will write in English if possible, but perhaps there may be no time.

We are all on our way to Agra, thirty-nine in all, including the members of the Provincial Committee and some Allahabad volunteers. Since he received the orders of removal, the Superintendent was kindness itself to us. He must have heaved a sigh of relief at our departure as of some great trouble. On the last day he said: 'You are an awful nuisance. I should get an allowance of Rs50 for each one of you.' We are being removed, for fear that we might influence the prison population and bring them to a knowledge of their slavery and ignorance.

PART VI

Brahmacharya: the Virtue of Chastity; Caste, and Hindu-Muslim Unity; Monoculture in Education; the Untouchables; Hinduism

BRAHMACHARYA

If it is contended that birth control is necessary for the nation because of over-population, I dispute the proposition. It has never been proved. In my opinion by a proper land system, better agriculture and a supplementary industry, this country is capable of supporting twice as many people as there are in it to-day.

What, then, is Brahmacharya? It means that men and women should refrain from carnal knowledge of each other. That is to say, they should not touch each other with a carnal thought, they should not think of it even in their dreams. Their mutual glances should be free from all suggestion of carnality. The hidden strength that God has given us should be conserved by rigid self-discipline, and transmitted into energy and power—not merely of body, but also of mind and soul.

But what is the spectacle that we actually see around us? Men and women, old and young, without exception, are caught in the meshes of sensuality. Blinded for the most part by lust, they lose all sense of right and wrong. I have myself seen even boys and girls behaving as if they were mad under its fatal influence. I too have behaved likewise under similar influences, and it could not well be otherwise. For the sake of a momentary pleasure, we sacrifice in an instant all the stock of vital energy that we have laboriously accumulated. The infatuation over, we find ourselves in a miserable condition. The next morning we feel hopelessly weak and tired, and the mind refuses to do its work. Then in order to remedy the mischief, we consume large quantities of milk, bhasmas, yakutis and what not. We take all sorts of 'nervine tonics' and place ourselves at the doctor's mercy for repairing the waste, and for recovering the capacity for enjoyment. So the days pass and years, until at length old age comes upon us, and finds us utterly emasculated in body and in mind.

But the law of Nature is just the reverse of this. The older we grow the keener should our intellect be; the longer we live the greater should be our capacity to communicate the benefit of our accumulated experience to our fellow men. And such is indeed the case with those who have been true Brahmacharis. They know no fear of death, and they do not forget God even in the hour of death; nor do they indulge in vain desires. They die with a smile on their lips, and boldly face the day of judgment. They are true men and women; and of them alone can it be said that they have conserved their health.

We hardly realize the fact that incontinence is the root cause of most vanity, anger, fear and jealousy in the world. If our mind is not under our control, if we behave once or oftener every day more foolishly than even little children, what sins may we not commit consciously or unconsciously? How can we pause to think of the consequences of our actions, however vile or sinful they may be?

But you may ask, 'Who has ever seen a true Brahmachari in this sense? If all men should turn Brahmacharis, would not humanity be extinct and the whole world go to rack and ruin?' We will leave aside the religious aspect of this question and discuss it simply from the secular point of view. To my mind, these questions only betray our timidity and worse. We have not the strength of will to observe Brahmacharya, and therefore set about finding pretexts for evading our duty. The race of true Brahmacharis is by no means extinct; but if they were commonly to be met with, of what value would Brahmacharya be? Thousands of hardy labourers have to go and dig deep into the bowels of the earth in search for diamonds, and at length they get perhaps merely a handful of them out of heaps and heaps of rock. How much greater, then, should be the labour involved in the discovery of the infinitely more precious diamond of a Brahmachari? If the observance of Brahmacharya should mean the end of the world, that is none of our business. Are we God that we should be so anxious about its future? He who created it will surely see to its preservation. We need not trouble to inquire whether other people practise Brahmacharya or not. When we enter a trade or profession, do we ever pause to consider what the fate of the world would be if all men were to do likewise? The true Brahmachari will, in the long run, discover for himself answers to such questions.

But how can men engrossed in the cares of the material world put these ideas into practice? What about those who are married? What shall they do who have children? And what shall be done by those people who cannot control themselves? We have already seen what is the highest state for us to attain. We should keep this ideal constantly before us, and try to approach it to the utmost of our capacity. When little children are taught to write the letters of the alphabet, we show them the perfect shapes of the letters, and they try to reproduce them as best they can. In the same way, if we steadily work up to the ideal of Brahmacharya we may ultimately succeed in realizing it. What if we have married already? The law of Nature is that Brahmacharya may be broken only when the husband and wife feel a desire for progeny. Those, who, remembering this law, violate Brahmacharya once in four or five years, will not become slaves to lust, nor lose much of their stock of vital energy. But, alas! How rare are those men and women who yield to the sexual craving merely for the sake of offspring! The vast majority turn to sexual enjoyment merely to satisfy their carnal passion, with the result that children are born to them quite against their will. In the madness of sexual passion, they give no thought to the consequences of their acts. In this respect, men are even more to blame than women. The man is blinded so much by his lust that he never cares to remember that his wife is weak and unable to bear or rear up a child. In the West, indeed, people have transgressed all bounds. They indulge in sexual pleasures and devise measures in order to evade the responsibilities of parenthood. Many books have been written on this subject and a regular trade is being carried on in contraceptives. We are as yet free from this sin, but we do not shrink from imposing heavy burden of maternity on our women, and we are not concerned even to find that our children are weak, impotent and imbecile.

We are, in this respect far worse than even the lower animals; for in their case the male and the female are brought together solely with the object of breeding from them. Man and woman should regard it a sacred duty to keep apart from the moment of conception up to the time when the child is weaned. But we go on with our fatal merry-making blissfully forgetful of that sacred obligation. This almost incurable disease enfeebles our mind and leads us to an early grave, after making us drag a miserable existence for a short while. Married people should understand the true function of marriage, and should not violate Brahmacharya except with a view to progeny.

But this is so difficult under our present conditions of life. Our diet, our ways of life, our common talk, and our environments are all equally calculated to rouse animal passions; and sensuality is like a poison eating into our vitals. Some people may doubt the possibility of our being able to free ourselves from this bondage. This book is written not for those who go about with such doubting of heart, but only for those who are really in earnest, and who have the courage to take active steps for self-improvement. Those who are quite content with their present abject condition will find this tedious even to read; but I hope it will be of some service to those who have realized and are disgusted with their own miserable plight.

From all that has been said it follows that those who are still unmarried should try to remain so; but if they cannot help marrying, they should defer it as long as possible. Young men, for instance, should take a vow to remain unmarried till the age of twenty-five or thirty. We cannot consider here all the advantages other than physical which they will reap and which are as it were added unto the rest.

My request to those parents who read this chapter is that they should not tie a millstone round the necks of their children by marrying them young. They should look to the welfare of the rising generation, and not merely seek to pamper their own vanity. They should cast aside all silly notions of family pride or respectability, and cease to indulge in such heartless practices. Let them rather, if they are true well-wishers of their children, look to their physical, mental and moral improvement. What greater disservice can they do to their progeny than compel them to enter upon married life, with all its tremendous responsibilities and cares, while they are mere children?

Then again the true laws of health demand that the man who loses his wife, as well as the woman that loses her husband, should remain single ever after. There is a difference of opinion among medical men as to whether young men and women need ever let their vital energy escape, some answering the question in the affirmative, others in the negative. But while doctors thus disagree we must not give way to over-indulgence from an idea that we are supported by medical authority. I can affirm, without the slightest hesitation, from my own experience as well as that of others, that sexual enjoyment is not only not necessary for, but is positively injurious to health. All the strength of body and mind that has taken long to acquire is lost all at once by a single dissipation of the vital energy. It takes a long time to regain this lost vitality, and even then there is no saying that it can be thoroughly recovered. A broken mirror may be mended and made to do its work, but it can never be anything but a broken mirror.

As has already been pointed out, the preservation of our vitality is impossible without pure air, pure water, pure and wholesome food, as well as pure thoughts. So vital indeed is the relation between health and morals that we can never be perfectly healthy unless we lead a clean life. The earnest man, who, forgetting the errors of the past, begins to live a life of purity, will be able to reap the fruit of it straightaway. Those who practise true Brahmacharya even for a short period will see how their body and mind improve steadily in strength and power, and they will not at any cost be willing to part with this treasure. I have myself been guilty of lapses even after having fully understood the value of Brahmacharya, and have of course paid dearly for it. I am filled with shame and remorse when I think of the terrible contrast between my condition before and after these lapses. But from the errors of the past I have now learnt to preserve this treasure intact, and I fully hope, with God's grace to continue to preserve it in the future; for I have, in my own person, experienced the inestimable benefits of Brahmacharya. I was married early, and had become the father of children as a mere youth. When at length, I awoke to the reality of my situation, I found that I was steeped in ignorance about the fundamental laws of our being. I shall consider myself amply rewarded for writing this chapter if at least a single reader takes a warning from my failings and experiences, and profits thereby. Many people have told—and I also believe it—that I am full of energy and enthusiasm, and that I am by no means weak in mind; some even accuse me of strength bordering on obstinacy. Nevertheless there is still bodily and mental ill-health as a legacy of the past. And yet when compared with my friends, I may call myself healthy and strong. If even after twenty years of sensual enjoyment, I have been able to reach this state, how much better off should I have been if I had kept myself pure during those twenty years as well? It is my full conviction, that if only I had lived a life of unbroken Brahmacharya all through, my energy and enthusiasm would have been a thousandfold greater and I should have been able to devote them all to the furtherance of my country's cause as my own. If an imperfect Brahmachari like myself can reap such benefit, how much more wonderful must be the gain in power—physical, mental, as well as moral—that unbroken Brahmacharya can bring to us.

When so strict is the law of Brahmacharya what shall we say of those guilty of the unpardonable sin of illegitimate sexual enjoyment? The evil arising from adultery and prostitution is a vital question of religion and morality and cannot be fully dealt with in a treatise on health. Here we are only concerned to point out how thousands who are guilty of these sins are afflicted by venereal diseases. God is merciful in this that the punishment swiftly overtakes sinners. Their short span of life is spent in abject bondage to quacks in a futile quest after a remedy for their ills. If adultery and prostitution disappeared, at least half the present number of doctors would find their occupation gone. So inextricably indeed has venereal disease caught mankind in its clutches that thoughtful medical men have been forced to admit, that so long as adultery and prostitution continue, there is no hope for the human race, all the discoveries of curative medicine notwithstanding. The medicines for these diseases are so poisonous that although they may appear to have done some good for the time being, they give rise to other and still more terrible diseases which are transmitted from generation to generation.

No one need therefore despair. My Mahatmaship is worthless. It is due to my outward activities, due to my politics which is the least part of me and is therefore evanescent. What is of abiding worth is my insistence on truth, non-violence and Brahmacharya, which is the real part of me. That permanent part of me, however small, is not to be despised. It is my all. I prize even the failures and disillusionments which are but steps towards success.[1]

CASTE, AND HINDU-MUSLIM UNITY

I am one of those who do not consider caste to be a harmful institution. In its origin, caste was a wholesome custom and promoted national well-being. In my opinion, the idea that inter-dining and intermarrying is necessary for national growth, is a superstition borrowed from the West. Eating is a process just as vital as the other sanitary necessities of life. And if mankind had not, much to its harm, made of eating a fetish and indulgence, we would have performed the operation of eating in private even as one performs the other necessary functions of life in private. Indeed the highest culture in Hinduism regards eating in that light and there are thousands of Hindus still living who will not eat their food in the presence of anybody. I can recall the names of several cultured men and women who ate their food in entire privacy but who never had any ill will against anybody and who lived on the friendliest terms with all.

Intermarriage is a still more difficult question. If brothers and sisters can live on the friendliest footing without ever thinking of marrying each other, I can see no difficulty in my daughter regarding every Mohammedan as a brother and vice versa. I hold strong views on religion and on marriage. The greater restraint we exercise with regard to our appetites whether about eating or marrying, the better we become from a religious standpoint. I should despair of ever cultivating amicable relations with the world, if I had to recognize the right or the propriety of any young man offering his hand in marriage to my daughter or to regard it as necessary for me to dine with anybody and everybody. I claim that I am living on terms of friendliness with the whole world. I have never quarrelled with a single Mohammedan or Christian, but for years I have taken nothing but fruits in Mohammedan or Christian households. I would certainly decline to eat cooked foods from the

[1]. Extract from *Self-Restraint v. Self-Indulgence* by M. K. Gandhi, Navajivan Publishing House, 1947.

same plate with my son or to drink water out of a cup which his lips have touched and which has not been washed. But the restraint or the exclusiveness exercised in these matters by me has never affected the closest companionship with the Mohammedan or the Christian friends or my sons.

But interdining and intermarriage have never been a bar to disunion, quarrels and worse. The Pandavas and the Kauravas flew at one another's throats without compunction although they interdined and intermarried. The bitterness between the English and the Germans has not yet died out.

The fact is that intermarriage and interdining are not necessary factors in friendship and unity though they are often emblems thereof. But insistence on either the one or the other can easily become and is to-day a bar to Hindu-Mohammedan Unity. If we make ourselves believe that Hindus and Mohammedans cannot be one unless they interdine or intermarry, we would be creating an artificial barrier between us which it might be almost impossible to remove. And it would seriously interfere with the growing unity between Hindus and Mohammedans if, for example, Mohammedan youths consider it lawful to court Hindu girls. The Hindu parents will not, even if they suspected any such thing, freely admit Mohammedans to their homes as they have begun to do now. In my opinion, it is necessary for Hindu and Mohammedan young men to recognize this limitation.

I hold it to be utterly impossible for Hindus and Mohammedans to intermarry and yet retain intact each other's religion. And the true beauty of Hindu-Mohammedan Unity lies in each remaining true to his own religion and yet being true to each other. For, we are thinking of Hindus and Mohammedans even of the most orthodox type being unable to regard one another as natural enemies as they have done hitherto.

What then does the Hindu-Mohammedan Unity consist in and how can it be best promoted? The answer is simple. It consists in our having a common purpose, a common goal and common sorrows. It is best promoted by co-operating to reach the common goal, by sharing one another's sorrows and by mutual toleration. A common goal we have. We wish this great country of ours to be greater and self-governing. We have enough sorrows to share. And to-day seeing that the Mohammedans are deeply touched on the question of Khilafat and their case is just, nothing can be so powerful for winning Mohammedan friendship for the Hindu as to give his whole-hearted support to the Mohammedan claim. No amount of drinking out of the same cup or dining out of the same bowl can bind the two as this help in the Khilafat question.

And mutual toleration is a necessity for all time and for all races. We cannot live in peace if the Hindu will not tolerate the Mohammedan form of worship of God and his manners and customs or if the Mohammedans will be impatient of Hindu idolatry or cow-worship. It is not necessary for toleration that I must approve of what I tolerate. I heartily dislike drinking, meat-eating and smoking, but I tolerate all these in Hindus, Mohammedans and Christians even as I expect them to tolerate my abstinence from all these although they may dislike it. All the quarrels between the Hindus and the Mohammedans have arisen from each wanting to force the other to his view.[2]

At West Keroa a Muslim Maulana from Khulna came to discuss with Gandhiji the problem of communal harmony when he was having his lunch which he invited the visitor to share with him. But the latter refused, as it was food touched by a non-believer! There seemed no other reason. Gandhiji twitted him, saying he did not know that even the Muslim community was tainted by untouchability!

Three local Muslims came to Gandhiji in 1947 to request him to pray that God might make both the communities live in peace and brotherhood. They found him reading Abdullah Suhrawardy's collection of the sayings of the Prophet. At the evening prayer Gandhiji read out two of those sayings to the gathering. The first was: 'Be in this world like a traveller or like a passer-on, and reckon yourself as of the dead.' In the other saying the question was asked as to who was the best man and who the worst. The Prophet's reply was that he considered that man to be the best who lived longest and did good acts and he the worst who did bad acts. Making those sayings the text of his discourse at the evening prayer gathering, Gandhiji observed that a man should be judged by what he did and not by what he professed as against the doctrine put forward by some Muslim divines that a person may continue to indulge in bad acts with impunity so long as he subscribes

2. *Young India*, Vol. III.

to a particular creed that is claimed to be right. That applied to Hindus, Muslims and all alike. For the Hindus, the moral was that their Hinduism with all its magnificent spiritual heritage, would avail them nothing if they continued to harbour the inhuman practice of untouchability. The British might go but freedom would not come without complete removal of the blot of untouchability.

At another place the Press party that had come to cover Gandhiji's mission in Noakhali, had arranged a common dinner for Hindus and Muslims in their camp. Some of the rehabilitated refugees felt panicky and said that if they agreed to dine with the Muslims the Muslims might next ask that they should recite the Kalima and even give their daughters in marriage to them. Gandhiji tried to explain to them that the age-old touch-me-notism among the Hindus in regard to eating and drinking was an outmoded custom. It could not be continued indefinitely and it was high time that they discarded it. But he recognised that their fear was not groundless. He would not therefore, he said, lay down the rule for them but leave them to decide for themselves as they felt prompted. The common dinner in consequence was not held on the poor man's premises, where the Press party had camped, but at the place where Gandhiji was staying and where the morale of the people stood high as a result of his presence. Further, to set an object lesson to the Hindus, he sent a woman member of his party to attend it.

Addressing a gathering of the Muslims a couple of days later, Gandhiji told them that, whilst he and his companions did not believe in pollution by touch and personally he had not the slightest compunction in dining with anyone irrespective of caste or creed, it was for the Muslim brethren to bear with those who might not have overcome their scruples in that regard. 'I hold the custom to be wrong; in time it will go. But in the meantime Muslims must realise that interdining is not an essential feature of mutual love. Let it not obscure from you genuine love wherever you may find it. That in itself would help to bridge the gulf.'

Thus, like an expert physician, he varied his prescription according to the nature of each case. His non-violence was not static or rigid but a living dialectic, calling for adaptation and change with every change in circumstance.

At an evening prayer gathering Gandhiji was asked: 'If there is only one God why should there not be only one religion?'

'Because,' replied Gandhiji, 'everyone has his own conception of God. For instance, I believe myself to be a Hindu but I know I do not worship God in the same manner as many of the Hindus do.'

The next day at Kamalapur, he was asked: 'You advocate inter-caste marriage. Do you also favour marriage between Indians professing different religions. Should they declare themselves as belonging to no denomination, or can they continue their old religious practices and yet intermarry? If so, what form should the marriage ceremony take?'

Gandhiji's reply showed how far he had travelled from his earlier position on the question. Although he had not always held that view, he replied, he had long come to the conclusion that an inter-religious marriage was a welcome event whenever it took place. Marriage in his estimation was a sacred institution. Hence there must be mutual friendship, either party having equal respect for the religion of the other. There was no room in this for conversion. Hence the marriage ceremony could be performed by the priests belonging to either faith. But this could come about only when the communities had shed mutual enmity and cultivated equal regard for all religions of the world.

Was not the institution of civil marriage a negation of religion and did it not tend to laxity in faith?

He did not believe in civil marriages, replied Gandhiji. But he welcomed the institution of civil marriage as a much needed reform to clear the way for inter-religious marriages.

'You say, you are in favour of inter-religious marriages, but at the same time you say that each party should retain his or her own religion. Are there any instances of parties belonging to different religions keeping up their own religion after such marriage to the end of their lives?'

Gandhiji replied that he had no instances in mind where parties had clung to their respective faiths 'till the end of their lives' because the parties he had in mind were still living. He had, however, known men and women who professing different religions had married, each clinging to his or her own faith without abatement. But must people demand upon precedents always? he asked. Why should they not set up precedents of their own, so that the timid ones might shed their timidity?—*Ed.*

MONOCULTURE IN EDUCATION

English is to-day studied because of its commercial and so-called political value. Our boys think, and rightly in the present circumstances, that without English they cannot get Government service. Girls are taught English as a passport to marriage. I know several instances of women wanting to learn English so that they may be able to talk to Englishmen in English. I know husbands who are sorry that their wives cannot talk to them and their friends in English. I know families in which English is being made the mother tongue. Hundreds of youths believe that without a knowledge of English freedom for India is practically impossible. The canker has so eaten into society that, in many cases, the only meaning of Education is a knowledge of English. All these are for me signs of our slavery and degradation. It is unbearable to me that the vernaculars should be crushed and starved as they have been. I cannot tolerate the idea of parents writing to their children, or husbands writing to their wives, not in their own vernaculars, but in English. I hope I am as great a believer in free air as the great poet. I do not want my house to be walled in on all sides and my windows to be stuffed. I want the cultures of all lands to be blown about my house as freely as possible. But I refuse to be blown off my feet by any.[3]

THE UNTOUCHABLES

The Devil succeeds only by receiving help from his fellows. He always takes advantage of the weakest spots in our natures in order to gain mastery over us. Even so does the Government retain its control over us through our weaknesses or vices. And if we would render ourselves proof against its machinations, we must remove our weaknesses. It is for that reason that I have called non-co-operation a process of purification. As soon as that process is completed, this Government must fall to pieces for want of the necessary environment, just as mosquitoes cease to haunt a place whose cesspools are filled up and dried.

Has not a just Nemesis overtaken us for the crime of untouchability? Have we not reaped as we have sown? Have we not practised Dyerism and O'Dwyerism on our own kith and kin? We have segregated the *pariah* and we are in turn segregated in the British Colonies. We deny him the use of public wells; we throw the leavings of our plates at him. His very shadow pollutes us. Indeed there is no charge that the *pariah* cannot fling in our faces and which we do not fling in the faces of Englishmen.

How is this blot on Hinduism to be removed? 'Do unto

3. *Young India*, Vol. III.

others as you would that others should do unto you.' I have often told English officials that, if they are friends and servants of India, they should come down from their pedestal, cease to be patrons, demonstrate by their loving deeds that they are in every respect our friends, and believe us to be equals in the same sense they believe fellow Englishmen to be their equals. After the experiences of the Punjab and the Khilafat, I have gone a step further and asked them to repent and to change their hearts. Even so it is necessary for us Hindus to repent of the wrong we have done, to alter our behaviour towards those whom we have 'suppressed' by a system as devilish as we believe the English system of the government of India to be. We must not throw a few miserable schools at them: we must not adopt the air of superiority towards them. We must treat them as our blood brothers as they are in fact. We must return to them the inheritance of which we have robbed them. And this must not be the act of a few English-knowing reformers merely, but it must be a conscious voluntary effort on the part of the masses. We may not wait till eternity for this much-belated reformation. We must aim at bringing it about within this year of grace, probation, preparation, and tapasya. It is a reform not to follow Swaraj but to precede it.

Untouchability is not a sanction of religion, it is a device of Satan. The Devil has always quoted scriptures. But scriptures cannot transcend Reason and Truth. They are intended to purify Reason and illuminate Truth. I am not going to burn a spotless horse, because the Vedas are reported to have advised, tolerated, or sanctioned the sacrifice. For me the Vedas are divine and unwritten. 'The letter killeth.' It is the spirit that giveth the light. And the spirit of the Vedas is purity, truth, innocence, chastity, simplicity, forgiveness, godliness, and all that makes a man or woman noble and brave. There is neither nobility nor bravery in treating the great and uncomplaining scavengers of the nation as worse than dogs to be despised and spat upon. Would that God gave us the strength and the wisdom to become voluntary scavengers of the nation as the 'suppressed' classes are forced to be. There are Augean stables enough and to spare for us to clean.[4]

How am I to plead with those who regard any contact

4. *Young India*, Vol. III.

with the members of the suppressed community as entailing defilement and of which they cannot be cleansed without necessary ablutions, and who thus regard omission to perform the ablutions a sin? I can only place before them my innermost convictions.

I regard untouchability as the greatest blot on Hinduism. This idea was not brought home to me by my bitter experiences during the South African struggle. It is not due to the fact that I was once an agnostic. It is equally wrong to think, as some people do, that I have taken my views from my study of Christian religious literature. These views date as far back as the time when I was neither enamoured of, nor was acquainted with, the Bible or the followers of the Bible.

I was hardly yet twelve when this idea had dawned on me. A scavenger named Uka, an untouchable, used to attend our house for cleaning latrines. Often I would ask my mother why it was wrong to touch him, why I was forbidden to touch him. If I accidentally touched Uka, I was asked to perform the ablutions, and though I naturally obeyed, it was not without smilingly protesting that untouchability was not sanctioned by religion, that it was impossible that it should be so. I was a very dutiful and obedient child and so far as it was consistent with respect for parents, I often had tussles with them on this matter. I told my mother that she was entirely wrong in considering physical contact with Uka as sinful.

While at school I would often happen to touch the 'untouchables', and as I never would conceal the fact from my parents, my mother would tell me that the shortest cut to purification after the unholy touch was to cancel the touch by touching any Mussulman passing by. And simply out of reverence and regard for my mother I often did so, but never did so believing it to be a religious obligation. After some time we shifted to Porebander, where I made my first acquaintance with Sanskrit. I was not yet put to an English school, and my brother and I were placed in charge of a Brahman, who taught us Ramraksha and Vishnu Punjar. The texts 'jale Vishnuh', 'sthale Vishnuh' (there is the Lord (present) in water, there is the Lord (present) in earth) have never gone out of my memory. A motherly old dame used to live close by. Now it happened that I was very timid then, and would conjure up ghosts and goblins whenever the lights went out, and it was dark. The old mother, to disabuse me of fears, suggested that I should mutter the Ramraksha texts whenever I was afraid, and all evil spirits would fly away. This I did and, as I thought, with good effect. I could never believe then that there was any text in Ramraksha pointing to the contact of the 'untouchables' as a sin. I did not understand its meaning then, or understood it very imperfectly. But I was confident that Ramraksha, which could destroy all fears of ghosts, could not be countenancing any such thing as fear of contact with the 'untouchables'.

· The Ramayana used to be regularly read in our family. A Brahmin called Ladha Maharaj used to read it. He was stricken with leprosy, and he was confident that a regular reading of the Ramayana would cure him of leprosy, and, indeed, he was cured of it. 'How can the Ramayana', I thought to myself, 'in which one who is regarded nowadays as an untouchable took Rama across the Ganges in his boat, countenance the idea of any human beings being untouchable on the ground that they were polluted souls?' The fact that we addressed God as the 'purifier of the polluted' and by similar appellations, shows that it is a sin to regard anyone born in Hinduism as polluted or untouchable—that it is satanic to do so. I have hence been never tired of repeating that it is a great sin. I do not pretend that this thing had crystallized as a conviction in me at the age of twelve, but I do say that I did then regard untouchability as a sin. I narrate this story for the information of the Vaishnavas and Orthodox Hindus.

I have always claimed to be a Sanatani Hindu. It is not that I am quite innocent of the Scriptures. I am not a profound scholar of Sanskrit. I have read the Vedas and the Upanishads only in translations. Naturally therefore, mine is not a scholarly study of them. My knowledge of them is in no way profound, but I have studied them as I should do as a Hindu and I claim to have grasped their true spirit. By the time I had reached the age of 21, I had studied other religions also.

There was a time when I was wavering between Hinduism and Christianity. When I recovered my balance of mind, I felt that to me salvation was possible only through the Hindu religion and my faith in Hinduism grew deeper and more enlightened.

But even then I believed that untouchability was no part of Hinduism; and that, if it was, such Hinduism was not for me.

I believe that caste has saved Hinduism from disintegration. But like every other institution, it has suffered from excrescences. I consider the four divisions alone to be fundamental, natural, and essential. The innumerable sub-castes are sometimes a convenience, often a hindrance. The sooner there is fusion the better. The silent destruction and reconstruction to sub-castes have ever gone on and are bound to continue. Social pressure and public opinion can be trusted to deal with the problem. But I am certainly against any attempt at destroying the fundamental divisions. The caste system is not based on inequality, there is no question of inferiority, and so far as there is any such question arising, as in Madras, Maharashtra, or elsewhere, the tendency should undoubtedly be checked. But there appears to be no valid reason for ending the system because of its abuse. It lends itself easily to reformation. The spirit of democracy, which is fast spreading throughout India and the rest of the world, will, without a shadow of doubt, purge the institution of the idea of predominance and subordination.

The spirit of democracy is not a mechanical thing to be adjusted by abolition of forms. It requires change of the heart. If caste is a bar to the spread of the spirit, the existence of five religions in India—Hinduism, Islam, Christianity, Zoroastrianism, and Judaism—is equally a bar. The spirit of democracy requires the inculcation of the spirit of brotherhood, and I can find no difficulty in considering a Christian or a Mohammedan to be my brother in absolutely the same sense as a blood brother, and Hinduism that is responsible for the doctrine of the caste is also responsible for the inculcation of the essential brotherhood, not merely of man but even of all that lives.

One of my correspondents suggests that we should abolish the caste but adopt the class system of Europe—meaning thereby I suppose that the idea of heredity in caste should be rejected. I am inclined to think that the law of heredity is an eternal law and any attempt to alter that law must lead, as it has before led, to utter confusion. I can see very great use in considering a Brahmin to be always a Brahmin throughout his life. If he does not behave himself like a Brahmin, he will naturally cease to command the respect that is due to the real Brahmin. It is easy to imagine the innumerable difficulties if one were to set up a court of punishments and rewards, degradation and promotion. If Hindus believe, as they must believe in reincarnation, transmigration, they must know that nature will, without any possibility of mistake, adjust the balance by degrading a Brahmin, if he misbehaves himself, by reincarnating him in a lower division, and translating one who lives the life of a Brahmin in his present incarnation to Brahminhood in his next.[5]

From the foregoing it might be deduced that Gandhi favoured the four main Hindu caste divisions, set aloof from the untouchables. This, of course, was not so. By the end of his life, as the following extracts from Pyarelal's *The Last Phase* show, Gandhi was *totally* opposed to caste, even to the extent of teaching that marriages should be inter-caste, and devoted his life to the complete rejection of untouchability—*Ed.*

HINDUISM

In dealing with the problem of untouchability, I have asserted my claim to being a Sanatani Hindu with greater emphasis than hitherto, and yet there are things which are commonly done in the name of Hinduism, which I disregard. I have no desire to be called a Sanatani Hindu or any other, if I am not such. And I have certainly no desire to steal in a reform or an abuse under cover of a great faith.

It is therefore necessary for me once for all distinctly to give my meaning of Sanatana Hinduism. The word Sanatana is used in its natural sense.

I call myself a Sanatani Hindu, because,

(1) I believe in the Vedas, the Upanishads, the Puranas and all that goes by the name of Hindu scriptures, and therefore in avatars and rebirth.

(2) I believe in the Varnashrama dharma in a sense in my opinion strictly Vedic, but not in its present popular and crude sense.

5. *Young India*, Vol. III.

(3) I believe in the protection of the cow in its much larger sense than the popular.

(4) I do not disbelieve in idol-worship.

The reader will note that I have purposely refrained from using the word divine origin in reference to the Vedas or any other scriptures. For I do not believe in the exclusive divinity of the Vedas. I believe the Bible, the Koran, and the Zend Avesta to be as much divinely inspired as the Vedas. My belief in the Hindu scriptures does not require me to accept every word and every verse as divinely inspired. Nor do I claim to have any first-hand knowledge of these wonderful books. But I do claim to know and feel the truths of the essential teaching of the scriptures. I decline to be bound by any interpretation, however learned it may be, if it is repugnant to reason or moral sense. I do most emphatically repudiate the claim (if they advance any such) of the present Shankaracharyas and Shastris to give a correct interpretation of the Hindu scriptures. On the contrary, I believe that our present knowledge of these books is in a most chaotic state. I believe implicitly in the Hindu aphorism, that no one truly knows the Shastras who has not attained perfection in Innocence (*ahimsa*), Truth (*satya*) and Self-Control (Brahmacharya) and who has not renounced all acquisition or possession of wealth. I believe in the institution of Gurus, but in this age millions must go without a Guru, because it is a rare thing to find a combination of perfect purity and perfect learning. But one need not despair of ever knowing the truth of one's religion, because the fundamentals of Hinduism as of every great religion are unchangeable, and easily understood. Every Hindu believes in God and His Oneness, in rebirth and salvation. But that which distinguishes Hinduism from every other religion is its cow protection, more than its Varnashrama.

Varnashrama is, in my opinion, inherent in human nature, and Hinduism has simply reduced it to a science. It does attach to birth. A man cannot change his varna by choice. Not to abide by one's varna is to disregard the law of heredity. The division, however, into innumerable castes is an unwarranted liberty taken with the doctrine. The four divisions are all-sufficing.

I do not believe that interdining or even intermarriage necessarily deprives a man of his status that his birth has given him. The four divisions define a man's calling, they do not restrict or regulate social intercourse. The divisions define duties, they confer no privileges. It is, I hold, against the genius of Hinduism to arrogate to oneself a higher status or assign to another a lower. All are born to serve God's creation, a Brahman with his knowledge, a Kshatriya with his power of protection, a Vaishya with his commercial ability and a Shudra with bodily labour. This, however, does not mean that a Brahman for instance is absolved from bodily labour, or the duty of protecting himself and others. His birth makes a Brahman predominantly a man of knowledge, the fittest by heredity and training to impart it to others. There is nothing, again, to prevent the Shudra from acquiring all the knowledge he wishes. Only, he will best serve with his body and need not envy others their special qualities for service. But a Brahman who claims superiority by right of knowledge falls and has no knowledge. And so with the others who pride themselves upon their special qualities. Varnashrama is self-restraint and conservation and economy of energy.

Though therefore Varnashrama is not affected by interdining or intermarriage, Hinduism does most emphatically discourage interdining and intermarriage between divisions. Hinduism reached the highest limit of self-restraint. It is undoubtedly a religion of renunciation of the flesh, so that the spirit may be set free. It is no part of a Hindu's duty to dine with his son. And by restricting his choice of a bride to a particular group, he exercises rare self-restraint. Hinduism does not regard a married state as by any means essential for salvation. Marriage is a 'fall' even as birth is a 'fall'. Salvation is freedom from birth and hence death also. Prohibition against intermarriage and interdining is essential for a rapid evolution of the soul. But this self-denial is no test of varna. A Brahman may remain a Brahman, though he may dine with his Shudra brother, if he has not left off his duty of service by knowledge. It follows from what I have said above, that restraint in matters of marriage and dining is not based upon notions of superiority. A Hindu who refuses to dine with another from a sense of superiority misrepresents his dharma.

Unfortunately to-day, Hinduism seems to consist merely in eating and not eating. Once I horrified a pious Hindu by taking toast at a Mussulman's house. I saw that he was pained to see me pouring milk into a cup handed by a Mussulman friend, but his anguish knew no bounds when he saw me taking toast at the Mussulman's hands. Hinduism is in danger of losing its substance, if it resolves itself into a matter of elaborate rules as to what and with whom to eat. Abstemiousness from intoxicating drinks and drugs, and from all kinds of foods, especially meat, is undoubtedly a great aid to the evolution of the spirit, but it is by no means an end in itself. Many a man eating meat and with everybody, but living in the fear of God, is nearer his freedom than a man religiously abstaining from meat and many other things, but blaspheming God in every one of his acts.

The central fact of Hinduism however is cow protection. Cow protection to me is one of the most wonderful phenomena in human evolution. It takes the human being beyond his species. The cow to me means the entire sub-human world. Man through the cow is enjoined to realize his identity with all that lives. Why the cow was selected for apotheosis is obvious to me. The cow was in India the best companion. She was the giver of plenty. Not only did she give milk, but she also made agriculture possible. The cow is a poem of pity. One reads pity in the gentle animal. She is the mother to millions of Indian mankind. Protection of the cow means protection of the whole dumb creation of God. The ancient seer, whoever he was, began with the cow. The appeal of the lower order of creation is all the more forcible because it is speechless. Cow protection is the gift of Hinduism to the world. And Hinduism will live so long as there are Hindus to protect the cow.

The way to protect is to die for her. It is a denial of Hinduism and *ahimsa* to kill a human being to protect a cow. Hindus are enjoined to protect the cow by their tapas-ya, by self-purification, by self-sacrifice. The present-day cow protection has degenerated into a perpetual feud with the Mussulmans, whereas cow protection means conquering the Mussulmans by our love. A Mussulman friend sent me some time ago a book detailing the inhumanities practised by us on the cow and her progeny; how we bleed her to take the last drop of milk from her, how we starve her to emaciation, how we ill-treat the calves, how we deprive them of their portion of milk, how cruelly we treat the oxen, how we castrate them, how we beat them, how we overload them. If they had speech, they would bear witness to our crimes against them which would stagger the world. By every act of cruelty to our cattle, we disown God and Hinduism. I do not know that the condition of the cattle in any other part of the world is so bad as in unhappy India. We may not blame the Englishman for this. We may not plead poverty in our defence. Criminal negligence is the only cause of the miserable condition of our cattle. Our Panjrapoles, though they are an answer to our instinct of mercy, are a clumsy demonstration of its execution. Instead of being model dairy farms and great profitable national institutions, they are merely depots for receiving decrepit cattle.

Hindus will be judged not by their tilaks, not by the correct chanting of mantras, not by their pilgrimages, not by their most punctilious observance of caste rules but by their ability to protect the cow. Whilst professing the religion of cow protection, we have enslaved the cow and her progeny, and have become slaves ourselves.

It will now be understood why I consider myself a Sanatani Hindu. I yield to none in my regard for the cow. I have made the Khilafat cause my own, because I see that through its preservation full protection can be secured for the cow. I do not ask my Mussulman friends to save the cow in consideration of my service. My prayer ascends daily to God Almighty, that my service of a cause I hold to be just may appear so pleasing to Him, that he may change the hearts of the Mussulmans, and fill them with pity for their Hindu neighbours and make them save the animal the latter hold dear as life itself.

I can no more describe my feeling for Hinduism than for my own wife. She moves me as no other woman in the world can. Not that she has no faults; I daresay, she has many more than I see myself. But the feeling of an indissoluble bond is there. Even so I feel for and about Hinduism with all its faults and limitations.

Nothing elates me so much as the music of the Gita or the Ramayana by Tulasidas, the only two books in Hinduism I may be said to know. When I fancied I was taking my last breath, the Gita was my solace. I know the vice that is going on to-day in all the great Hindu shrines, but I love them in spite of their unspeakable failings. There is an interest which I take in them and which I take in no other.

I am a reformer through and through. But my zeal never takes me to the rejection of any of the essential things of Hinduism. I have said I do not disbelieve in idol worship. An idol does not excite any feeling of veneration in me. But I think that idol worship is part of human nature. We hanker after symbolism. Why should one be more composed in a church than elsewhere? Images are an aid to worship. No Hindu considers an image to be God. I do not consider idol worship a sin.

It is clear from the foregoing that Hinduism is not an exclusive religion. In it there is room for the worship of all the prophets of the world. It is not a missionary religion in the ordinary sense of the term. It has no doubt absorbed many tribes in its fold, but this absorption has been of an evolutionary, imperceptible character. Hinduism tells every one to worship God according to his own faith or dharma, and so it lives at peace with all the religions.

That being my conception of Hinduism, I have never been able to reconcile myself to untouchability. I have always regarded it as an excrescence. It is true that it has been handed down to us from generations, but so are many evil practices even to this day. I should be ashamed to think that dedication of girls to virtual prostitution was a part of Hinduism. Yet it is practised by Hindus in many parts of India. I consider it positive irreligion to sacrifice goats to Kali and do not consider it a part of Hinduism. Hinduism is a growth of ages. The very name, Hinduism, was given to the religion of the people of Hindustan by foreigners. There was no doubt at one time sacrifice of animals offered in the name of religion. But it is not religion, much less is it Hindu religion. And so also, it seems to me that when cow protection became an article of faith with our ancestors, those who persisted in eating beef were excommunicated. The civil strife must have been fierce. Social boycott was applied not only to the recalcitrants, but their sins were visited upon their children also. The practice which had probably its origin in good intentions hardened into usage, and even verses crept into our sacred books giving the practice a permanence wholly undeserved and still less justified. Whether my theory is correct or not, untouchability is repugnant to reason and to the instinct of mercy, pity or love. A religion that establishes the worship of the cow cannot possibly countenance or warrant a cruel and inhuman boycott of human beings. And I should be content to be torn to pieces rather than disown the suppressed classes. Hindus will certainly never deserve freedom, nor get it if they allow their noble religion to be disgraced by the retention of the taint of untouchability. And as I love Hinduism dearer than life itself, the taint has become for me an intolerable burden. Let us not deny God by denying to a fifth of our race the right of association on an equal footing.[6]

A deputation of the Scheduled Castes came to Gandhi and asked his advice as to whether they should aim at 'elevating' themselves to the status of the so-called high castes by securing special concessions for themselves as a class or whether their effort should be directed to the eradication of untouchability root-and-branch so that all distinction between caste and outcaste would become a thing of the past?

Gandhiji answered that he naturally preferred the second course; classless and casteless society was his ideal. When untouchability was really gone, there would be no caste. All would be Hindus pure and simple. On the other hand, if Harijans set about organising themselves separately to secure exclusive privileges for themselves, it would precipitate a class conflict. Apart from the evils inherent in such a conflict, it would be an unequal fight in which, as far as he could see, the odds would weigh heavily against them. Besides, such a course would perpetuate the 'bar-sinister' by creating a vested interest in 'untouchability' which it was their object to eradicate. His advice to the Harijans, therefore, was that they should abolish all caste distinctions among themselves and observe the laws of cleanliness better than the so-called caste Hindus. Instead of working for separate treatment for themselves, they should 'endeavour to merge themselves in the ocean of Hindu humanity. That is the only possible way to free India.'

To the castemen, on the other hand, his advice was that they should prove that they had really obliterated caste by their readiness to take up all those occupations which the 'untouchables' engaged in. Thus, they should be ready to do a scavenger's work. But it must be done in an intelligent, clean and sanitary manner; not in a mechanical, slothful and sluggish manner. The system of cleaning closets would then automatically be transformed. In England real Bhangis were famous engineers and sanitarians. He had seen European households where the Bhangis had a perfectly clean way of dealing with the human excreta. They were provided with cane baskets in which the pails were carried. One could easily mistake them for 'dinner-baskets'! Needless to say, the Harijans would then live in the same streets as others without any segregation and enjoy the same municipal and civil amenities as the rest.

The problem of removal of untouchability in Gandhiji's hands thus assumed the form of double education. 'Touchables' had to be taught 'patiently by practice and example that untouchability is a sin against humanity and to be atoned for, and the untouchables that they should cease to fear the touchables and not show untouchability amongst themselves.' The untouchables had further to get rid of the evil customs and practices rampant in their midst, e.g. drink, eating of carrion, unclean and insanitary habits, so that no-one might be able to point the finger of scorn at them. To realise the goal of this two-fold education, he had set up an all-India organisation, the Harijan Sevak Sangh, conceived essentially as a 'society of penitents' to enable Hindu society to atone for its sin against the so-called untouchables. Its function being to discharge a debt rather than confer a privilege, its executive was manned exclusively by those who had to do the atonement.

'How can caste Hindus look after the interests of the Harijans? How can they realise the feelings of the classes who have suffered so long at their hands?' Gandhiji was finally asked.

'By caste Hindus voluntarily becoming scavengers not only in name but in action,' replied Gandhiji. 'If the caste Hindus discharged their duty fully and properly, Harijans would rise at a bound and Hinduism, purified of its taint, would leave a rich legacy to the world.'—*Ed.*

PART VII

Extracts from Gandhi's Diary kept during his residence in Delhi after India had achieved Dominion Status up to the time of his Assassination

---

10th September 1947

Is it not our shame as a nation that there should be any refugee problem at all? Qaid-e-Azam Jinnah, Liaquatsaheb and other Pakistan leaders have proclaimed in common with Pandit Nehru and Sardar Patel that the minorities will be treated in the respective dominions with the same consideration as the majorities. Was this said by each to tickle the world with sweet words, or was it meant to show to the world that we mean what we say and that we will die in the attempt to redeem the world. If so, why are the Hindus and Sikhs and the proud Amils and Bhaibunds driven to leave Pakistan which is their home? What has happened in Quetta, Nawabshah and Karachi? The tales one hears and reads from western Pakistan are heartbreaking. It will not do for either party to plead helplessness and say it is all the work of *goondas*. Each dominion is bound to take full responsibility for the acts of those who live in either dominion. 'Theirs is not to reason why; theirs but to do and die.' No longer do we work willy-nilly under the crushing weight of imperialism. But this does not mean that there will now be no rule of law if we are to face the world squarely in the face. Are the Union ministers to declare their bankruptcy and shamelessly own to the world that the people of Delhi or the refugees will not cheerfully and voluntarily obey the rule of law? I would like the Ministers to break in the attempt to wean the people from their madness rather than bend.

12th September 1947

Anger breeds revenge and the spirit of revenge is to-day responsible for all the horrible happenings here and elsewhere. What good will it do the Muslims to avenge the happenings in Delhi or for the Sikhs and the Hindus to avenge cruelties on our co-religionists in the Frontier and West Punjab? If a man or a group of men go mad, should everyone follow suit? I warn the Hindus and Sikhs that by killing and loot and arson they are destroying their own religions. I claim to be a student of religion and I know that no religion teaches madness. Islam is no exception. I implore you all to stop your insane actions at once. Let not future generations say that we lost the sweet bread of freedom because we could not digest it. Remember that unless we stop this madness the name of India will be mud in the eyes of the world.

15th September 1947
During the night as I heard what should have been the soothing sound of gentle life-giving rain, my mind went out to the thousands of refugees lying about in the open camps in Delhi. I was sleeping snugly in a veranda protecting me on all sides. But for the cruel hand of man against his brother, these thousands of men, women and children would not be shelterless and in many cases foodless. In some places they could not but be in knee-deep water. Was it all inevitable? The answer from within was an emphatic No. Was this the first fruit of freedom, just a month-old baby? These thoughts have haunted me throughout these last twenty hours. My silence has been a blessing. It has made me inquire within. Have the citizens of Delhi gone mad? Have they no humanity left in them? Have love of the country and its freedom no appeal for them? I must be pardoned for putting the first blame on the Hindus and Sikhs. Could they not be men enough to stem the tide of hatred? I would urge the Muslims of Delhi to shed all fear, trust God and discover all the arms in their possession which the Hindus and Sikhs fear they have. Not that the former too do not have any. The question is one of degree. Either the minority rely upon God and His creature man to do the right thing, or rely upon their firearms to defend themselves against those whom they must not trust.

My advice is precise and firm. Its soundness is manifest. Trust your Government to defend every citizen against wrong-doers, however well armed they may be. Further, trust it to demand and get damages for every member of the community wrongfully dispossessed. All that neither Government can do is to resurrect the dead. The people of Delhi will make it difficult to demand justice from the Pakistan Government. Those who seek justice must do justice, must have clean hands. Let the Hindus and Sikhs take the right step and invite the Muslims who have been driven out of their homes to return. If they can take this courageous step worthy from every point of view, they immediately reduce the refugee problem to its simplest terms. They will command recognition from Pakistan, nay from the whole world. They will save Delhi and India from disgrace and ruin. For me, transfer of millions of Hindus and Sikhs and Muslims is unthinkable. It is wrong. The wrong of Pakistan will be undone by the right of a resolute non-transfer of population. I hope I shall have the courage to stand by it, even though mine may be a solitary voice in its favour.

19th September 1947
I visited the Hindu pocket in Kucha Tarachand surrounded on all sides by Muslims. The spokesman recited in highly exaggerated language the woes of the Hindus and ended by saying that the whole of the locality should be denuded of all the Muslims who were mostly Leaguers and who had carried on a wild agitation against the Hindus. He maintained that the Hindus should do exactly as the Muslims in Pakistan were reported to be doing.

I replied that I could not associate myself with the contention that India should drive out all its Muslim population to Pakistan as the Muslims of Pakistan were driving out all non-Muslims. Two wrongs cannot make one right. I therefore invited my audience to listen to my advice and act bravely and fearlessly and be proud to live in the midst of a large Muslim population.

I then went to the *Anathalaya* in Pataudi House and advised the responsible parties to bring back the orphans who had been removed out of fright. I was told that there was a shower of bullets from the adjoining Muslim houses killing one child and wounding another. This was about the 7th of September. Maulana Ahmad Said and other Muslim friends who were accompanying me said that the neighbouring Muslims would see to it that no harm befell the inmates. The next place was near the house of Shri Bhargava who is the sole Hindu living in the midst of Muslims. It was packed with Muslims. I hope that the Muslims will fulfil my dream as a lad of twelve that the Hindus, Muslims and the other Indians will live together as brothers and friends. And finally I ask you to join me in a prayer that God will fulfil that dream, or take me away and save me from witnessing the awful tragedy of one part of India being inhabited by the Muslims only and the other part by the Hindus.

21st September 1947

I am not going to argue with this objector. I realize the anger that rages in people's hearts to-day. The atmosphere is so surcharged that I think it right to respect even one objector, but by no means does this mean that I give up God or His worship in my heart. Prayer demands a pure atmosphere. One thing that everyone should take to heart from such objections is that those who are anxious to serve must have endless patience and tolerance. One must never seek to impose one's views on others.

The Hindus greet me with *Mahatma Gandhiki Jai*, but they little know that to-day there can be no victory for me, nor do I wish to live if the Hindus, Muslims and Sikhs cannot live at peace with one another. I am doing my level best to drive home the truth that there is strength in unity and weakness in disunion. Just as a tree that does not bear fruit withers, so also will my body be useless if my service cannot bear the expected fruit. Whilst this is true, it is equally true that one is bound to work without attachment to fruit. Detachment is more fruitful than attachment. I am merely explaining the logic of facts. A body that has outlived its usefulness will perish giving place to a new one. The soul is imperishable and continues to take on new forms for working out its salvation through acts of service.

23rd September 1947

I am told that there are still left over 18,000 Hindus and Sikhs in Rawalpindi and 30,000 in the Wah Camp. I will repeat my advice that they should all be prepared to die rather than leave their homes. The art of dying bravely and with honour does not need any special training, save a living faith in God. Then there will be no abductions and no forcible conversions. I know that you are anxious

I should go to the Punjab at the earliest moment. I want to do so. But if I failed in Delhi, it is impossible for me to succeed in Pakistan. For I want to go to all the parts and provinces of Pakistan under the protection of no escort save God. I will go as a friend of the Muslims as of others. My life will be at their disposal. I hope that I may cheerfully die at the hands of anyone who chooses to take my life. Then I will have done as I have advised all to do.

26th September 1947

There was a time when India listened to me. To-day I am a back number. I have been told I have no place in the new order, where we want machines, navy, air force and what not. I can never be a party to that. If you can have the courage to say that you will retain freedom with the help of the same force with which you have won it, I am your man. My physical incapacity and my depression will vanish in a moment. The Muslims are reported to have said *hanske liya Pakistan, larke lenge Hindustan*. If I had my way, I would never let them have it by force of arms. Some dream of converting the whole of India to Islam. That will never happen through war. Pakistan can never destroy Hinduism. The Hindus alone can destroy themselves and their faith. Similarly, if Islam is destroyed, it will be destroyed by the Muslims in Pakistan, not by the Hindus in Hindustan.

3rd October 1947

To-day I am getting news of *satyagraha* being started in many places. Often I wonder whether the so-called *satyagraha* is not really *duragraha*. Whether it is strikes in mills or railways or post offices or movement in some of the states, it seems as if it is a question of seizing power. A virulent poison is leavening society to-day and every opportunity for attaining their object is seized by those who do not stop to consider that means and ends are convertible terms.

I would like to refer to the fact that I am even getting letters asking me to bless people's work or the starting of movements. In my opinion every good work carries within it its own blessings and does not need mine or anyone's backing. A good man who was doing good work and who came to me understood my proposition at once. Truth is always self-evident and it is everyone's duty to abide by it at all costs. But those who resort to *satyagraha* should search their hearts and find out whether it is Truth that they are seeking. If not, then insistence becomes a mockery. I affirm that those who are seeking to get what is not in reality theirs cannot possibly abide by *ahimsa*, and Truth cannot be found without it.

7th October 1947

Many people come and talk to me and leave literature with me to the effect that the popular ministers are acting in an autocratic fashion like their British predecessors. I have not talked to the ministers in this connection. But I am quite clear that nothing for which you have criticized the British Government shall happen in the régime of responsible ministries. Under the British rule the Viceroy could issue ordinances for making laws and executing them. There was a hue and cry against the combination of judicial and executive functions. Nothing has happened since to warrant a change in the opinion. There should be no ordinance rule. Your legislative assemblies should be your only law-makers. Ministers are liable to be changed at will. Their acts should be subject to review by the courts. They should do all in their power to make justice cheap, expeditious and incorruptible. For that purpose *Panchayat Raj* has been suggested. It is not possible for a high court to reach *lakhs* and *lakhs* of people. Only extraordinary situations require emergency legislation. Legislative assemblies, even though the procedure may entail some delay, must not be superseded by the executive. I have no concrete example in mind. I have based my remarks upon the correspondence I have received from various provinces. Therefore, while I appeal to the people not to take the law into their own hands, I appeal to the ministers to beware of lapsing into the old ways which they have condemned.

20th October 1947

It is my painful duty to draw attention to another menace, if it be one. A Britisher writes in an open letter: 'To whom it may concern':

> 'Several of us are living in a lonely spot in a disturbed area. We are pure British and for years we have devoted ourselves at great personal sacrifice to the welfare of the people of this country. . . . We now find that a secret

word has gone out that all the British left in India are to be murdered. I read in the newspapers Pandit Nehru's assurance that the Government will protect the persons and property of all loyal citizens of the State. But there is no protection for persons living in little country places or almost none. None at all for us. It is a physical impossibility.'

There is much else in this open letter which can be quoted with advantage. I have reproduced enough to warn us of the lurking danger. Of course, it may be only a scare and there may be nothing beyond it. There may be no secret circular.

There is, however, prudence in not disregarding such warnings. I am hoping that the writer's fears are wholly groundless. I agree with him that all promise of protection by authority in isolated places is vain. It simply cannot be done, no matter how efficient the military and police machine may be, which, it must be admitted it is not at present. Protection must come first from within, i.e. from rock-like faith in God and secondly from the goodwill of the neighbouring population. If neither is present, the best and the safest way is to leave India's inhospitable shore. Things have not come to such a pass. The duty of all of us is to regard with special attention all the Britishers who choose to remain in India as its faithful servants. They must be free from every kind of insult or disregard. The Press and public bodies have to be circumspect in this as in many other respects if we are to render a good account of ourselves as a free and self-respecting nation. Those who respect themselves cannot make good the claim if they will not respect their neighbours however few or insignificant they may be.

21st October 1947

I have heard of another sad incident. It is not a communal murder. The victim is a Hindu government officer. A soldier shot him dead, because he would not act as he was directed. This tendency to use a gun on the slightest pretext is a grave portent. There are barbarous people in the world, to whom life has no value. They shoot dead human beings as they would shoot down birds or beasts. Is free India to be in this category? Man has not the power to create life, hence he has no right to take it. Yet the Muslims murder the Hindus and Sikhs and vice versa. When this cruel game is finished, the blood lust is bound to result in the Muslims slaughtering the Muslims, and the Hindus and Sikhs slaughtering themselves. I hope they will never reach that savage state. That is their fate unless both the states pull themselves together and set things right before it is too late.

30th October 1947

This evening when as usual before the prayer meeting the audience was asked if there was any objector to the Koran verses being recited as part of the prayer, one member spoke up and persisted in his objection. Gandhiji had made it clear that if there was such objection, he would neither have public prayer nor the after-prayer speech on current events. Consequently, he sent word that there would be neither prayer nor speech before the public. But the gathering would not disperse without seeing Gandhiji. He, therefore, went to the rostrum and said a few words on the reason for abstention and the working of *ahimsa* as he understood it:

It is unseemly for anyone to object to the prayer, especially when it is on a private lawn. Nevertheless, my *ahimsa* warns me against disregarding even one objector when an overwhelming majority are likely to overawe one person into silence. It would be otherwise if the whole audience objected. It would then be my duty to have the prayer even at the risk of being molested. There is also the further consideration that the majority should not be disappointed for the sake of one objector. The remedy is simple. If the majority restrain themselves and entertain no anger against, or evil design on, the solitary objector, it will be my duty to hold the prayer. The possibility, however, is that if the whole audience is non-violent in intention and action, the objector will restrain himself. Such I hold to be the working of non-violence. I further hold that truth and non-violence are not the monopoly of a few adepts. All universal rules of conduct known as God's commandments are simple and easy to understand and carry out if the will is there. They only appear to be difficult because of the inertia which governs mankind. Man is a progressive being. There is nothing at a standstill in nature. Only God is motionless for He was, is, and will be the same yesterday, to-day and to-morrow, and yet is ever moving. We need not, however, worry ourselves over the attributes of God. We have to realize that we are ever progressing. Hence, I hold that if mankind is to live, it has to come growingly under the sway of truth and non-violence. It is in view of these two fundamental rules of conduct that I and you have to work and live.

3rd November 1947

If two quantities of poison mix together, who will decide which was first on the field, and if such a decision could be arrived at, what end would it serve? We know this, however, that a virus has spread throughout the western Pakistan area and that it has not as yet been recognized as such by the powers that be. So far as the Union is concerned, it has been confined to a small part of it. Would to God that the virus would remain under isolation and control! There would then be cause for every hope that it would be expelled in due time and that soon from both parts.

In view of the fact that Dr Rajendraprasad has called a meeting of the Premiers or their representatives and others to help and advise him in the matter of food control, I feel that I should devote this evening to that very important question. Nothing that I have heard during these days has moved me from the stand I have taken up from the beginning, that the control should be entirely removed at the earliest moment possible, certainly not later than six months hence. Not a day passes but letters and wires come to me, some from important persons, declaring emphatically that both the controls should be removed. I propose to omit the other, i.e. cloth control, for the time being.

Control gives rise to fraud, suppression of truth, intensification of the black market and to artificial scarcity. Above all, it unmans the people and deprives them of initiative, it undoes the teaching of self-help they have been learning for a generation. It makes them spoon-fed. This is a tragedy next only, if indeed not equal, to the fratricide on a vast scale and the insane exchange of population resulting in unnecessary deaths, starvation and want of proper residence and clothing more poignant for the coming inclement weather. The second is certainly more spectacular. We dare not forget the first because it is not spectacular.

This food control is one of the vicious legacies of the last world war. Control then was probably inevitable because a very large quantity of cereals and other foodstuffs were exported outside. This unnatural export was bound to create a man-made scarcity and lead to rationing in spite of its many drawbacks. Now there need be no export which we cannot avoid if we wish to. We would help the starving parts of the world, if we do not expect outside help for India in the way of food.

I have seen during my lifetime covering two generations several God-sent famines, but have no recollection of an occasion when rationing was even thought of.

To-day, thank God, the monsoons have not failed us. There is, therefore, no real scarcity of food. There are enough cereals, pulses and oil seeds in the villages of India. The artificial control of prices, the growers do not, cannot understand. They, therefore, refuse willingly to part with their stock at a price much lower than they command in the open market. This naked fact needs no demonstration. It does not require statistics or desk-work civilians buried in their red-tape files to produce elaborate reports and essays to prove that there is scarcity. It is to be hoped that no one will frighten us by trotting out before us the bogey of over-population.

13th November 1947

Freedom without equality for all, irrespective of race or religion, is not worth having for the Congress. In other words, the Congress and any government representative of the Congress must remain a purely democratic, popular body, leaving every individual to follow that form of religion which best appeals to him without any interference from the state. There is so much in common between people living in the same state under the same flag owing undivided allegiance to it. There is so much in common between man and man that it is a marvel that there can be any quarrel on the ground of religion. Any creed or dogma which coerces others into following one uniform practice is a religion only in name, for a religion worth the name does not admit of any coercion. Anything that is done under coercion has only a short lease of life. It is bound to die. It must be a matter of pride to you, whether you are four-anna Congress members or not, that you have in your midst an institution without a rival which disdains to become a theocratic state, and which always believes and lives up to the belief that the state of your conception must be a secular, democratic state having perfect harmony between the different units composing the state. When I think of the plight of the Muslims in the Union, how in many places life has become difficult for them and how there is a continuing exodus of the Muslims from the Union, I wonder whether the people who are responsible for creating such a state of things could ever become a credit to the Congress. I therefore hope that during the year which has just commenced, the Hindus and Sikhs will so behave as to enable every Muslim, whether a boy or a girl, to feel that he or she is as safe and free as the tallest Hindu or Sikh.

14th November 1947
I am taking the *bhajan* of the evening as my text for my discourse. When I was fasting in the Aga Khan Palace which was converted into a prison to accommodate Devi Sarojini Naidu, Mirabehn, Mahadevbhai and myself, this *bhajan* gripped me. I do not wish to go into the causes of the fast. Its relevance simply is that I was sustained throughout the twenty-one days not by the quantity of water I drank, or for some days by the quantity of orange juice I took, or by the extraordinary medical care and attention I was receiving, but by enthroning in my heart God whom I know as Rama. I was so much enamoured of the lines of the *bhajan*, but whose words I had then forgotten, that I asked my associates to send a telegram for the exact words of the *bhajan*. To my joy I received the full text of the *bhajan* in the reply telegram. Its refrain is that *Ramanama* is everything, and that before it the other gods are of no consequence. I wish to recall this instructive episode from my life in order to emphasize to my audience the fact that the momentous session of the A.I.C.C. which is to meet in New Delhi to-morrow, i.e. Saturday, should carry on their deliberations with God in their hearts. This they are bound to do as they are representative of Congressmen, and as such they would not be worth their salt if their chiefs, the Congressmen, had God in their hearts instead of Satan.

16th November 1947

It is the fashion nowadays to use the word *satyagraha* for any kind of resistance, armed or otherwise. This looseness harms the community and degrades *satyagraha*. If, therefore, you understand all the implications of *satyagraha* and know that the living God of Truth and Love is with the *satyagrahi*, you will have no hesitation in believing that it is invincible. I am sorry to say what I do about the Hindu Mahasabha and the Rashtriya Swayamsevak Sangh. I would be glad to find that I am wrong. I have seen the chief of the Rashtriya Swayamsevak Sangh. I have attended a meeting of the members of the R.S.S. Since then I have been upbraided for having gone to the meeting and have had many letters of complaints about the organization.

17th November 1947

'A man becomes what he thinks,' says an *Upanishad mantra*. Experience of wise men testifies to the truth of the aphorism. The world will thus become what its wise men think. An idle thought is no thought. It would be a serious mistake to say that the world will become as the unthinking multitude act. They will not think. Independence should mean democracy. Democracy demands that every citizen has the opportunity of receiving wisdom as distinguished from a knowledge of facts so-called. South Africa has many wise men and women as it has also many able soldiers who are equally able farmers. It will be a tragedy for the world if they do not rise superior to their debilitating surroundings and give a proper lead to their country on this vexed and vexing problem of White supremacy. Is it not by this time a played-out game?

I must keep you for a moment over the much-debated question of control. Must the voice of the people be drowned by the noise of the pundits who claim to know all about the virtue of controls? Would that our ministers who are drawn from the people and are of the people listened to the voice of the people rather than of the controllers of the red tape which, they know, did them infinite harm when they were in the wilderness! The pundits then ruled with a vengeance. Must they do so even now? Will not the people have any opportunity of committing mistakes and learning by them? Do the ministers not know that they have the power to resume control wherever necessary, if decontrol is found to have been harmful to the people, in any instance out of the samples, by no means exhaustive, that I am giving below? The list before me confounds my simple mind. There may be virtue in some of them. All I contend is that the science, if it is one, of controls requires a dispassionate examination and then education of the people in the secret of controls in general or specified controls. Without examining the merits of the list I have received I pick out a few of the samples given to me: Control on Exchange, Investment, Capital Issues, Opening branches of Banks and their investments, Insurance investments, all Import and Export of every kind of commodity, Cereals, Sugar, *Gur*, Cane and Syrup, *Vanaspati*, Textiles, including Woollens, Power Alcohols, Petrol and Kerosene, Paper, Cement, Steel, Mica, Manganese, Coal, Transport, Installation of Plant, Machinery, Factories, Distribution of cars in certain provinces and Tea plantation.

21st November 1947
A member of the audience asks me: What is a Hindu? What is the origin of the word? Is there any Hinduism?

These are pertinent questions for the time. I am no historian, I lay claim to no learning. But I have read in an authentic book on Hinduism that the word 'Hindu' did not occur in the Vedas but when Alexander the Great invaded India, the inhabitants of the country to the east of the Sindhu, which is known by the English-speaking Indians as the Indus, were described as Hindus. The letter 'S' had become 'H' in Greek. The religion of these inhabitants became Hinduism and as they knew it, it was a most tolerant religion. It gave shelter to the early Christians who had fled from persecution, also to the Jews known as Heni-Israel, as also to the Parsis. I am proud to belong to that Hinduism which is all-inclusive, and which stands for tolerance. Aryan scholars swear by what they call the Vedic religion and Hindustan is otherwise known as Aryavarta. I have no such aspiration. Hindustan of my conception is all-sufficing for me. It certainly includes the Vedas, but it includes also much more. I can detect no inconsistency in declaring that I can, without in any way whatsoever impairing the dignity of Hinduism, pay equal homage to the best of Islam, Christianity, Zoroastrianism and Judaism. Such Hinduism will live as long as the sun shines. Tulsidas has summed it up in one *doha*: 'The root of religion is embedded in Mercy, whereas egotism is rooted in love of the body. Tulsi says that Mercy should never be abandoned, even though the body perishes.'

Finally I feel bound to refer to a case of persecution of the Roman Catholics near Gurgaon, which was brought to my notice. The village in question where it took place is known as Kanhai, about twenty-five miles from Delhi. One of my visitors was an Indian Roman Catholic chaplain and the other was a catechist belonging to a village. They produced to me a letter from the Roman Catholics in the village relating the story of persecution at the hands of the Hindus. This was curious enough in *urdu*. I understand that the inhabitants of that part of the country, whether they are Hindus or others, can only speak Hindustani and write in the *urdu* script. The informants told me that the Roman Catholics there had been threatened if they did not remove themselves from their village. I hope that it was an idle threat and that these Christian brothers and sisters will be left to follow their own faith and avocation without let or hindrance. Surely, they are not less entitled to their freedom than they were under the British régime, now that there is freedom from political bondage. That freedom can never be confined to Hindus only in the Union and the Muslims only in Pakistan. I have in one of my speeches already told you that when the mad fury against the Muslims has abated, it is likely to be vented on others; but when I made the remark I was not prepared for such an early verification of my forebodings. The fury against the Muslims has not yet completely abated. So far as I know, these Christians are utterly inoffensive. It is suggested that their offence consists in being Christians, more so because they eat beef and pork. As a matter of curiosity I asked the chaplain whether there was any truth in the remark, and I was told that these Roman Catholics, of their own accord, have abjured beef and pork not only now, but long ago. If this kind of unreasoning prejudice persist, the future for independent India is dismal. The chaplain himself has recently had his bicycle taken away from him when he was at Rewari, and he narrowly escaped death. Is this agony to end only with the extinction of all the non-Hindus and non-Sikhs?

I have no desire to live to witness such a dissolution of

India, and I would ask you to join me in the wish and prayer that good sense will return to the Hindus and Sikhs of the Union.

24th December 1947

To-morrow, Christmas Day, is a festival for the Christians as *Deepavali* is for the Hindus. I do not think that either festival is meant for indulgence in drinks, dances and merry-making. These are holy days making one examine oneself and do better next year. I offer greetings to all Christian friends in India and outside and hope that they will enforce in their own lives the teachings of Jesus Christ. I warn the Hindus, Muslims and Sikhs against entertaining any ill-will towards the Christians, who are a minority in India. Nor should they entertain any wish about converting them to Hinduism, Islam or Sikhism. I do not believe in such conversions. I want the Christians to be good Christians, the Muslims to be good Muslims, the Sikhs to be good Sikhs and the Hindus to be good Hindus under all circumstances. That to me is real conversion.

I have seen in the newspapers that in view of the fact that State patronage to Christianity or any other religion will not be given, 75 per cent of the churches in India will have to be closed down. Religion can never be served through money. The Christians should rejoice that an artificial prop is being removed. God is Omnipresent. Our bodies are the real temples rather than buildings of stone. The best place for congregational worship for any religion in my opinion is in the open with the sky above as the canopy and mother earth below for the floor. Every individual is the protector of his own religion against the whole world.

27th December 1947

The Panchayat should now see to cattle improvement. They should show steady increase in the milk yield. Our cattle have become a burden on the land for want of care. It is gross ignorance to blame the Muslims for cow slaughter. I hold that it is the Hindus who kill the cattle by inches through ill-treatment. Slow death by torture is far worse than outright killing.

The Panchayat should also see to an increase in the quantity of foodstuff grown in their village. That is to be accomplished by properly manuring the soil. The Compost Con-

ference recently held in Delhi under the inspiration of
Shrimati Mirabehn has told us how the excreta of animals
and human beings mixed with rubbish can be turned into
valuable manure. This manure increases the fertility of the
soil. Then they must see to the cleanliness of their village
and its inhabitants. They must be clean and healthy in
body and mind.

I hope that they will have no cinema house. People say
that the cinema can be a potent means of education. That
may come true some day, but at the moment I see how
much harm the cinema is doing.

6th January 1948

With reference to news from Bombay that dock labourers
and others are thinking of going on strike, I appeal to all
concerned, whether they belong to the Congress, the Social-
ist Party—if the latter can be counted apart from the
Congress—or the Communist Party to desist. This is no
time for strikes. Such strikes are harmful to all concerned
and to the country as a whole.

7th January 1948

I have received a note in which the writer says he has
undertaken a fast which will be continued. I consider the
fast to be wrong. I am of the opinion that during my lifetime those who undertake such fasts should consult me.

I have seen in the newspapers that the students in Delhi
propose to organize a strike on the 9th instant. I told them
yesterday that this is no time for strikes. Strikes by students
I consider generally to be wrong. I have conducted many
strikes during my life, more or less successfully. But I can
tell you that all strikes are not right and certainly not non-
violent. If the students will listen to me, they will give up
the idea of the proposed strike.

12th January 1948

One fasts for health's sake under laws governing health,
fasts as a penance for a wrong done and felt as such. In
these fasts, the fasting one need not believe in *ahimsa*.
There is, however, a fast which a votary of non-violence
sometimes feels impelled to undertake by way of protest
against some wrong done by society and this he does when

he as a votary of *ahimsa* has no other remedy left. Such an occasion has come my way.

When on September 9th I returned to Delhi from Calcutta, it was to proceed to the west of Punjab. But that was not to be. Gay Delhi looked a city of the dead. As I alighted from the train I observed gloom on every face I saw. Even the Sardar, whom humour and the joy that humour gives never desert, was no exception this time. The cause of it I did not know. He was on the platform to receive me. He lost no time in giving me the sad news of the disturbances that had taken place in the Metropolis of the Union. At once I saw that I had to be in Delhi and 'do or die'. There is apparent calm brought about by prompt military and police action. But there is storm within the breast. It may burst forth any day. This I count as no fulfilment of the vow to 'do' which alone can keep me from death, and incomparable friends. I yearn for heart friendship between the Hindus, Sikhs and Muslims. It subsisted between them the other day. To-day it is non-existent. It is a state that no Indian patriot worthy of the name can contemplate with equanimity. Though the Voice within has been beckoning for a long time, I have been shutting my ears to it, lest it may be the voice of Satan, otherwise called my weakness. I never like to feel resourceless; a *satyagrahi* never should. Fasting is his last resort in the place of the sword—his or other's. I have no answer to return to the Muslim friends who see me from day to day as to what they should do. My impotence has been gnawing at me of late. It will go immediately the fast is undertaken. I have been brooding over it for the last three days. The final conclusion has flashed upon me and it makes me happy. No man, if he is pure, has anything more precious to give than his life. I hope and pray that I have that purity in me to justify the step.

I ask you all to bless the effort and to pray for me and with me. The fast begins from the first meal to-morrow. The period is indefinite and I may drink water with or without salts and sour limes. It will end when and if I am satisfied that there is a reunion of hearts of all the communities brought about without any outside pressure, and from an awakened sense of duty. The reward will be the regaining of India's dwindling prestige and her fast-fading sovereignty over the heart of Asia and thereby, the world.

I flatter myself with the belief that the loss of her soul by India will mean the loss of the hope of the aching, storm-tossed and hungry world. Let no friend, or foe, if there be one, be angry with me. There are friends who do not believe in the method of the fast for the reclamation of the human mind. They will bear with me and extend me the same liberty of action that they claim for themselves. With God as my supreme and sole counsellor, I felt that I must take the decision without any other adviser. If I have made a mistake and discover it, I shall have no hesitation in proclaiming it from the house-top and retracing my faulty step. There is little chance of my making such a discovery. If there is clear indication, as I claim there is, of the Inner Voice, it will not be gainsaid. I plead for all absence of argument and inevitable endorsement of the step. If the whole of India responds or at least Delhi does, the fast might be soon ended.

But whether it ends soon or late or never, let there be no softness in dealing with what may be termed as a crisis. Critics have regarded some of my previous fasts as coercive and held that on merits the verdict would have gone against my stand but for the pressure exercised by the fasts. What value can an adverse verdict have when the purpose is demonstrably sound? A pure fast, like duty, is its own reward. I do not embark upon it for the sake of the result it may bring. I do so because I must. Hence, I urge everybody dispassionately to examine the purpose and let me die, if I must, in peace which I hope is ensured. Death for me would be a glorious deliverance rather than that I should be a helpless witness of the destruction of India, Hinduism, Sikhism and Islam. That destruction is certain if Pakistan ensures no equality of status and security of life and property for all professing the various faiths of the world and if India copies her. Only when Islam dies in the two Indias, not in the world. But Hinduism and Sikhism have no world outside India. Those who differ from me will be honoured by me for their resistance however implacable. Let my fast quicken conscience, not deaden it. Just contemplate the rot that has set in in beloved India and you will rejoice to think that there is a humble son of hers who is strong enough and possibly pure enough to take the happy step. If he is neither, he is a burden on earth. The sooner he disappears and clears the Indian atmosphere of the burden the better for him and all concerned.

I would beg of all friends not to rush to Birla House nor try to dissuade me or be anxious for me. I am in God's hands. Rather, they should turn the searchlights inwards, for this is essentially a testing time for all of us. Those who remain at their post of duty and perform it diligently and well, now more so than hitherto, will help me and the cause in every way. The fast is a process of self-purification.

13th January 1948

I must warn you against being surprised that I have walked to the prayer ground as usual. A fast weakens nobody during the first twenty-four hours after a meal. It generally does good to those who fast occasionally for twenty-four hours.

To-morrow it may be difficult for me to walk to the prayer ground. But if you are eager to attend the prayers all the same, you can come and the girls will recite the prayers with you even though I am not present.

You ask me whom I consider blameworthy for the fast. I blame no individual or community. I do believe, however, that if the Hindus and Sikhs insist on turning out the Muslims from Delhi, they will be betraying India and their own faiths. And that hurts me.

If Delhi becomes peaceful in the real sense of the term, I will then break the fast. Delhi is the Capital of India. The ruin or downfall of Delhi I would regard as the ruin of India and Pakistan. I want Delhi to be safe for all Muslims, even for one like Shaheed Suhrawardy, who is looked upon as the chief of *goondas*. Let all proved *goondas* be rounded up. But I am witness to the fact that Shaheedsaheb has worked for peace in Calcutta in all sincerity. He has pulled out the Muslims from Hindus' houses which they had forcibly occupied. He is living with me. He will willingly join the prayer, but I will not expose him to the risk of being insulted. I want him, as I do every Muslim, to feel as safe in Delhi as the tallest of you.

I do not mind how long it takes for real peace to be established. Whether it takes one day or one month, it is immaterial. No one should say or do anything to lure me into giving up my fast prematurely. The object should not be to save my life. It should be to save India and her honour. I shall feel happy and proud when I see that India's place is not lowered as it has become by the recent happenings which I have no wish to recall.

14th January 1948

I have come to the prayer meeting in spite of the doctor's objections. But from to-morrow I shall probably not be able to walk to the prayer ground. I have the strength to-day and I use it though the doctors have advised me to conserve it. I am in God's hands. If He wants me to live I shall not die. I do not want my faith in God to weaken.

Before I ever knew anything of politics in my early youth, I dreamt the dream of communal unity of the heart. I shall jump in the evening of my life, like a child, to feel that the dream has been realized in this life. The wish for living the full span of life, portrayed by the seers of old and which they permit us to set down at 125 years, will then revive. Who would not risk sacrificing his life for the realization of such a dream? Then we shall have real Swaraj. Then, though legally and geographically we may still be two states, in daily life no one will think that we were separate states. The vista before me seems to me to be, as it must be to you, too glorious to be true. Yet like a child in a famous picture, drawn by a famous painter, I shall not be happy till I have got it. I live and want to live for no lesser goal. Let the seekers from Pakistan help me to come as near the goal as it is humanly possible. A goal ceases to be one, when it is reached. The nearest approach is always possible. What I have said holds good irrespective of whether others do it or not. It is open to every individual to purify himself or herself so as to render him or her fit for that land of promise. I remember to have read, I forget whether in the Delhi Fort or the Agra Fort, when I visited them in 1896, a verse on one of the gates, which when translated reads: 'If there is paradise on earth, it is here, it is here, it is here.' That fort with all its magnificence at its best, was no paradise in my estimation. But I should love to see that verse with justice inscribed on the gates of Pakistan at all the entrances. In such paradise, whether it is in the Union or in Pakistan, there will be neither paupers nor beggars, nor high nor low, neither millionaire employers nor half-starved employees, nor intoxicating drinks or drugs. There will be the same respect for women as vouchsafed to men, and the chastity and purity of men and women will be jealously guarded. Where every woman except one's wife will be treated by men of all religions as mother, sister or daughter according to her age. Where there will be no untouchability and where there will be equal respect for all faiths. They will be all proudly, joyously and voluntarily bread labourers. I hope everyone who listens to me or reads these lines will forgive me if stretched on my bed and basking in the sun, inhaling life-giving sunshine, I allow myself to indulge in this ecstasy. Let this assure the doubters and sceptics that I have not the slightest desire that the fast should be ended as quickly as possible. It matters little if the ecstatic wishes of a fool like me are never realized and the fast is never broken. I am content to wait as long as it may be necessary, but it will hurt me to think that people have acted merely in order to save me. I claim that God has inspired this fast and it will be broken only when and if He wishes it. No human agency has ever been known to thwart, nor will it ever thwart the Divine Will.

16th January 1948

I did not expect I would be able to speak to you to-day but you will be pleased to learn that if anything, my voice is less feeble to-day than yesterday. I cannot explain it except for the grace of God. I have never felt so well on the fourth day of a fast in the past. If all of you continue to participate in the process of self-purification, I shall probably have the strength to speak to you till the end. I am in no hurry to break the fast. Hurry would spoil matters. I do not want anyone to come and tell me that things have been set right while the process is incomplete. If Delhi becomes peaceful in the real sense of the term, it will have its repercussions all over the country. I have no wish to live unless peace reigns in the two Dominions.

It is never a light matter for any responsible Cabinet to alter a deliberate, settled policy. Yet our Cabinet, responsible in every sense of the term, has with equal deliberation yet promptness unsettled their settled fact. They deserve the warmest thanks from the whole country, from Kashmir to Cape Comorin and from Karachi to the Assam frontier. And I know that all the nations of the earth will proclaim this gesture as one which only a large-hearted Cabinet like ours could rise to. This is no policy of appeasement of the

Muslims. This is a policy, if you like, of self-appeasement. No Cabinet worthy of being representative of a large mass of mankind can afford to take any step merely because it is likely to win the hasty applause of an unthinking public. In the midst of insanity, should not our best representatives retain sanity and bravely prevent a wreck of the ship of state under their management? What, then, was the actuating motive? It was my fast. It changed the whole outlook. Without the fast, they could not go beyond what the law permitted and required them to do. But the present gesture on the part of the Government of India is one of unmixed goodwill. It has put the Pakistan Government on its honour. It ought to lead to an honourable settlement not only of the Kashmir question but of all the differences between the two Dominions. Friendship should replace the present enmity. Demands of equity supersede the letter of the law. There is a homely maxim of law which has been in practice for centuries in England that when common law seems to fail, equity comes to the rescue. Not long ago there were even separate courts for the administration of law and of equity. Considered in this setting, there is no room for questioning the utter justice of this act of the Union Government. If we want a precedent, there is a striking one at our disposal in the form of what is popularly known as the MacDonald Award. That award was really the unanimous judgment of not only the members of the British Cabinet, but also of the majority of the members of the Second Round Table Conference. It was undone overnight as a result of the fast undertaken in the Yeravda prison.

I have been asked to end the fast because of this great act of the Union Government. I wish I could persuade myself to do so. I know that the medical friends who, of their own volition and at considerable sacrifice, meticulously examine me from day to day are getting more and more anxious as the fast is prolonged. Because of defective kidney function they dread not so much my instantaneous collapse as permanent after-effects of any further prolongation. I did not embark upon the fast after consultation with medical men, be they however able. My sole guide, even dictator, was God, the Infallible and Omnipotent. If He has any further use for this frail body of mine, He will keep it in spite of the prognostications of medical men and women. I am in His hands. Therefore, I hope you will believe me when I say that I dread neither death nor permanent injury, even if I survive. But I do feel that this warning of medical friends should, if the country has any use for me, hurry the people up to close their ranks. And like brave men and women, that we ought to be under hard-earned freedom, we should trust even those whom we may suspect as our enemies. Brave people disdain distrust. The letter of my vow will be satisfied if the Hindus, Muslims and Sikhs of Delhi bring about a unison, which not even a conflagration around them in all the other parts of India or Pakistan will be strong enough to break. Happily, the people in both the Dominions seem to have instinctively realized that the fittest answer to the fast should be a complete friendship between the two Dominions, such that members of all communities should be able to go to either Dominion without the slightest fear of molestation. Self-purification demands nothing less. It will be wrong for the rest of the two Dominions to put a heavy strain upon Delhi. After all, the inhabitants of the Union are not superhuman. In the name of the people, our Government has taken a liberal step without counting the cost. What will be Pakistan's counter gesture? The ways are many if there is the will. Is it there?

17th January 1948

I repeat what I have said before—nothing is to be done under pressure of the fast. I have observed before that things done under pressure of a fast have been undone after the fast is over. If any such thing happens, it would be a tragedy of the highest degree. There is no occasion for it at any time. What a spiritual fast does expect is cleansing of the heart. The cleansing, if it is honest, does not cease to be when the cause which induced it ceases. The cleansing of a wall seen in the form of a whitewash does not cease when the dear one has come and gone. This material cleansing is bound to require renovation after some time. Cleansing of the heart once achieved only dies with one's death. Apart from this legitimate and laudable pressure, the fast has no other function which can be described as proper.

18th January 1948

I embarked on the fast in the name of Truth whose familiar name is God. Without living Truth God is nowhere.

In the name of God we have indulged in lies, massacres of people, without caring whether they were innocent or guilty, men or women, children or infants. We have indulged in abductions, forcible conversions and we have done all this shamelessly. I am not aware if anybody has done these things in the name of Truth. With that same name on my lips I have broken the fast. The agony of our people was unbearable. Rashtrapati Dr Rajendrababu brought over a hundred people representing the Hindus, Muslims, Sikhs, representatives of the Hindu Mahasabha, the Rashtriya Swayamsevak Sangh and representatives of refugees from the Punjab, the Frontier Province and Sind. In this very representative company were present Zahid Hussainsaheb, the High Commissioner for Pakistan, the Chief Commissioner of Delhi and the Deputy Commissioner, General Shah Nawazkhan, representing the Azad Hind Fouj (I.N.A.). Pandit Nehru, sitting like a statue, was of course there, as also Maulanassaheb. Dr Rajendrababu read a document in Hindustani signed by these representatives, asking me not to put any further strain on them and end the agony by breaking the fast. Telegrams after telegrams have come from Pakistan and the Indian Union urging me to do the same. I could not resist the counsel of all these friends. I could not disbelieve their pledge that come what may, there would be complete friendship between the Hindus, Muslims, Sikhs, Christians, Parsis and Jews, a friendship not to be broken. To break that friendship would be to break the nation.

As I write, comforting telegrams are deluging me. How I wish that God will keep me fit enough and sane enough to render the service of humanity that lies in front of me! If the solemn pledge made to-day is fulfilled, I assure you that it will revive with redoubled force my intense wish and prayer before God that I should be enabled to live the full span of life doing service of humanity till the last moment. That span according to learned opinion is at least one hundred and twenty-five years, some say one hundred and thirty-three. The letter of my vow has been fulfilled early, beyond expectation, through the great goodwill of all the citizens of Delhi, including the Hindu Mahasabha leaders and the Rashtriya Swayamsevak Sangh. The result could not be otherwise when I find that thousands of refugees and others have been fasting since yesterday. Signed

assurances of heart friendship have been pouring in upon
me from thousands. Telegraphic blessings have come from
all over the world. Can there be a better sign of God's
hand in this act of mine? But beyond the letter of fulfilment
of my solemn vow lies its spirit without which the letter
killeth. The spirit of the vow is sincere friendship between
the Hindus, Muslims and Sikhs of the Union and a similar
friendship in Pakistan. If the first is assured, the second
must follow, as sure as day follows night. If there is darkness in the Union, it would be folly to expect light in
Pakistan. But if the night in the Union is dispelled beyond
the shadow of a doubt, it cannot be otherwise in Pakistan,
nor are signs wanting in that direction. Numerous messages
have come from Pakistan, not one of dissent. May God, who
is Truth, guide us as He has visibly guided us during all
these six days.

19th January 1948

In this age of senseless imitation my warning is that it
would be foolish for anybody to embark on such a fast
expecting identical results in an identically short space of
time. If anyone does, he will face severe disappointment
and will discredit what is a hoary and infallible institution.
Two severe qualifications are necessary—a living faith in
God and a felt peremptory call from Him. I am tempted to
add a third, but it is superfluous. A peremptory call from
God within presupposes the rightness, timeliness, and propriety of the cause for which the fast is taken. It follows
that a long previous preparation is required. Let no one,
therefore, lightly embark on such a fast.

21st January 1948

I am going to speak about yesterday's bomb explosion. I
have been receiving anxious inquiries and praise for being
unruffled at the accident. I thought it was military practice
and therefore nothing to worry about. I did not realize
until after the prayers that it was a bomb explosion and
that the bomb was meant against me. God only knows how
I would have behaved in front of a bomb aimed at me and
exploding. Therefore, I deserve no praise. I would deserve
a certificate only if I fell as a result of such an explosion
and yet retained a smile on my face and no malice against
the doer. What I want to say is that no one should look

down upon the misguided youth who threw the bomb. He probably looks upon me as an enemy of Hinduism. After all, has not the Gita said that whenever there is an evil-minded person damaging religion, God sends someone to put an end to his life? That celebrated verse has a special meaning. The youth should realize that those who differ from him are not necessarily evil. The evil has no life apart from the toleration of good people. No one should believe that he or she is so perfect that he or she was sent by God to punish evil doers, as the accused seems to flatter himself he is.

26th January 1948

This day, 26th January, is Independence Day. This observance was quite appropriate when we were fighting for Independence we had not seen nor handled. Now! We have handled it and we seem to be disillusioned. At least I am, even if you are not.

What are we celebrating to-day? Surely not our disillusionment. We are entitled to celebrate the hope that the worst is over and that we are on the road to showing the lowliest villager that it means his freedom from serfdom and that he is no longer a serf born to serve the cities and towns of India, but that he is destined to exploit the city dwellers for the advertisement of the finished fruits of well-thought-out labours, that he is the salt of the Indian earth, that it means also equality of all classes and creeds, never the domination and superiority of the major community over a minor, however insignificant it may be in number or influence. Let us not defer the hope and make the heart sick. Yet what are the strikes and a variety of lawlessness but a deferring of the hope? These are symptoms of our sickness and weakness. Let labour realize its dignity and strength. Capital has neither dignity nor strength compared to labour. These the man in the street also has. In a well-ordered democratic society there is no room, no occasion for lawlessness or strikes. In such a society there are ample lawful means for vindicating justice. Violence, veiled or unveiled must be taboo. Strikes in Cawnpore, coal-mines or elsewhere mean material loss to the whole society not excluding the strikers themselves. I need not be reminded that this declamation does not lie well in the mouth of one like me who has been responsible for so many successful strikes. If there be such critics they ought not to forget that then there was neither independence nor the kind of legislation we have now. I wonder if we can remain free from the fever of power politics or the bid for power which afflicts the political world, the East and the West. Before leaving this topic of the day, let us permit ourselves to hope that though geographically and politically India is divided into two, at heart we shall ever be friends and brothers helping and respecting one another and be one for the outside world.[1]

1. Extracts from *Delhi Diary* (Prayer Speeches from 10.9.47 to 30.1.48), by M. K. Gandhi, Ahmedabad, Navajivan Publishing House, March 1948. Pp. 4, 7-8, 15-16, 22-3, 27-8, 33-4, 40-1, 58-9, 70-1, 101-3, 123-4, 133-5, 168-70, 174-5, 178-9, 193-4, 195-6, 281-2, 289-90, 314, 316, 330-3, 335, 336, 338, 339, 341-3, 348-52, 356-8, 359-60, 365-6, 380-1.

PART VIII

Correspondence between Mahatma Gandhi and Lord Linlithgow, Mira Behn, Pandit Nehru, Lord Mountbatten, Sardar Patel, M. A. Abdullah and Lord Ismay

---

CORRESPONDENCE WITH LORD LINLITHGOW AND THE GOVERNMENT OF INDIA

EARLIER CORRESPONDENCE ABOUT AUGUST DISTURBANCES

The Aga Khan's Palace
Yeravda

Dear Lord Linlithgow,   *14th August 1942*

The Government of India were wrong in precipitating the crisis. The Government resolution justifying this step is full of distortions and misrepresentations. That you have the approval of your Indian 'colleagues' can have no significance, except this that in India you can always command such services. That co-operation is an additional justification for the demand of withdrawal irrespective of what people and parties may say.

The Government of India should have waited at least till the time that I inaugurated mass action. I had publicly stated that I fully contemplated sending you a letter before taking concrete action. It was to be an appeal to you for an impartial examination of the Congress case. As you know the Congress has readily filled in every omission that has been discovered in the conception of its demand. So could I have dealt with every difficulty if you had given me the opportunity. The precipitate action of the Government leads one to think that they were afraid that the extreme caution and gradualness with which the Congress was moving towards direct action might make world opinion veer round to the Congress as it had already begun doing, and expose the hollowness of grounds for the Government rejection of the Congress demand. They should surely have waited for an authentic report of my speeches on Friday and on Saturday night after the passing of the resolution by the A.I.C.C. You would have found in them that I would not hastily begin action. You should have taken advantage of the interval foreshadowed in them and explored every possibility of satisfying the Congress demand.

The resolution says: 'The Government of India have waited patiently in the hope that wiser counsels might prevail. They have been disappointed in that hope.' I suppose 'wiser counsels' here mean abandonment of its demand by the Congress. Why should the abandonment of a demand legitimate at all times be hoped for by a government pledged to guarantee independence to India? Is it a challenge that could only be met by immediate repression instead of patient reasoning with the demanding party? I venture to suggest that it is a long draft upon the credulity of mankind to say that the acceptance of the demand 'would plunge India into confusion'. Anyway the summary rejection of the demand has plunged the nation and the Government into confusion. The Congress was making every effort to identify India with the allied cause.

The Government resolution says: 'The Governor-General-in-Council has been aware, too, for some days past, of dangerous preparations by the Congress party for unlawful and in some cases violent activities, directed among other things to interruption of communications and public utility services, the organization of strikes, tampering with the loyalty of Government servants and interference with defence measures including recruitment.' This is a gross distortion of the reality. Violence was never contemplated at any stage. A definition of what could be included in non-violent action has been interpreted in a sinister and subtle manner as if the Congress was preparing for violent action. Everything was openly discussed among Congress circles, for nothing was to be done secretly. And why is it tampering with your loyalty if I ask you to give up a job that is harming the British people? Instead of publishing behind the backs of principal Congressmen the misleading paragraph, the Government of India, immediately they came to know of the 'preparations', should have brought to book the parties concerned with the preparations. That would have been the appropriate course. By their unsupported allegations in the resolution, they have laid themselves open to the charge of unfair dealing.

The Congress movement was intended to evoke in the people the measure of sacrifice sufficient to compel attention. It was intended to demonstrate what measure of popular support it had. Was it wise at this time of the day to seek to suppress a popular movement avowedly nonviolent?

The Government resolution further says: 'The Congress is not India's mouthpiece. Yet in the interests of securing their own dominance and in pursuit of their totalitarian policy, its leaders have consistently impeded the efforts made to bring India to full nationhood.' It is a gross libel thus to accuse the oldest national organization of India. This language lies ill in the mouth of a government which has, as can be proved from public records, consistently thwarted every national effort for attaining freedom and sought to suppress the Congress by hook or by crook.

The Government of India have not condescended to consider the Congress offer that if simultaneously with the declaration of the independence of India, they could not trust the Congress to form a stable provisional government, they should ask the Muslim League to do so and that any national government formed by the League would be loyally accepted by the Congress. Such an offer is hardly consistent with the charge of totalitarianism against the Congress. Let me examine the Government offer. 'It is that as soon as hostilities cease, India shall devise for herself, with full freedom of decision and on a basis embracing all and not only a single party, the form of government which she regards as most suited to her conditions.' Has this offer any reality about it? All parties have not agreed now. Will it be any more possible after the war, and if the parties have to act before independence is in their hands? Parties grow up like mushrooms, for without proving their representative character, the Government will welcome them as they have done in the past, if the parties oppose the Congress and its activities, though they may do lip homage to independence, frustration is inherent in the Government offer. Hence the logical cry of withdrawal first. Only after the end of the British power and a fundamental change in the political status of India from bondage to freedom, will the formation of a truly representative government, whether provisional or permanent, be possible. The living burial of the author of the demand has not resolved the deadlock. It has aggravated it.

Then the resolution proceeds: 'The suggestion put forward by the Congress party that the millions of India uncertain as to the future are ready, despite the sad lessons of so many martyr countries, to throw themselves into the arms of the invaders, is one that the Government of India cannot accept as a true representation of the feeling of the people of this great country.' I do not know about the millions. But I can give my own evidence in support of the Congress statement. It is open to the Government not to believe the Congress evidence. No imperial power likes to be told that it is in peril. It is because the Congress is anxious for Great Britain to avoid the fate that has overtaken other imperial powers that it asked her to shed imperialism voluntarily by declaring India independent. The Congress has not approached the movement with any but the friendliest motive. The Congress seeks to kill imperialism as much for the sake of the British people and humanity as for India. Notwithstanding assertions to the contrary, I maintain that the Congress has no interest of its own apart from that of the whole of India and the world.

The following passage from the peroration in the resolution is interesting. 'But on them (the Government) there lies the task of defending India, of maintaining India's capacity to wage war, of safeguarding India's interests, of holding the balance between the different sections of her people without fear or favour.' All I can say is that it is a mockery of truth after the experience of Malaya, Singapore and Burma. It is sad to find the Government of India claiming to hold the 'balance' between the parties for which it is itself demonstrably responsible.

One thing more. The declared cause is common between the Government of India and us. To put it in the most concrete terms, it is the protection of the freedom of China and Russia. The Government of India think that the freedom of India is not necessary for winning the cause. I think exactly the opposite. I have taken Jawaharlal Nehru as my measuring rod. His personal contacts make him feel much more the misery of the impending ruin of China and Russia than I can, and may I say than even you can. In that misery he tried to forget his old quarrel with imperialism. He dreads much more than I do the success of Nazism and Fascism. I argued with him for days together. He fought against my position with a passion which I have no words to describe. But the logic of facts overwhelmed him. He yielded when he saw clearly that without the freedom of India that of the other two was in great jeopardy. Surely you are wrong in having imprisoned such a powerful friend and ally.

If notwithstanding the common cause, the Government's answer to the Congress demand is hasty repression, they will not wonder if I draw the inference that it was not so much the Allied cause that weighed with the British Government, as the unexpressed determination to cling to the possession of India as an indispensable part of imperial policy. This determination led to the rejection of the Congress demand and precipitated repression.

The present mutual slaughter on a scale never before known to history is suffocating enough. But the slaughter of truth accompanying the butchery and enforced by the falsity of which the resolution is reeking adds strength to the Congress position.

It causes me deep pain to have to send you this letter. But however much I dislike your action, I remain the same friend you have known me. I would still plead for a reconsideration of the Government of India's whole policy. Do not disregard this pleading of one who claims to be a sincere friend of the British people.

Heaven guide you!

I am,

Yours sincerely,

M. K. GANDHI

The Viceroy's House

New Delhi

22nd August 1942

Dear Mr Gandhi,

Thank you very much for your letter dated the 14th August which reached me only a day or two ago.

I have read, I need not say, what you have been good enough to say in your letter with very close attention, and I have given full weight to your views. But I fear in the result that it would not be possible for me either to accept the criticisms which you advance of the resolution of the Governor-General-in-Council or your request that the whole policy of the Government of India should be reconsidered.

Yours sincerely,

M. K. Gandhi, Esq. LINLITHGOW

Secretary, Government of India (H.D.), 23.9.42
New Delhi.

Sir,

In spite of the chorus of approval sung by the Indian councillors and others, of the present government policy in dealing with the Congress, I venture to assert that had the Government but awaited my contemplated letter to H.E. the Viceroy and the result thereafter, no calamity would have overtaken the country. The reported deplorable destruction would have most certainly been avoided.

In spite of all that has been said to the contrary, I claim that the Congress policy still remains unequivocally non-violent. The wholesale arrest of the Congress leaders seem to have made the people wild with rage to the point of losing self-control. I feel that the Government, not the Congress, are responsible for the destruction that has taken place. The only right course for the Government seems to me to be to release the Congress leaders; to withdraw all repressive measures and explore ways and means of conciliation. Surely the Government have ample resources to deal with any overt act of violence. Repression can only breed discontent and bitterness.

Since I am permitted to receive newspapers, I feel that I owe it to the Government to give my reaction to the sad happenings in the country. If the Government think that as a prisoner I have no right to address such communications, they have but to say so and I will not repeat the mistake.

I am,

Yours, etc.,

M. K. GANDHI

CORRESPONDENCE WITH LORD LINLITHGOW
LEADING TO THE FAST AND AFTER

Personal *Detention Camp*
New Year's Eve, 1942

Dear Lord Linlithgow,

This is a very personal letter. Contrary to the Biblical injunction I have allowed many suns to set on a quarrel I have harboured against you. But I must not allow the old year to expire without disburdening myself of what is rankling in my breast against you. I have thought we were friends and should still love to think so. However what has happened since the 9th of August last makes me wonder whether you still regard me as a friend. I have perhaps not come in such close touch with any occupant of your *gadi* as with you.

Your arrest of me, the communiqué you issued thereafter, your reply to Rajaji and the reasons given therefore, Mr Amery's attack on me and much else I can catalogue to show that at some stage or other you must have suspected my bona fides. Mention of other Congressmen in the same connection is by the way. I seem to be the *fons et origo* of all the evil imputed to the Congress. If I have not ceased to be your friend why did you not, before taking drastic action, send for me, tell me of your suspicions and make yourself sure of your facts?

I am quite capable of seeing myself as others see me. But in this case I have failed hopelessly. I find that all the statements made about me in Government quarters in this connection contain palpable departures from truth.

I have so much fallen from grace that I could not establish contact with a dying friend. I mean Prof. Bhansali who is fasting in regard to the Chimur affair!

And I am expected to condemn the so-called violence of some people reputed to be Congressmen, although I have no data for such condemnation save the heavily censored reports of newspapers. I must own that I thoroughly distrust these reports. I could write much more, but I must not lengthen my tale of woe. I am sure what I have said is enough to enable you to fill in details.

You know I returned to India from South Africa at the end of 1914 with a mission which came to me in 1906, namely, to spread truth and non-violence among mankind in the place of violence and falsehood in all walks of life. The law of *satyagraha* knows no defeat. Prison is one of the many ways of spreading the message. But it has its limits. You have placed me in a palace where every reasonable creature comfort is ensured. I have freely partaken of the latter purely as a matter of duty, never as a pleasure, in the hope that some day those who have the power will realize that they have wronged innocent men. I have given myself six months. The period is drawing to a close. So is my patience. The law of *satyagraha* as I know it prescribes a remedy in such moments of trial. In a sentence it is, 'Crucify the flesh by fasting'. That same law forbids its use except as a last resort. I do not want to use it if I can avoid it.

This is a way to avoid it. Convince me of my error or errors, and I shall make ample amends. You can send for me or send someone who knows your mind and can carry conviction. There are many other ways if you have the will.

May I expect an early reply?

May the New Year bring peace to us all!

I am,

Your sincere friend,

M. K. GANDHI

Personal

The Viceroy's House
New Delhi

Dear Mr Gandhi,   *13th January 1943*

Thank you for your personal letter of 31st December, which I have just received. I fully accept its personal character, and I welcome its frankness. And my reply will be, as you would wish it to be, as frank and as entirely personal as your letter itself.

I was glad to have your letter, for, to be as open with you as our previous relations justify, I have been profoundly depressed during recent months first by the policy that was adopted by the Congress in August, secondly, because while that policy gave rise, as it was obvious it must, throughout the country to violence and crime (I say nothing of the risks to India from outside aggression) no word of condemnation for that violence and crime should have come from you, or from the Working Committee. When you were first at Poona I knew that you were not receiving newspapers, and I accepted that as explaining your silence. When arrangements were made that you and the Working Committee should have such newspapers as you desired I felt certain that the details those newspapers contained of what was happening would shock and distress you as much as it has us all, and that you would be anxious to make your condemnation of it categorical and widely known. But that was not the case; and it has been a real disappointment to me, all the more when I think of these murders, the burning alive of police officials, the wrecking of trains, the destruction of property, the misleading of these young students, which has done so much harm to India's good name, and to the Congress Party. You may take it from me that the newspaper accounts you mention are well founded—I only wish they were not, for the story is a bad one. I well know the immense weight of your great authority in the Congress movement and with the Party and those who follow its lead, and I wish I could feel, again speaking very frankly, that a heavy responsibility did not rest on you. (And unhappily, while the initial responsibility rests with the leaders, others have to bear the consequences, whether as law breakers, with the results that that involves, or as the victims.)

But if I am right in reading your letter to mean that in the light of what has happened you wish to retrace your steps and dissociate yourself from the policy of last summer, you have only to let me know and I will at once consider the matter further. And if I have failed to understand your object you must not hesitate to let me know without delay in what respect I have done so, and tell me what positive suggestion you wish to put to me. You know me well enough after these many years to believe that I shall be only too concerned to read with the same close attention as ever any message which I receive from you, to give it the fullest weight and approach it with the deepest anxiety to understand your feelings and your motives.

Yours sincerely,
LINLITHGOW

Personal   *Detention Camp*
                                            19th January 1943

Dear Lord Linlithgow,

I received your kind letter of 13th instant yesterday at 2.30 p.m. I had almost despaired of ever hearing from you. Please excuse my impatience.

Your letter gladdens me to find that I have not lost caste with you.

My letter of 31st December was a growl against you. Yours is a counter-growl. It means that you maintain that you were right in arresting me and you were sorry for the omissions of which in your opinion, I was guilty.

The inference you draw from my letter is, I am afraid, not correct. I have reread my letter in the light of your interpretation, but have failed to find your meaning in it.

I wanted to fast and should still want to if nothing comes out of our correspondence and I have to be a helpless witness to what is going on in the country including the privations of the millions owing to the universal scarcity stalking the land.

If I do not accept your interpretation of my letter, you want me to make a positive suggestion. This, I might be able to do, only if you put me among the members of the Working Committee of the Congress.

If I could be convinced of my error or worse, of which you are evidently aware, I should need to consult nobody, so far as my own action is concerned, to make a full and open confession and make ample amends. But I have not any conviction of error. I wonder if you saw my letter to the Secretary to the Government of India (H.D.) of 23rd September 1942. I adhere to what I have said in it and in my letter to you of 14th August 1942.

Of course I deplore the happenings that have taken place since 9th August last. But have I not laid the whole blame for them at the door of the Government of India? Moreover, I could not express any opinion on events which I cannot influence or control and of which I have but a one-sided account. You are bound *prima facie* to accept the accuracy of reports that may be placed before you by your departmental heads. But you will not expect me to do so. Such reports have, before now, often proved fallible. It was for that reason that in my letter of 31st December, I pleaded with you to convince me of the correctness of the information on which your conviction was based. You will perhaps appreciate my fundamental difficulty in making the statement you have expected me to make.

This, however, I can say from the housetop, that I am as confirmed a believer in non-violence as I have ever been. You may not know that any violence on the part of Congress workers, I have condemned openly and unequivocally. I have even done public penance more than once. I must not weary you with examples. The point I wish to make is that on every such occasion I was a free man.

This time the retracing, as I have submitted, lies with the Government. You will forgive me for expressing an opinion challenging yours. I am certain that nothing but good would have resulted if you had stayed your hand and granted me the interview which I had announced, on the night of the 8th August I was to seek. But that was not to be.

Here, may I remind you that the Government of India have before now owned their mistakes, as for instance, in the Punjab when the late General Dyer was condemned, in the U.P. when a corner of a mosque in Cawnpore was restored, and in Bengal when Partition was annulled. All these things were done in spite of great and previous mob violence.

To sum up:

(1) If you want me to act singly, convince me that I was wrong and I will make ample amends.

(2) If you want me to make any proposal on behalf of the Congress you should put me among the Congress Working Committee members.

I do plead with you to make up your mind to end the impasse.

If I am obscure or have not answered your letter fully, please point out the omissions and I shall make an attempt to give you satisfaction.

I have no mental reservation.

I find that my letters to you are sent through the Government of Bombay. This procedure must involve some loss of time. As time is of the essence in this matter, perhaps you will issue instructions that my letters to you may be sent directly by the Superintendent of this camp.

I am,

Your sincere friend,

M. K. GANDHI

The Viceroy's House
New Delhi
25th January 1943

Dear Mr Gandhi,

Many thanks for your personal letter of the 19th January, which I have just received, and which I need not say I have read with close care and attention. But I am still, I fear, rather in the dark. I made clear to you in my last letter that, however reluctantly, the course of events, and my familiarity with what has been taking place, has left me no choice but to regard the Congress movement, and you as its authorized and fully empowered spokesman at the time of the decision of last August, as responsible for the sad campaign of violence and crime, and revolutionary activity which has done so much harm, and so much injury to India's credit, since last August. I note what you say about non-violence. I am very glad to read your unequivocal condemnation of violence and I am well aware of the importance which you have given to that article of your creed in the past. But the events of these last months, and even the events that are happening to-day, show that it has not met with the full support of certain at any rate of your followers, and the mere fact that they may have fallen short of an ideal which you have advocated is no answer to the relations of those who have lost their lives, and to those themselves who have lost their property or suffered severe injury as a result of violent activities on the part of Congress and its supporters. And I cannot I fear accept as an answer your suggestion that 'the whole blame' has been laid by you yourself at the door of the Government of India. We are dealing with facts in this matter, and they have to be faced. And while, as I made clear in my last letter, I am very anxious to have from you anything that you may have to say or any specific proposition that you may have to make, the position remains that it is not the Government of India, but Congress and yourself that are on their justification in this matter.

If therefore you are anxious to inform me that you repudiate or dissociate yourself from the resolution of the 9th August and the policy which that resolution represents, and if you can give me appropriate assurances as regards the future, I shall, I need not say, be very ready to consider the matter further. It is of course very necessary to be clear on that point, and you will not, I know, take it amiss that I should make that clear in the plainest possible words.

I will ask the Governor of Bombay to arrange that any communication from you should be sent through him, which will I trust reduce delay in its transmission.

Yours sincerely,
LINLITHGOW

Detention Camp
29th January 1943

Dear Lord Linlithgow,

I must thank you warmly for your prompt reply to my letter of 19th instant. I wish I could agree with you that your letter is clear. I am sure you do not wish to imply by clearness simply that you hold a particular opinion strongly. I have pleaded and would continue to plead till the last breath that you should at least make an attempt to convince me of the validity of the opinion you hold, that the August resolution of the Congress is responsible for the popular violence that broke out on the 9th August last and after, even though it broke out after the wholesale arrest of principal Congress workers. Was not the drastic and unwarranted action of the Government responsible for the reported violence? You have not even said what part of the August resolution is bad or offensive in your opinion. That resolution is in no way a retraction by the Congress of its policy of non-violence. It is definitely against Fascism in every shape or form. It tenders co-operation in the war effort under circumstances which alone can make effective and nation-wide co-operation possible.

Is all this open to reproach?

Objection may be raised to that clause of the resolution which contemplated civil disobedience. But that itself cannot constitute an objection since the principle of civil disobedience is implicitly conceded in what is known as the 'Gandhi-Irwin Pact'. Even that civil disobedience was not to be started before knowing the result of the meeting for which I was to seek from you an appointment.

Then, take the unproved and in my opinion unprovable charges hurled against the Congress and me by so responsible a Minister as the Secretary of State for India.

Surely I can say with safety that it is for Government to justify their action by solid evidence, not by mere *ipse dixit*.

But you throw in my face the facts of murders by persons reputed to be Congressmen. I see the fact of murders as clearly, I hope, as you do. My answer is that the Government goaded the people to the point of madness. They started leonine violence in the shape of the arrests already referred to. That violence is not any the less so, because it is organized on a scale so gigantic that it displaces the Mosaic law of tooth for tooth by that of ten thousand for one— not to mention the corollary of the Mosaic law, i.e. of non-resistance as enunciated by Jesus Christ. I cannot interpret in any other manner the repressive measures of the all-powerful Government of India.

Add to this tale of woe the privations of the poor millions

due to India-wide scarcity which I cannot help thinking might have been largely mitigated, if not altogether prevented, had there been a bona fide national government responsible to a popularly elected assembly.

If then I cannot get soothing balm for my pain, I must resort to the law prescribed for *satyagrahis*, namely, a fast according to capacity. I must commence after the early morning breakfast of the 9th February, a fast for twenty-one days ending on the morning of the 2nd March. Usually, during my fasts, I take water with the addition of salts. But nowadays, my system refuses water. This time therefore I propose to add juices of citrus fruits to make water drinkable. For, my wish is not to fast unto death but to survive the ordeal, if God so wills. This fast can be ended sooner by the Government giving the needed relief.

I am not marking this letter personal, as I did the two previous ones. They were in no way confidential. They were mere personal appeals.

I am,
Your sincere friend,
M. K. GANDHI

PS.—The following was inadvertently omitted: The Government have evidently ignored or overlooked the very material fact that the Congress, by its August resolution, asked nothing for itself. All its demands were for the whole people. As you should be aware, the Congress was willing and prepared for the Government inviting Qaid-i-Azam Jinnah to form a national government subject to such agreed adjustments as may be necessary for the duration of the war, such government being responsible to a duly elected assembly. Being isolated from the Working Committee, except Shrimati Sarojini Devi, I do not know its present mind. But the Committee is not likely to have changed its mind.

M. K. GANDHI

The Viceroy's House
New Delhi
5th February 1943

Dear Mr Gandhi,

Many thanks for your letter of 29th January which I have just received. I have read it, as always, with great care and with every anxiety to follow your mind and to do full justice to your argument. But I fear that my view of the responsibility of Congress and of yourself personally for the lamentable disorders of last autumn remains unchanged.

In my last letter I said that my knowledge of the facts left me no choice but to regard the Congress movement and you as its authorized and fully empowered leader at the time of the decision of last August, as responsible for the campaign of violence and crime that subsequently broke out. In reply you have reiterated your request that I should attempt to convince you that my opinion is correct. I would readily have responded earlier to that request were it not that your letters gave no indication, such as I should have been entitled to expect, that you sought the information with an open mind. In each of them you have expressed profound distrust of the published reports of the recent happenings, although in your last letter, on the basis of the same information, you have not hesitated to lay the whole blame for them on the Government of India. In the same letter you have stated that I cannot expect you to accept the accuracy of the official reports on which I rely. It is not therefore clear to me how you expect or even desire me to convince you of anything. But in fact, the Government of India have never made any secret of their reasons for holding the Congress and its leaders responsible for the deplorable acts of violence, sabotage and terrorism that have occurred since the Congress resolution of the 8th August declared a 'mass struggle' in support of its demands, appointed you as its leader and authorized all Congressmen to act for themselves in the event of interference with the leadership of the movement. A body which passes a resolution in such terms is hardly entitled to disclaim responsibility for any events that follow it. There is evidence that you and your friends expected this policy to lead to violence; and that you were prepared to condone it; and that the violence that ensued formed part of a concerted plan, conceived long before the arrest of Congress leaders. The general nature of the case against the Congress has been publicly stated by the Home Member, Government of India, in his speech in the Central Legislative Assembly on the 15th September last, and if you need further information I would refer you to it. I enclose a complete copy in case the press versions that you must have seen were not sufficient. I need only add that all the mass of evidence that has since come to light has confirmed the conclusions then reached. I have ample information that the campaign of sabotage has been conducted under secret instructions circulated in the name of the A.I.C.C., that well-known congressmen have organized and freely taken part in acts of violence and murder; and that even now an underground Congress organization exists in which, among others, the wife of a member of the Congress Working Committee plays a prominent part, and which is actively engaged in planning the bomb outrages and other acts of terrorism that have disgusted the whole country. If we do not act on all this information or make it more publicly known it is because the time is not yet ripe; but you may rest assured that the charges against the Congress will have to be met sooner or later and it will then be for you and your colleagues to clear yourselves before the world if you can. And if in the meanwhile you yourself, by any action such as you now appear to be contemplating, attempt to find an easy way out, the judgment will go against you by default.

I have read with surprise your statement that the principle of civil disobedience is implicitly conceded in the Delhi Settlement of the 5th March 1931, which you refer to as the 'Gandhi-Irwin Pact'. I have again looked at the document. Its basis was that civil disobedience would be 'effectively discontinued' and that certain 'reciprocal action' would be taken by Government. It was inherent in such a document that it should take notice of the existence of civil disobedience. But I can find nothing in it to suggest that civil disobedience was recognized as being in any circumstances legitimate. And I cannot make it too plain that it is not so regarded by my Government.

To accept the point of view which you put forward would be to concede that the authorized government of the country, on which lies the responsibility for maintaining peace and good order, should allow subversive and revolutionary movements described by you yourself as open rebellion, to take place unchallenged; that they should allow preparations for violence, for the interruption of communications, for attacks on innocent persons, for the murder of police officers and others to proceed unchecked. My Government and I are open indeed to the charge that we should have taken drastic action at an earlier stage against you and against the Congress leaders. But my anxiety and that of my Government has throughout been to give you, and to give the Congress organization, every possible opportunity to withdraw from the position which you have decided to take up. Your statements of last June and July, the original resolution of the Working Committee of the 14th July, and your declaration on the same day that there was no room left for negotiations, and that after all it was an open rebellion, are all of them grave and significant, even without your final exhortation to 'do or die'. But with a patience that was perhaps misplaced, it was decided to wait until the resolution of the All India Congress Committee made it clear that there could be no further toleration of the Congress attitude if Government was to discharge its responsibility to the people of India.

Let me in conclusion say how greatly I regret, having regard to your health and your age, the decision that you tell me that you now have it in mind to take. I hope and pray that wiser counsels may yet prevail with you. But the decision whether or not to undertake a fast with its attendant risks is clearly one that must be taken by you alone and the responsibility for which and for its consequences must rest on you alone. I trust sincerely that in the light of what I have said you may think better of your resolution and I would welcome a decision on your part to think better of it, not only because of my own natural reluctance to see you wilfully risk your life, but because I regard the use of a fast for political purposes as a form of political blackmail (*himsa*) for which there can be no moral justification, and understood from your own previous writings that this was also your view.

Yours sincerely,

M. K. Gandhi, Esq.   LINLITHGOW

The Viceroy's House
New Delhi

Dear Mr Gandhi,   *5th February 1943*

In your letter of 29th January to H.E. you mentioned that you were not marking that letter personal like your two earlier letters, but that those two earlier letters were in no way confidential, and were a mere personal appeal. As you would no doubt have expected H.E. had hitherto attached to the word 'personal' its normal conventional meaning, and had accordingly given the same marking to his replies. He assumes in the light of what you say that you would have no objection to his publishing these letters with his replies to them despite the fact of their personal marking. Perhaps you would be so kind as to let me know.

Yours sincerely,

M. K. Gandhi, Esq.   G. LAITHWAITE

Detention Camp

Dear Sir Gilbert,   *7th February 1943*

I was delighted to see your signature after such a lapse of time. When I said that the two personal letters were not confidential I certainly meant what you say. But I meant also that though they were not confidential on my part, if His Excellency wanted to treat them as such, being personal, he was free to do so, and therefore equally free to regard his two replies also as such. In that case he could have the four letters withheld from publication. So far as I am concerned my request of course is that the whole correspondence beginning with my letter of 14th August last, and including my letter to the Secretary to the Government of India, Home Department, should be published.

Yours sincerely,

M. K. GANDHI

Detention Camp

Dear Lord Linlithgow,   *7th February 1943*

I have to thank you for your long reply dated 5th instant to my letter of 29th January last.

I would take your last point first, namely, the contemplated fast which begins on 9th instant. Your letter, from a *satyagrahi*'s standpoint, is an invitation to fast. No doubt the responsibility for the step and its consequences will be solely mine. You have allowed an expression to slip from your pen for which I was unprepared. In the concluding sentence of the second paragraph you describe the step as an attempt 'to find an easy way out'. That you, as a friend, can impute such a base and cowardly motive to me passes comprehension. You have also described it as 'a form of political blackmail', and you quote my previous writings on the subject against me. I abide by my writings. I hold that there is nothing inconsistent in them with the contemplated step. I wonder whether you have yourself read those writings.

I do claim that I approached you with an open mind when I asked you to convince me of my error. A 'profound distrust' of the published reports is in no way inconsistent with my having an open mind.

You say that there is evidence that I (I leave my friends out for the moment) 'expected this policy to lead to violence', that I was 'prepared to condone it', and that 'the violence that ensued formed part of a concerted plan conceived long before the arrest of Congress leaders'. I have seen no evidence in support of such a serious charge. You admit that part of the evidence has yet to be published. The speech of the Home Member, of which you have favoured me with a copy, may be taken as the opening speech of the prosecution counsel and nothing more. It contains unsupported imputations against Congressmen. Of course he has described the violent outburst in graphic language. But he has not said why it took place when it did. You have condemned men and women before trying them and hearing their defence. Surely there is nothing wrong in my asking you to show me the evidence on which you hold them guilty. What you say in your letter carries no conviction. Proof should correspond to the canons of English jurisprudence.

If the wife of a member of the Working Committee is actively engaged in 'planning the bomb outrages and other acts of terrorism' she should be tried before a court of law, and punished if found guilty. The lady you refer to could only have done the things attributed to her after the wholesale arrests of 9th August last which I have dared to describe as leonine violence.

You say that the time is not yet ripe to publish the charges against the Congress. Have you ever thought of the possibility of their being found baseless when they are put before an impartial tribunal, or that some of the condemned persons might have died in the meanwhile, or that some of the evidence that the living can produce might become unavailable?

I reiterate the statement that the principle of civil disobedience is implicitly conceded in the settlement of 5th March 1931, arrived at between the then Viceroy on behalf of the Government of India and myself on behalf of the Congress. I hope you know that the principal Congressmen were discharged before that settlement was even thought of. Certain reparations were made to Congressmen under that settlement. Civil disobedience was discontinued only on certain conditions being fulfilled by the Government. That by itself was, in my opinion, an acknowledgment of its legitimacy, of course under given circumstances. It therefore seems somewhat strange to find you maintain that civil disobedience cannot be recognized as being in any circumstances legitimate 'by your Government'. You ignore the practice of the British Government which has recognized its legitimacy under the name of 'passive resistance'.

Lastly you read into my letter a meaning which is wholly inconsistent with my declaration, in one of them, of adherence to unadulterated non-violence. For, you say in your letter under reply, that 'acceptance of my point of view would be to concede that the authorized Government of the country on which lies the responsibility for maintaining peace and good order, should allow movements to take place that would admit preparations for violence, interruption of communications, for attacks on innocent persons, for murders of police officers and others, to proceed unchecked'. I must be a strange friend of yours whom you believe to be capable of asking for recognition of such things as lawful.

I have not attempted an exhaustive reply to the views and statements attributed to me. This is not the place nor the time for such reply. I have only picked out those things which in my opinion demanded an immediate answer. You have left me no loophole for escaping the ordeal I have set before myself. I begin it on 9th instant with the clearest possible conscience. Despite your description of it as 'a form of political blackmail', it is on my part meant to be an appeal to the Highest Tribunal for justice which I have failed to secure from you. If I do not survive the ordeal I shall go to the judgment seat with the fullest faith in my innocence. Posterity will judge between you as representative of an all-powerful Government and me as a humble man who has tried to serve his country and humanity through it.

My last letter was written against time and therefore a material paragraph went in as postscript. I now send herewith a fair copy typed by Pyarelal who has taken Mahadeo Desai's place. You will find the postscript paragraph restored to the place where it should have been.

I am,

Your sincere friend,

M. K. GANDHI

(Received by Post)
Confidential

Home Department
New Delhi

Dear Mr Gandhi,   *7th February 1943*

The Government of India have been informed by His Excellency the Viceroy of your intention as communicated to him of undertaking a fast for twenty-one days in certain circumstances. They have carefully considered the position, and the conclusions they have reached in the light of such consideration are set out in the statement of which a copy is enclosed, which they would propose, in the event of your maintaining your present intention, to release in due course to the press.

1. The Government of India, as you will see from their statement, would be very reluctant to see you fast, and I am instructed to inform you that, as the statement makes clear, they would propose that, should you persist in your intention, you will be set at liberty for the purpose, and for the duration, of your fast as from the time of its commencement. During the period of your fast there will be no objection to your proceeding where you wish, though the Government of India trust that you will be able to arrange for your accommodation away from the Aga Khan's Palace.

2. Should you for any reason find yourself unable to take advantage of these arrangements, a decision which the Government of India would greatly regret, they will of course suitably amend the statement of which a copy is now enclosed before it issues. But they wish to repeat, with all earnestness, their anxiety and their hope that the considerations which have carried so much weight with them will equally carry weight with you, and that you will not pursue your present tentative proposal. In that event

no occasion will of course arise for the issue of any statement of any kind.

Yours sincerely,

R. TOTTENHAM

PS. *8th February*—In view of the urgency of the matter the text of this letter was telegraphed to the Governor's Secretary yesterday for communication to you to-day.

Detention Camp

Dear Sir Richard,   *8th February 1943*

I have carefully studied your letter. I am sorry to say that there is nothing in the correspondence which has taken place between His Excellency and myself or your letter, to warrant a recalling of my intention to fast. I have mentioned in my letters to His Excellency the conditions which can induce prevention or suspension of the step.

If the temporary release is offered for my convenience, I do not need it. I shall be quite content to take my fast as a *détenu* or prisoner. If it is for the convenience of the Government I am sorry I am unable to suit them much as I should like to do so. I can say this much that I, as a prisoner, shall avoid, as far as is humanly possible, every cause of inconvenience to the Government save what is inherent in the fast itself. The impending fast has not been conceived to be taken as a free man. Circumstances may arise, as they have done before now, when I may have to fast as a free man. If therefore I am released, there will be no fast in terms of my correspondence above mentioned. I shall have to survey the situation *de novo* and decide what I should do. I have no desire to be released under false pretences. In spite of all that has been said against me, I have not to belie the vow of Truth and Non-violence which alone makes life liveable for me. I say this, if it is only for my own satisfaction. It does me good to reiterate openly my faith when outer darkness surrounds me, as it does just now.

I must not hustle the Government into a decision on this letter. I understand that your letter has been dictated through the telephone. In order to give the Government enough time, I shall suspend the fast, if necessary, to Wednesday next, 10th instant.

So far as the statement proposed to be issued by the Government is concerned, and of which you have favoured me with a copy, I can have no opinion. But if I might have I must say that it does me an injustice. The proper course would be to publish the full correspondence and let the public judge for themselves.

Your sincerely,

M . K . GANDHI

Detention Camp

Dear Lord Linlithgow,   27th September 1943

On the eve of your departure from India I would like to send you a word.

Of all the high functionaries I have had the honour of knowing none has been the cause of such deep sorrow to me as you have been. It has cut me to the quick to have to think of you as having countenanced untruth, and that regarding one whom you at one time considered as your friend. I hope and pray that God will some day put it into your heart to realize that you, a representative of a great nation, had been led into a grievous error.

With good wishes,

I still remain,
Your friend,

M . K . GANDHI

Personal   Viceroy's Camp India
                                                (Simla)
Dear Mr Gandhi,   7th October 1943

I have received your letter of 27th September. I am indeed sorry that your feelings about any deeds or words of mine should be as you describe. But I must be allowed, as gently as I may, to make plain to you that I am quite unable to accept your interpretation of the events in question.

As for the corrective virtues of time and reflection evidently these are ubiquitous in their operation, and wisely to be rejected by no man.

Yours sincerely,

M. K. Gandhi, Esq.   LINLITHGOW
Received on 15th October 1943.

CORRESPONDENCE WITH MIRA BEHN[1]

Chi. Mira,   *4th April 1927*

Though you absolve me from having to write to you I cannot deny myself the joy of writing to you every Monday. Writing love letters is a recreation, not a task one would seek an excuse to shirk. I am better though still weak.

Dr Mehta came all the way from Bombay to examine the body. He is emphatically of opinion that all touring should be given up for some months to come. He does not forbid reading in the bed or even occasional letters to friends. If I take full rest he thinks that I would regain most of the lost strength but never be strong enough to undertake the exacting tours such as the one that came to an abrupt end on the 25th ultimo. We shall see. If the tour is finally cancelled, I must take my rest at the Ashram. I shall come to a decision to-day or to-morrow. The probability is that it will be cancelled. Even so I shall not move out before Tuesday next week.

But why are you having these attacks? Is it mere spiritual agony or has the climate also anything to do with it? If you need a bracing climate you must move out. How do you find the climate there? . . .

                                        With love,

Chi. Mira,   *27th April 1927*

I have your cheerful letter. If you can realize every word of what you have written, all your trouble is over and also my anxiety. We really live through and in our work. We perish through our perishable bodies, if instead of using them as temporary instruments, we identify ourselves with them.

The more I observe and study things, the more convinced I become that sorrow over separation and death is perhaps the greatest delusion. To realize that it is a delusion is to become free. There is no death, no separation of the substance. And yet the tragedy of it is that though we love friends for the substance we recognize in them, we deplore the destruction of the insubstantial that covers the substance for the time being. Whereas real friendship

[1]. The letters in this section are taken from *Gandhi's Letters to a Disciple* (Madeleine Slade), London, Gollancz, 1951.

should be used to reach the whole through the fragment. You seem to have got the truth for the moment. Let it abide for ever.

With love,

Unrevised   *Nandi Hills*
                                            2nd May 1927

Chi. Mira,

I wrote to you a p.c. in Hindi just to tell you that I was thinking constantly of you and to see whether you could read and understand my Hindi. Do not be alarmed. I do not propose to write to you always in Hindi. But if you can follow my Hindi, I do want now and then to write my extra letters in Hindi i.e., if you like the idea, not otherwise.

Now for your disturbing wire. I wonder what in my letters has prompted it. You can have no notion of the energy I have already regained. I have written for N.J.[2] four articles this week. For Y.I. I wrote three last week. I am really doing almost the normal work for the papers now. And I do a fair amount of love letters.

But all this is nothing compared to the result of medical examination yesterday. The pressure dropped from 188 to 155, and 155 to 160 is the normal for my age. I have been walking for the last three days over 1 mile per day in two periods, each extending to 30 minutes. This is more than Amboli. So there is now no anxiety about my health. There can be no question now of leaving Nandi. It would be foolish to think of leaving it till my previous strength is attained, if it can be at all, or till the season for Nandi ends, which it does about July.

I observe from your wire that in spite of your previous letter of attainment of peace, the pendulum has swung back and that you are again perturbed. This does not surprise me. If our lucid moments were lasting, nothing further will remain to be done. Unfortunately or fortunately, we have to pass through many an ebb and flow before we settle down to real peace.

I have therefore left you free to do as you please. Better certainly if you can keep your peace and stay. Equally certainly come away if you cannot keep your peace. Only in any decision you come to, please eliminate the question of my health. For if you come, you would

2. *Navajivan*, the Gujarati counterpart of *Young India*.

find little difference between me as you saw me in Kangri and me as I am now. Dive deep into yourself then and find out, if you can, where you are and act accordingly irrespective of what I would like you to do. Or put it another way. I would like you to do what your inner spirit tells you to do.

With love,

Unrevised

Sunday
8th May, 1927

Chi. Mira,

I hope you are getting all the letters I have been writing to you of late. Probably one letter every other day on an average.

I have your further letter. But I see you will be some time before you regain your balance. I do not mind the ups and downs so long as you retain the elasticity. My own opinion is this—it will be perfectly natural for you to come to me wherever I am *after* finishing your allotted task, whenever that happens. An ordinary person may not give up a self-imposed programme. But if you become highly emotional and your nerves remain under tension, you should come even though your course may not be finished.

Naturally I am anxious for you to finish your course. I should not like to have to think that it was beyond you. But your health is more precious to me than your studies or any other preparation.

You must not think of coming to me for my health. For it is good and I cannot be looked after better even if you came. If I needed your nursing, I should wire for you. But such an event will not happen, if only because I have got into the habit of taking nursing from anybody and I train new nurses to my requirements. There are more nurses than I need here. So if you come in the hope of doing some personal service, you would feel idle and yawning.

Now for the necessity of personal touch. My own opinion is that it is necessary in the preliminary stages. And then the touch comes through joint work. You come in daily touch with me by doing my work as if it was your own. And this can, must and will outlast the existence of this physical body of mine. You are, and will be, in touch whether I am alive or dead. And that is what I want you to be. You have come to me not for me, but for my ideals in so far as I live them. You *now* know how far I live the ideals I set forth. It is now for you to work out those ideals and practise them to greater perfection than has been given to me to do. He or she who does that will be my first heir and representative. I want you to be the first, if only because you studied me from a distance and made your choice. And when, in the course of the work, God brings us physically together, it is well, but it is well also when He keeps us apart in pursuance of the common object.

But this is counsel of perfection. Having listened to it and understood it, you are free to do as you choose. If you cannot contain yourself, you must come, and not feel that I shall be displeased. I should be displeased if you did violence to yourself and became prostrate.

With love,

Shrimati Mira behn
Satyagraha Ashram
Sabarmati

Chi. Mira,   *28th September 1927*

I could not restrain myself from sending you a love message on reaching here. I felt very sad after letting you go. I have been very severe with you, but I could not do otherwise. I had to perform an operation and I steadied myself for it. Now let us hope all would go on smoothly, and that all the weakness is gone.

I have your two missing letters just now, but of that later. I am writing this against the posting time. You won't worry about me on any account whatsoever.

With love,

(Postcard)
Chi. Mira,   *29th September 1927*

This is merely to tell you I can't dismiss you from my mind. Every surgeon has soothing ointment after a severe operation. This is my ointment, . . .

Chi. Mira,   *8th October 1927*

I am not going to write to you everyday. For I fancy you do not need any soothing ointment. The wound must be healed by this time. And your letter from the Ashram reassures me.

Yes, you may take up the dairy work or whatever you like. How about your food? . . .

With love,

Chi. Mira,   8th April 1929

I sent you a letter yesterday from Hyderabad (Deccan). I am nearing Bezwada, but still away from it. We are in a little village without a telegraphic office. The post from Bezwada has been brought here. So I have two letters from you, 2nd and 3rd. If you cannot be radically cured, you must take a change. You can go to a seaside or to a hillside.

If you can hold out till June, you might perhaps go with me to Almora. So far as I am aware, there is to be an Almora programme in June. You will have to travel 2nd class though, I should dread to put you in a 3rd class compartment in your weak state. But this is all building castles in the air. The immediate thing is for you to get well. To spend lavishly on fruit is real economy. You cannot keep good health without fresh fruit. Lemons are the prince among fruits. Dr Rajabali told me, one lemon was equal to six oranges. I can well believe it. But you must have all the fruit you fancy. Raw green leaf is good but it must be eaten sparingly, not more than one tola at a time and then too only if it does not upset the system . . . Your primary concern is not to discover a cheap diet, but it is to be able to live in villages without needing a yearly exodus to the hills. Your attention must, therefore, be concentrated on making your experiment a success, no matter how much it costs you to live. I am going to wire you as soon as I am at a wiring station. How nice it is to be without a wiring office at either end! I know that I need not wire. If I was really poor, I could not wire. But I am not going to act mechanically. When that faith comes, I shall cease to think of wiring. It is enough for the time being that I am not fretting, even though I get letters about your illness and though I have no telegraph office here.

I seem to be flourishing on my diet, 3rd class travelling and continuous engagements. I wonder myself that I have not yet collapsed. Of course, I snatch plenty of rest and the happy knack of sleeping at will saves me. Truth is that God saves me so long as He wants me in this body. The moment His wants are satisfied, no precautions on my part will save me.

Of course, you will locate Bezwada on the map. There are five or six districts to cover.

Love,

5.30 a.m.

Chi. Mira,   5th May 1929

I have your letter and your wire. It distresses me to have to send you 'no' for my answer. I am rarely for two nights at one place. The heat is daily increasing. There is no rest, no adequate arrangement for food except for me. And as I do not take milk, there is rarely good milk obtainable. There are no oranges as I have cut down my fruit requirement. In this state to bring you here in your present condition is too great a risk and too great a strain on the Reception Committee, which has to find motor accommodation. The most strenuous part of the tour commences from Nellore. I cannot procure for you all the comforts I must give you, without putting an undue strain on everybody about me. I am sure you do not want to do this. You will, therefore, hold yourself in patience till 23rd May, after which I shall gladly take charge of you. This does not mean that I am myself put to any inconvenience. So many look after me and what is more, I insist on my requirements being met. I have to, if I am to finish the tour without collapsing. You need not, therefore, feel the slightest anxiety about me. I am in first class health. But I am a big enough morsel for the people. Now all are waiting for me to be ready for the journey.

Love,

Yeravda

Chi. Mira,   12th May 1930

Yours is the first letter I take up to write from the mail, and that on the silence day.

I have been quite happy and have been making up for arrears of rest. The nights here are cool and as I am permitted to sleep right under the sky, I have refreshing sleep. About the change made in the manner of taking the diet, you will learn from my general letter.

It was a great treat to receive the wheel so thoughtfully sent and with things so carefully packed in it. The carding bow, the Superintendent tells me, was lost on the way by the friends who brought it. I am in no hurry for it, as you have sent me a liberal quantity of slivers.

. . . I am giving as much time as I can to the *takli*. I find that I have no speed on it at all. I hardly get thirty rounds in one hour. For the first day I gave nearly seven hours to reach 160 rounds. I was washed out at the end of the performance. I must learn the trick of getting more speed . . .

I hope you had good news from mother about her health and otherwise.

The prison officials are kind and attentive.

Love,

Chi. Mira,   *13th December 1930*

Your p.c. was duly received. The absence of any further news from you, I take to mean perfect restoration. After each illness you are soon well, because the treatment followed is natural, but every sickness leaves behind it a legacy of weakness unless the system is allowed full rest and the mind relieved of tension. I suppose the mental control is the most difficult. For this the sovereign remedy is the application of the Gita. Each time mind suffers a shock, there is a failure in application. Let good news as well as bad pass over you like water over a duck's back. When we hear any, our duty is merely to find out whether any action is necessary and if it is, to do as an instrument in the hands of Nature without being affected by or attached to the result. This detachment appears a scientific necessity when we remember that in bringing about a result more than one instrument is employed. Who shall dare say 'I have done it'? I know you know all this. Nevertheless, I drive the truth home, so that from the brain it may percolate to the heart. So long as it remains in the brain only, it is a dead weight on it. Any truth received by the brain must immediately be sent down to the heart. When it is not, it suffers abortion and then it lies on the brain as so much poisonous matter. What poisons the brain poisons the whole system. Hence the necessity of using the brain as it should be merely as a transmitting station. Whatever is there received is either transmitted to the heart for immediate action or it is rejected there and then as being unfit for transmission.

Failure of the brain to perform this function properly is the cause of almost all the ills that flesh is heir to as also for mental exhaustion. If the brain simply performed its function, there need never be any brain-fag. So whenever we suffer from illness generally there is not only a dietetic error but there is also a failure on the part of the brain to function properly. The author of the *Gita* evidently saw this and gave the world the sovereign remedy in the clearest possible language. Whenever therefore anything preys upon your mind, you should meditate on the central teaching of the *Gita* and throw off the burden. Let us hope there never will be a recurrence of the terrible constipation.

Whenever you are ill, you will not hesitate to write to me at once without waiting for the weekly letter day.

Love,

Chi. Mira,   *3rd January* 1931

I have read the two renderings you have sent me of the first verse of the morning prayer. For use and perhaps conveying the meaning. I prefer my rendering. If you find any obscurity anywhere, please tell me. The 2nd I sent you by the last mail. Here is the 3rd.

'In the early morning I bow to Him who is beyond darkness, who is like the sun, who is perfect, ancient, called Purushottam (the best among men) and in whom (through the veil of darkness) we fancy the whole universe as appearing even as (in darkness) we imagine a rope to be a snake.'

The idea is that the universe is not real in the sense of being permanent, it is neither a thing to be hankered after nor feared because it is supposed to be God's creation. As a matter of fact, it is a creation of our imagination even as the snake in the rope is. The real universe like the real rope is there. We perceive either when the veil is lifted and darkness gone—compare 'And with the morn, those angel faces smile which I have loved long since and lost awhile.' The three verses go together and I think are Shankar's composition. You do know of Shankar, do you not? Five more days and I shall have finished the translation of the preface. My suggestion is that I continue to send you the verses and the *bhajans* with such comments as then occur to me. You should for your own satisfaction, with the help of whoever comes your way, translate the weekly notes on the *Gita*. The plan I am now following is well thought out i.e., that of looking through the translation of the whole *Gita* in the light of my rendering and translating the notes. The attempt may lead to something good of which we have no knowledge today. If I begin the translation of the weekly notes, the above plan may fall through altogether. It would not be right. Of my food experiment, you will learn everything from Narandas. The assurance, that the moment I find it necessary I shall revert to milk, should remove all cause for anxiety.

I was sorry to learn about Romain Rolland's health. Do please send him my love and tell him I often think of him and pray that he may be long spared in the service of humanity.

Love,

Chi. Mira,   *24th June 1931*

You are on the brain. I look about me, and miss you. I open the *charkha* and miss you. So on and so forth. But what is the use? You have done the right thing. You have left your home, your people and all that people prize most, not to serve me personally, but to serve the cause I stand for. All the time you were squandering your love on me personally, I felt guilty of misappropriation. And I exploded on the slightest pretext. Now that you are not with me, my anger turns itself upon me for having given you all those terrible scoldings. But I was on a bed of hot ashes all the while I was accepting your service. You will truly serve me by joyously serving the cause. 'Cheer boys cheer, no more of idle sorrow.'

Love,

Y.M.

Chi. Mira,   *13th May 1932*

In the hope that you would get this on or before Monday I write in reply to your unexpected letter received to-day.

It is well if you do without the fountain pen. But what we must aim at is the correct attitude. This brings about lasting and drastic changes. A detailed local treatment must go hand in hand with a penetrating search after the root cause, the desire to possess. It is possible to conceive a person not being poor in spirit though he may have nothing, because he is jealous of those who possess. He has nothing, but feels the deprivation. Another may have by him a golden footstool which he is seen using in order to save his feet from treading on hot ashes, but which he converts into cash for the poor the very next moment and feels the delight of dispossession. This is not to criticize what you have done but to enforce it, if it is at all necessary or possible.

Your left hand writing is certainly steadier than mine. You will in a short time write as well with the left as you do with the right hand . . .

Magan wheel has caused me trouble, but I am gaining mastery over it. Groundnuts are gone. Vallabhbhai and Mahadev frightened me and I have allowed myself to be frightened. My weight has gone up to 105½ again.

Love from us all,

11.30 p.m.

Chi. Mira,   *23rd September 1932*

The thought of you corrodes me. I wish you could be at peace. Do write daily and wire to-morrow your condition. I am taking the fast very well.

. . . Be steady and strong. Have faith in God. Shall send you daily report through Mahadev. May not be able myself to write.

Love,

24th September 1932

(Letter from Mahadev saying Bapu was doing fairly well. And across the top of the paper Bapu writes in his own hand the following words:)

My dearest child,

You are not to break. You must be seeing God's Grace pouring in abundance as perhaps never before.

Love,

Chi. Mira,

Your letter comes with unfailing regularity.

You will find many more gems in the *Quran*. Some of them are penetrating . . . Whose translation are you reading?

My weight and health keep steady. I tried bread for two

days and then fell back on fruit, milk and a vegetable. I pour my milk over the vegetable which is just now alternately marrow and pumpkin. These are the only two vegetables to be had just now in the prison garden. And I try to restrict myself just to the vegetables grown there. They seem to suit the body quite well. The monotony does not worry me.

I see with the comparative coolness of weather, you are improving. I hope the improvement will be steady.

The seven years seem like a dream. As I recall the terrible scoldings I tremble. And I derive such comfort as is possible from the fact that it was love that was scolding. But I know that there was a better way. As I look back upon the past I realize that my love was impatient. To that extent it was ignorant. Enlightened love is ever patient. Ignorant love is a crude translation of the word *moh* in Sanskrit. I shall learn to be patient. As I watch myself in little things, I know that I have not yet acquired the measure of patience which true love demands. That patience shall come.

You remember Shanti, the Chinese young man? I had a wire from him during the fast and now I have a penitent letter from him. Poor boy! He could not keep his vows and so kept silent. He is father of many children. He gives a desolate picture of China and is impatient to come back to India by way of penance for the past. His English has improved wonderfully.

If Kisan is there love to you both.

26th October 1932

This is going in a special envelope which I hope you will get.

Dictated　　　　　　　　　　　　　　　*Parnakuti*
　　　　　　　　　　　　　　　　　　　Poona
Chi. Mira,　　　　　　　　　　　　　*7th June 1933*

I must not write. The last letter that I wrote to you caused much strain upon the hand. I am, therefore, dictating this letter in reply to yours of the 5th inst.

You say that the brief sentence I wrote at the end of the letter written by Mahadev gave you pangs. It is won-

derful how we create misery for ourselves where there is
not even the slightest cause. My sentence had reference
to your fever, which you yourself had said was due to
over-anxiety on your part. You had explicitly mentioned
that you were ill-able to bear the separation . . . There
was no thought whatsoever that you should live out of
sight even when it was possible for you to be with me,
that is if we were both not imprisoned. Of course, in that
case, you would be most naturally with me. But to be out of
prison is not my natural life. My natural life is that of a
prisoner and therefore I suggest that you should learn to
do without my physical presence. Is not this as clear as
daylight?

I do not like this loss of weight by you. There is something radically wrong in your carrying this load of anxiety
on your shoulders. It is incompatible with a living faith in
a living God. As days pass I feel this Living Presence in
every fibre of my veins. Without that feeling I should be
demented. There are so many things that are calculated
to disturb my peace of mind. So many events happen that
would, without the realization of that Presence, shake me
to the very foundation. But they pass me by leaving me
practically untouched. I want you to share that reality with
me. Then you would not be disturbed because you could
not be physically near me. Remember that no heroic effort
is necessary in order to be able to bear such enforced
separation as you and I have to put up with. Millions of
human beings do so without any effort. Do not make the
mistake of thinking that they bear such separation because
their nature is not sensitive to such things. If we would
examine them we would find that they are just as sensitive
as you and I are likely to be. Only they have a natural
faith in God of which they have not even the knowledge.
Ours is, besides theirs, a laboured faith. Hence we have to
put forth a Herculean effort to bear the separation. Anyway that is my analysis of your mentality. If it is not
true you will make your own analysis and somehow or
other cure yourself of the terrible anxiety. Carefully ponder
over Krishna's discourse in the second chapter of the Gita.
Then go on to the twelfth chapter, and see whether you
cannot find real peace and calmness of mind. Do not try
to give me a detailed reply to this argument of mine. I do

not want you to go through that strain. I have advanced the argument simply to soothe you if at all I can. I know that argument is vain when one's whole being is in rebellion against itself. Perhaps the painful process through which you are passing is preliminary to the coming realization of the living Presence of God. May it be so. Anyway do not again allow the thought to cross your mind that there is any question whatsoever of your having to live in separation from me when we both find ourselves out of prison.

Now about myself. I am flourishing. Rebuilding the body at the age of 64 must be a slow process, and I see that it will be slower than I had expected. Yet recovery is steady . . .

You complain of sultry weather. Here we have delicious cool weather. Of course, Poona is ideal in the rainy season.

Devadas will be married to Lakshmi on the 16th: that is the date when the religious ceremony will be gone through. But as this will be a marriage in breach of the present Hindu usage, there will be also a civil registration on the 21st.

Love,

Chi. Mira,

At 6 a.m. I entered upon the fast. It is now 7 a.m. I hope that you would not be disturbed during the week. There is no cause for uneasiness. But what is the use of my saying all this? Ere this reaches the fast would have been twice over.

Many changes are taking place in my mind just now. The corruption in Congress is preying on me as it has never before done. I am conferring with friends as to the advisability of leaving the Congress and pursuing its ideals outside it. It is good that the corruption agitates me. I shall take no hasty step. but there it is. And I feel that the girls' institution here should be closed unless I am prepared to sit down in Wardha or Vinoba takes the sole responsibility of its management. He will think over it during the fast. These are the two things that are uppermost in my mind.

The rest you will have from Mahadev or Pyarelal.

Your work there is certainly voluminous. You are putting forth extraordinary energy. What more can you do? Take your time. Do not get ill.

Love,

Wardha
7th August 1934

I have not been able to write to Maxwell. Sorry.

Chi. Mira,

Your letter disturbs me in more senses than one. You are not yet well. If life in Segaon does not suit you, you must leave in time and not as you had to in Bihar where there was a collapse. I may or may not know my limits. But you certainly do need to be cautioned, again and again. You must not become a wreck. And may this illness again be due to separation from me, though this time there are no such antecedent circumstances as there were last time.

Love,

Delhi
Chi. Mira,   *23rd March 1936*

I have your letter of 28th.

Of course you will incur the expense of a latrine. It may be well to dig up a bath room also side by side as we had in Sabarmati.

I would not want you to go to a seaside, if your hut on an apology for a hill serves the same purpose.

I hope we shall reach Wardha on 15th June Monday, if not on the 14th. My effort would be to reach there on a speaking day. That can only be Sunday. But if I cannot manage, I shall be satisfied to reach there even on Monday.

You must have by now heard about Harilal's[3] acceptance of Islam. If he had no selfish purpose behind, I should have nothing to say against the step. But I very much fear that there is no other motive behind this step. Let us see what happens now.

We descend to Bangalore city to-morrow.

Love,

3. Harilal: Gandhi's son—*Ed.*

Sevagram, Wardha
Chi. Mira,   *22nd May 1941*
Your letter. An inquiry has come from London whether the report is true that you have sevèred all connection with me and are living away from me !!! How wish is father to thought!

As you say if something drastic has to happen, it will do so even on some pretext appearing altogether flimsy.

Most of the reports you read in the papers are patent lies, manufactured for pushing up sales. I am not going to Ahmedabad, nor touring, nor going to Simla. And yet any of these things may come to pass though at present unexpected. But these newspaper men will be able to say, 'you see we were right.'

War news continues to be sensational. The news about the destruction in England is heart-rending. The Houses of Parliament, the Abbey, the Cathedral seemed to be immortal. And yet there is no end . . .

Love,

Sevagram
Chi. Mira,   *25th January 1942*
Your letter. Your pathetic note was received in Kashi. I could not understand why you should have felt so grieved at our not meeting, as I went.[4] You had met me in the morning, had you not? But even if you had not, you should be now above these outward demonstrations of affection which is a permanent thing independent of outward manifestations. Let your work be your sole absorption.

I am glad you are keeping fit.

. . . I am all right.

Love,

Sevagram
Chi. Mira,   *19th August 1946*
This is merely to ask you how you would arrange the latrines for the Ashram and the village. Subsoil water being so near the surface, medical men who gathered here

4. Never in all these years had I not touched Bapu's feet before he left for a journey; but on this occasion he had departed before I realized what was happening. (Note by Mira Behn—*Ed.*)

yesterday voted for septic tanks. I know you are averse to the idea. Send me your own opinion and a description of the preparation of compost. I forgot if you include night-soil also as they do in Indore. Anyway give me an accurate description for me to print or show to medical friends.

Don't recommence work unless you are quite fit. You have ample to do in Mussoorie.

It is raining as I write.

Love,

(As from Kazirkhil, Ramganj Post, Noakhali District)

Camp: Chandipur
Chi. Mira,   4th January 1947

Your registered letter is in front of me. The news will be given to you by Parashuram together with this letter. I simply dictate to say that the position you adumbrate is the correct thing. Everything depends upon one's purity in thought, word and deed, using the word 'purity' in its widest sense. Then there may be no cause for even so much as a headache. Only get hold of this fundamental fact. We often loosely use the word 'purity' and excuse all sorts of lapses. Do not even worry how I am faring or what I am doing here. If I succeed in emptying myself utterly, God will possess me. Then I know that everything will come true, but it is a serious question when I shall have reduced myself to zero. Think of 'I' and 'O' in juxtaposition and you shall have the whole problem of life in two signs. In this process you have helped me considerably for, though at a distance, you seem to be doing your duty to the fullest extent possible in your field of work.

This was dictated four days ago when I was resting in bed. But it remained untyped. Meantime your other letter and samples of Khadi have been received. Have you any khadi to spare for sale? I make this enquiry for the sake of the refugees. Do not overdo things. Do not overwork. Be careful for nothing. The pilgrimage on foot commences to-morrow. There may be then no letter to you. A bulletin will be sent to you. This I am scribbling in the early morning. 'Blessed are they that expect nothing.'

Love,

Calcutta

Chi. Mira, *20th August 1947*

Your two letters and wire. I hope you got mine at Pratapnagar. All your letters were received.

So you have not gained by your stay in the Himalayan Hills. You are evidently unable to build up your body.

I suggest your giving up all activities including cow-keeping.

What about the buildings you have erected and the ground taken? You can certainly come back to me and stay at will. Have no irons in the fire until your body is like true steel. I hold that it can be like that if the conditions are fulfilled.

I hope the examination of your heart will prove satisfactory.

I am fixed up here for the time being. Then the intention is to go to Noakhali. When that time will come I do not know.

This letter has taken me two hours to finish. There were many interruptions.

I had expressed the intention to pass my days in Pakistan, no promise.

Love,

Shri Mira behn,
Birla House,
New Delhi.

Birla House
New Delhi

Chi. Mira, *16th January 1948*

I got your letter yesterday. Evidently when you wrote it, you had no knowledge of this, my greatest fast.[5] Whether it will ultimately prove so or not is neither your concern nor mine. Our concern is the act itself not the result of the action. The fast commenced as usual with service, part of which was singing of 'When I survey.' It was well sung by Sushila. There were some good friends at the service. The company was impromptu. No one was invited. I am dictating this immediately after the 3.30 a.m. prayer while I am-

5. 'It will end when and if I am satisfied that there is a reunion of hearts of all the communities brought about without any outside pressure, and from an awakened sense of duty.' (From Gandhi's statement of January 12, 1948.—*Ed.*)

taking my meal such as a fasting man with prescribed food can take. Don't be shocked. The food consists of 8 ozs. of hot water sipped with difficulty. You sip it as poison, well knowing that in result it is nectar. It revives me whenever I take it. Strange to say this time I am able to take about 8 meals of this poison-tasting, but nectar-like meal. Yet I claim to be fasting and credulous people accept it! What a strange world!

Your description . . . It is enough to make one despair of the cow, the mother of prosperity, receiving her due in a country accused of cow-worship. There is no Swaraj in such a land.

Your describing the Ashram as 'Pashulok' is a magnificent idea. It is poetic. Don't ever write Pashulok Ashram. Ashram—Pashulok, with a dash in between, is good. Though now that I am thinking over it a little more deeply, Pashulok Ashram perhaps better represents your idea. Since, however, it is your excellent idea, that is to be carried out, your choice is to be final.

Don't rush here because I am fasting. The yagna, 279 as I have called it, demands that everyone, wherever he or she is, should perform his or her duty. If an appreciable number do this, I must survive the ordeal. Trust God and be where you are . . .

CORRESPONDENCE WITH
SARDAR PATEL, M. A. ABDULLAH
AND PANDIT NEHRU[6]

GANDHIJI TO SARDAR PATEL

One of them (the Khaksars) wept bitterly. He said that the officials had told them that in any case they would have to go, therefore, nothing further would happen. In spite of it, that very night Muslims in the mosque were fired upon. Many were killed. An old man of seventy received seven bullets. It is not known how many of the casualties died and how many survived. The mosque was surrounded. For three days the Khaksars had to suffer the torture of hunger and thirst. They could not even go out

6. The letters in this section are extracts from Gandhi's correspondence in The Last Phase, Vol. II by Pyarelal, Ahmedabad, Navajivan Publishing House, 1956.

to attend to nature's needs.

I was staggered to hear all this. I rebuked him: 'All that is impossible. The Sardar has only to-day told me that it was when the Khaksars refused to vacate the mosque under any circumstances and the Muslim elders themselves suggested that police officials emptied the premises after obtaining the permission of the Imam. No force was used. Only tear gas was used and no-one was killed. I cannot therefore swallow what you say.' Their reply was: 'We know our statements can count for nothing when your Sardar tells you something different. Well, the Khaksars are dead and gone, what is the use of asking for justice now? Truth will not remain hidden.' I said: 'If I discover that wrong has been done, I will not shelter even my dearest one. There is nothing more I can say to you now. But you can depend upon me to do my duty.' Now, if there is anything in it, please let me know.

SARDAR PATEL TO GANDHIJI   *11th August 1947*
The Khaksars are bothering you for nothing. In your letter . . . from Delhi you mentioned about (alleged) firing and the resulting casualties in a Delhi mosque. The whole story about firing is a fabrication and no Khaksar has died of bullet wounds. A number of Khaksars had established themselves in the mosque and were plotting to stage a demonstration during the celebration of independence day (15th August). Their plan was not to allow the Congress flag to be flown and to create a disturbance and indulge in violence. The Commissioner (a Muslim) therefore used tear gas in the mosque and arrested them. Nothing besides this has happened. Some Khaksars have come with your letter to-day. Their complaint also is utterly baseless. I have sent them to the Commissioner. The Khaksars want Delhi and Agra to be included in Pakistan, also Ajmer. To that end they want to establish a front in Delhi and create disturbance. These people do not want to allow the Commissioner to remain in Delhi. They take sanctuary in mosques. Local Muslims are not giving them any support.

FROM THE LEADER OF THE KHAKSARS
In your so-called prayer meetings which you so hypocritically begin with Koran and Gita there is not a single utterance of yours about political matters not streaked

with bitterness, perversion of truth or revenge against the Musalmans . . . and it is double clear now . . . that you are the enemy . . . of the entire ten crore Muslims of India. My two months' personal investigation of the State killings of Bihar conclusively proved that these were planned under your immediate and sole direction.

Murshidabad
M. A. ABDULLAH TO GANDHIJI *15th February 1947*
I miss here nothing except your valuable and instructive association, which I enjoyed so long at Noakhali. This district has a lot of historical backgrounds (monuments?) and I propose to pay visits to all of them in the near future. Noakhali was known for 'perjury and forgery' and this district has the old historical legacy of 'insincerity, hypocrisy and treachery . . .' I have been wondering how the world gets on when truth in almost all spheres of life has become such a rare phenomenon!

Noakhali
GANDHIJI TO M. A. ABDULLAH *18th February 1947*
When all parties become displeased with one it is generally a sure sign of one's having done one's duty. May it be so with you.

Noakhali
GANDHIJI TO M. A. ABDULLAH *20th February 1947*
According to the letter under reply there is not much to choose between the two districts. I suppose a police officer, having to deal with crimes, will naturally spot first the weakness of the society to which he goes. It flatters me to think that you will miss my association in Berhampore. I am sure that that would be a temporary phase only, and in any case it can be well made up by correspondence.

GANDHIJI TO PANDIT NEHRU *24th August 1947*
Punjabis in Calcutta have been pressing me to go to the Punjab at once. They tell me a terrible story. Thousands have been killed! A few thousand girls have been kidnapped! Hindus cannot live in the Pakistan area, nor Muslims in the other portion. Add to this the information that the two wings of the army took sides and worked havoc! Can any of this be true?

When do you think I should go to the Punjab, if at all?
I have still work in Calcutta, then in Noakhali and Bihar.
But everything can be laid aside to go to the Punjab if it
is proved to be necessary.

PANDIT NEHRU TO GANDHIJI   25th August 1947
In my last letter I gave you some idea of conditions in
the Punjab. This second visit has depressed me even more
. . . Normally even after the worst riots most people stick
to their homes. Now with the coming of Pakistan the urge
to get out of it has added to the normal urge to escape
from a dangerous zone. On both sides of the border in the
Punjab people are affected in this way and mass migrations
are taking place on a vast scale. These are largely spontaneous. Inevitably this is resulting and will result in misery
for hundreds, of thousands of people. It will mean also a
tremendous burden on all Governments concerned, Provincial and Central, on both sides . . .
The Muslims of Amritsar district, that is the survivors,
told me that 50,000 of them had perished in the district.
This is certainly wild exaggeration. But we should not be
surprised if anything up to 10,000 were killed in Eastern
Punjab . . . There has been widespread killing on both
sides and large numbers of refugees have been massacred.
In Eastern Punjab probably the Akali Sikhs have indulged
in killing more than anyone else. Worse than the killing
have been the horrible outrages on women on both sides.
It is said and rightly that Lahore and Amritsar are quiet.
The fact is that there are not many people left there to be
killed. That is to say that Lahore has become almost entirely
a Muslim city and Amritsar a Hindu-Sikh city . . .
More and more, both in the East and West Punjab,
habitually lawless elements are coming to the front and
they are not prepared to listen to the leaders. There are
internal conflicts also in both Provinces. In Western
Punjab there is conflict between Mamdot, the Chief Minister,
and Feroz Khan Noon. Noon appears to be encouraging the
wilder elements in the League. In Eastern Punjab there is a
good deal of stress and strain between the Sikhs and Hindus.
The Akalis, or some of them, do not hesitate to talk in terms
of establishing a Sikh State as a result of this turmoil.
Their logic is not very good, but there is little doubt that
many of them have vague hopes that something advan-

tageous to them might happen if trouble continued. Some
of these think that they can force India to go to war with
Pakistan. In such a war they imagine that Pakistan is bound
to be defeated and then Sikhistan will emerge.

Master Tara Singh and Giani Kartar Singh, however, have
been trying to get peace restored. Their influence does not
seem to go as far as many people imagined. The wilder
elements among the Akalis have joined hands with some
of the R.S.S. people.

GANDHIJI TO PANDIT NEHRU   30th August 1947

About my going to the Punjab, I won't move without
your and Vallabhbhai's wish. I want to say, however, that
everyday pressure is being put upon me to rush to the
Punjab before it is too late. If you wish I would send you all
that comes to me in that way so as to enable you to come to
a true judgment.

If I am not going to the Punjab, would I be of much use
in Delhi as an Adviser or consultant? I fancy I am not
built that way. My advice has value only when I am
actually working at a particular thing. I can only disturb
when I give academic advice as on food, clothing, the use
of the military. The more I think, the more I sense the
truth of this opinion. Left to myself, I would probably
rush to the Punjab and if necessary break myself in the
attempt to stop the warring elements from committing
suicide. From a letter I just have from Lord Mountbatten
I get the same impression. He would welcome my immediate going to the Punjab.

On this side I have work which must help you all.

EARLIER CORRESPONDENCE
WITH NEHRU[7]

LETTER FROM GANDHI TO NEHRU
                                    24th October 1940

('If you are ready you may now ceremonially declare
your civil disobedience. I would suggest your choosing a

[7]. The letters in this section are taken from *Nehru, The First
Sixty Years* Vol. II, edited by Dorothy Norman, London, The
Bodley Head, 1965.

village for your audience. I do not suppose they will allow you to repeat your speech. They were not ready with their plans so far as Vinoba was concerned. But should they let you free I suggest your following the plan laid down for Vinoba. But if you feel otherwise, you will follow your own course. Only I would like you to give me your programme. You will fix your own date so as to leave me time for announcing the date and place. It may be that they won't let you even fulfil your very first programme. I am prepared for every such step on the part of the Government. Whilst I would make use of every legitimate method seeking publicity for our programme my reliance is on regulated thought producing its own effect. If this is hard for you to believe, I would ask you to suspend judgment and watch results. I know you will yourself be patient and ask our people on your side to do likewise. I know what strain you are bearing in giving me your loyalty. I prize it beyond measure. I hope it will be found to have been well-placed for it is "do or die". There is no turning back. Our case is invulnerable. There is no giving in. Only I must be allowed to go my way in demonstrating the power of non-violence when it is unadulterated.')

Gandhi stated in 1940: 'Nehru wants industrialization, because he thinks that if it is socialized, it (will) be free from the evils of capitalism. My own view is that the evils are inherent in industrialism, and no amount of socialization can eradicate them.'

FROM GANDHI LETTER TO NEHRU
5th October 1945

'The first thing I want to write about is the difference of outlook between us. If the difference is fundamental then I feel that the public should also be made aware of it. It would be detrimental to our work for Swaraj to keep them in the dark. I have said that I still stand by the system of Government envisaged in Hind Swaraj. These are not mere words. All the experience gained by me since 1908 when I wrote the booklet has confirmed the truth of my belief. Therefore if I am left alone in it I shall not mind, for I can only bear witness to the truth as I see it. I have not Hind Swaraj before me as I write. It is really better for me to draw the picture anew in my own words.

And whether it is the same as I drew in Hind Swaraj or not is immaterial for both you and me. It is not necessary to prove the rightness of what I said then. It is essential only to know what I feel to-day. I am convinced that if India is to attain true freedom and through India the world also, then sooner or later the fact must be recognized that people will have to live in villages, not in towns, in huts, not in palaces. Crowds of people will never be able to live at peace with each other in towns and palaces. They will then have no recourse but to resort to both violence and untruth. I hold that without truth and non-violence there can be nothing but destruction for humanity. We can realize truth and non-violence only in the simplicity of village life and this simplicity can best be found in the *charkha* and all that the *charkha* connotes. I must not fear if the world to-day is going the wrong way. It may be that India too will go that way and like the proverbial moth burn itself eventually in the flame round which it dances more and more furiously. But it is my bounden duty up to my last breath to try to protect India and through India the entire world from such a doom. The essence of what I have said is that man should rest content with what are his real needs and become self-sufficient. If he does not have this control he cannot save himself. After all the world is made up of individuals just as it is (of) drops that constitute the ocean. I have said nothing new. This is a well known truth.

But I do not think I have stated this in Hind Swaraj. While I admire modern science, I find that it is the old looked at in the true light of modern science which should be reclothed and refashioned aright. You must not imagine that I am envisaging our village life as it is to-day. The village of my dreams is still in my mind. After all every man lives in the world of his dreams. My ideal village will contain intelligent human beings. They will not live in dirt and darkness as animals. Men and women will be free and able to hold their own against any one in the world. There will be neither plague, nor cholera nor small pox; no one will be idle, no one will wallow in luxury. Everyone will have to contribute his quota of manual labour. I do not want to draw a large scale picture in detail. It is possible to envisage railways, post and telegraph offices, etc. For me it is material to obtain the real article and the rest will fit into the picture afterwards. If I let go the real thing, all else goes.

On the last day of the Working Committee it was decided that this matter should be fully discussed and the position clarified after a two or three days session. I should like this. But whether the Working Committee sits or not I want our position vis-à-vis each other to be clearly understood by us for two reasons. Firstly, the bond that unites us is not only political work. It is immeasurably deeper and quite unbreakable. Therefore it is that I earnestly desire that in the political field also we should understand each other clearly. Secondly neither of us thinks himself useless. We both live for the cause of India's freedom and we would both gladly die for it. We are not in need of the world's praise. Whether we get praise or blame is immaterial to us. There is no room for praise in service. I want to live to one hundred and twenty-five for the service of India but I must admit that I am now an old man. You are much younger in comparison and I have therefore named you as my heir. I must, however, understand my heir and my heir should understand me. Then alone shall I be content.'

Poona

FROM GANDHI LETTER TO NEHRU

13th November 1945

'Our talk of (yesterday) made me glad. I am sorry it could not be longer. I feel it cannot be finished in a single sitting, but will necessitate frequent meetings between us. I am so constituted that, if only I were physically fit to run about, I would myself overtake you, wherever you might be, and return after a couple of days' heart-to-heart talk with you. I have done so before. It is necessary that we understand each other well and that others also should clearly understand where we stand. It would not matter if ultimately we might have to agree to differ so long as we remained one at heart as we are to-day. The impression that I have gathered from our yesterday's talk is that there is not much difference in our outlook. To test this I put down below the gist of what I have understood. Please correct me if there is any discrepancy.

(1) The real question, according to you, is how to bring about man's highest intellectual, economic. political and

moral development. I agree entirely.

(2) In this there should be an equal right and opportunity for all.

(3) In other words, there should be equality between the town-dwellers and the villagers in the standard of food and drink, clothing and other living conditions. In order to achieve this equality to-day people should be able to produce for themselves the necessaries of life i.e. clothing, food-stuffs, dwellings and lighting and water.

(4) Man is not born to live in isolation but is essentially a social animal independent and interdependent. No one can or should ride on another's back. If we try to work out the necessary conditions for such a life, we are forced to the conclusion that the unit of society should be a village, or call it a small and manageable group of people who would, in the ideal, be self-sufficient (in the matter of their vital requirements) as a unit and bound together in bonds of mutual co-operation and inter-dependence.'

CORRESPONDENCE WITH LORD ISMAY AND LORD MOUNTBATTEN[8]

Bhangi Colony
New Delhi
Dear Lord Ismay,   *5th April 1947*

Pandit Nehru gave me what you have described as an outline of a scheme. What I read is merely a copy of the points I hurriedly dictated, whereas, as I understood from H.E. the Viceroy, you were to prepare a draft agreement after the line of the points I had dictated. Of course you were at liberty to amend them, add to them and omit what you wished to omit.

I had a chat with Pandit Nehru twice during the day, the second time when he handed a copy of the outline at 5 p.m.

The seventh point should read thus: 'Within the framework hereof Mr Jinnah will be perfectly free to present for acceptance a scheme of Pakistan even before the transfer of power, provided however, that he is successful in his appeal to reason and not to the force of arms which

[8] The letters in this section are taken from *The Last Phase*, Vol. II.

he abjures for all time for this purpose. Thus, there will be no compulsion in this matter over a Province or a part thereof.'

What I could not recall yesterday I now recall.

The eighth will read as follows: 'In the Assembly the Congress has a decisive majority. But the Congress shall never use that majority against the League policy simply because of its identification with the League but will give its hearty support to every measure brought forward by the League Government, provided that it is in the interest of the whole of India. Whether it is in such interest or not shall be decided by Lord Mountbatten as man and not in his representative capacity.'

I have finished dictating this at 8.45 p.m. I am anxious that it reaches you to-night. Therefore, I have only made manifest correction and addition. The outline is by no means complete. When a draft agreement is prepared, many other points which should occur to any draftsman will have to be covered.

I must add that Pandit Nehru has at least one vital objection to the outline. But I will not tax you with its mention here. If the outline appears workable to H.E. I would like to wait on him once more and discuss Pandit Nehru's objections. Before putting it before Q. A. Jinnah I would like to show it to a few friends.

Yours sincerely,
M. K. GANDHI

Lord Ismay.

(The following were the points referred to in the above for a draft agreement dictated by Gandhiji to Lord Ismay.)

1. Mr Jinnah to be given the option of forming a Cabinet.

2. The selection of the Cabinet is left entirely to Mr Jinnah. The members may be all Moslems, or all non-Moslems, or they may be representatives of all classes and creeds of the Indian people.

3. If Mr Jinnah accepted this offer, the Congress would guarantee to co-operate freely and sincerely, so long as all the measures that Mr Jinnah's Cabinet bring forward are in the interests of the Indian people as a whole.

4. The sole referee of what is or is not in the interests of India as a whole will be Lord Mountbatten, in his personal capacity.

5. Mr Jinnah must stipulate, on behalf of the League or of any other parties represented in the Cabinet formed by him that, so far as he or they are concerned, they will do their utmost to preserve peace throughout India.

6. There shall be no National Guards or any other form of private army.

7. Within the framework hereof Mr Jinnah will be perfectly free to present for acceptance a scheme of Pakistan even before the transfer of power, provided however, that he is successful in his appeal to reason and not to the force of arms which he abjures for all time for this purpose. Thus, there will be no compulsion in this matter over a Province or a part thereof.

8. In the Assembly the Congress has a decisive majority. But the Congress shall never use that majority against the League policy simply because of its identification with the League but will give its hearty support to every measure brought forward by the League Government, provided that it is in the interest of the whole of India. Whether it is in such interest or not shall be decided by Lord Mountbatten as man and not in his representative capacity.

9. If Mr Jinnah rejects this offer, the same offer to be made *mutatis mutandis* to Congress.

Bhangi Colony
Reading Road, New Delhi
Dear Friend,   *7th April 1947*

I have pressing letters from friends in the Punjab asking me to go there even if it be for a few days. Pandit Nehru agrees. Nevertheless I would like you to guide me too.

Then Noakhali calls. If wires received by me during the last two days are to be relied upon, there is increasing lawlessness in Noakhali. Attempts at roasting people alive have been traced twice, and loot etc. is going on. You will see my public statement in the Press.

This outbreak of violence is not a mere detail. If it cannot be dealt with now, it won't be fourteen months hence.

Yours sincerely,
M . K . GANDHI

The Viceroy's House
New Delhi

Dear Mr Gandhi   *7th April 1947*

Many thanks for your letter of to-day. I find it difficult to advise you. Though the root causes of the disturbances in the Punjab still exist there has been a considerable measure of success in dealing with immediate disturbances, and I doubt whether you ought to exhaust yourself by undertaking any tour in the Punjab at this time of the year.

I quite agree that those outbreaks of violence are not a mere detail. What we have to secure is a settlement between the parties at the centre and, if possible, a combined front against violence. It is the effort to find a solution which will occupy all my efforts in the near future, and I know I can rely on help from you wherever you may be.

I enjoyed meeting you so much and found all you had to say of the greatest interest.

Yours sincerely,

M. K. Gandhi, Esq.   MOUNTBATTEN OF BURMA

Bhangi Colony
Reading Road, New Delhi

Dear Friend,   *11th April 1947*

I had several short talks with Pandit Nehru, and an hour's talk with him alone, and then with several members of the Working Committee last night about the formula I had sketched before you, and which I had filled in for them with all the implications. I am sorry to say that I failed to carry any of them with me except Badshah Khan.

I do not know that having failed to carry both the head and heart of Pandit Nehru with me I would have wanted to carry the matter further. But Panditji was so good that he would not be satisfied until the whole plan was discussed with the few members of the Congress Working Committee who were present.

I felt sorry that I could not convince them of the correctness of my plan from every point of view. Nor could they dislodge me from my position although I had not closed my mind against every argument. Thus I have to ask you to omit me from your consideration.

Congressmen who are in the Interim Government are

stalwarts, seasoned servants of the nation and, therefore, so far as the Congress point of view is concerned, they will be complete advisers.

I would still love to take the place that the late C. F. Andrews took. He represented no one but himself. And if you ever need my service on its merit, it will be always at your disposal.

In the circumstances above mentioned, subject to your consent, I propose, if possible, to leave to-morrow for Patna.

I have not forgotten the book about tribal expeditions. I have not yet been able to lay my hands on it for I cannot recall the name of the author nor the year in which I read the book. As I told you it was years ago in S. Africa that I came across it. My search will continue wherever I am and as soon as I trace it, it shall be sent to you.

I must also confess a slip of memory I am answerable for in the course of our talks. I was wrong in connecting Sir Francis Mudie with the late Pandit Nehru. The incident I referred to was in connection with Muddiman, not Mudie. The charge, almost universally believed by Congressmen against the present Governor of Sindh remains unaltered— in spite of my slip of memory.

I hope these constant interviews are not proving an unbearable strain.

                                        Yours sincerely,
H.E. the Viceroy.   M. K. GANDHI

                                   On the train to Patna
Dear Friend,   8th May 1947
    It strikes me that I should summarise what I said and wanted to say and left unfinished for want of time, at our last Sunday's meeting.

                            I

Whatever may be said to the contrary, it would be a blunder of first magnitude for the British to be party in any way whatsoever to the division of India. If it has to come, let it come after the British withdrawal, as a result of understanding between the parties or [of] an armed conflict which according to Quaid-i-Azam Jinnah is taboo. Protection of minorities can be guaranteed by establishing a court of arbitration in the event of difference of opinion among contending parties.

2. Meantime the Interim Government should be composed either of Congressmen or those whose names the Congress chooses or of Muslim League men or those whom the League chooses. The dual control of to-day, lacking team work and team spirit, is harmful for the country. The parties exhaust themselves in the effort to retain their seat and to placate you. Want of team spirit demoralises the Government and imperils the integrity of the services so essential for good and efficient Government.

3. Referendum at this stage in the Frontier (or any Province for that matter) is a dangerous thing in itself. You have to deal with the material that faces you. In any case nothing should or can be done over Dr Khan Saheb's head as Premier. Note that this paragraph is relevant only if division is at all to be countenanced.

4. I feel sure that partition of the Punjab and Bengal is wrong in every case and a needless irritant for the League. This as well as all innovation can come after the British withdrawal not before, except always for mutual agreement. Whilst the British power is functioning in India, it must be held principally responsible for the preservation of peace in the country. That machine seems to be cracking under the existing strain which is caused by the raising of various hopes that cannot or must not be fulfilled. These have no place during the remaining thirteen months. This period can be most profitably shortened if the minds of all were focused on the sole task of withdrawal. You and you alone can do it to the exclusion of all other activity so far as the British occupation is concerned.

5. Your task as undisputed master of naval warfare, great as it was, was nothing compared to what you are called to do now. The single-mindedness and clarity that gave you success are much more required in this work.

6. If you are not to leave a legacy of chaos behind, you have to make your choice and leave the Government of the whole of India including the States to one party. The Constituent Assembly has to provide for the governance even of that part of India which is not represented by the Muslim League or some States.

7. Non-partition of the Punjab and Bengal does not mean that the minorities in these Provinces are to be neglected. In both the Provinces they are large and powerful enough

to arrest and demand attention. If the popular Governments cannot placate them the Governors should during the inter-regnum actively interfere.

8. The intransmissibility of paramountcy is a vicious doctrine, if it means that they [the States] can become sovereign and a menace for Independent India. All the power wherever exercised by the British in India must automatically descend to the successor. Thus the people of the States become as much part of Independent India as the people of British India. The present Princes are puppets created or tolerated for the upkeep and prestige of the British power. The unchecked powers exercised by them over their people is probably the worst blot on the British Crown. The Princes under the new regime can exercise only such powers as trustees can and as can be given to them by the Constituent Assembly. It follows that they cannot maintain private armies or arms factories. Such ability and statescraft as they possess must be at the disposal of the Republic and must be used for the good of their people and the people as a whole. I have merely stated what should be done with the States. It is not for me to show in this letter how this can be done.

9. Similarly difficult but not so baffling is the question of the Civil Service. Its members should be taught from now to accommodate themselves to the new régime. They may not be partisans taking sides. The slightest trace of communalism among them should be severely dealt with. The English element in it should know that they owe loyalty to the new régime rather than to the old and therefore to Great Britain. The habit of regarding themselves as rulers and therefore superiors must give place to the spirit of true service of the people.

II

10. I had a very pleasant two hours and three-quarters with Quaid-i-Azam Jinnah on Tuesday last. We talked about the joint statement on non-violence. He was agreeably emphatic over his belief in non-violence. He has reiterated it in the Press statement which was drafted by him.

11. We did talk about Pakistan cum partition. I told him that my opposition to Pakistan persisted as before and suggested that in view of his declaration of faith in non-violence he should try to convert his opponents by reason-

ing with them and not by show of force. He was, however, quite firm that the question of Pakistan was not open to discussion. Logically, for a believer in non-violence, nothing, not even the existence of God could be outside its scope.

Rajkumari Amrit Kaur saw the first eight paragraphs, the purport of which she was to give to Pandit Nehru with whom I was to send you this letter. But, I could not finish it in New Delhi. I finished it on the train.

I hope you and Her Excellency are enjoying your hard-earned rest.

Yours sincerely,

H.E. the Viceroy,   M. K. GANDHI
Simla.

URGENT   *New Delhi*
27/28th June 1947

Dear Friend,

I sent you a note in the afternoon. The time after the evening prayer and walk I wish to devote to talking to you on certain matters I was able to touch but could not develop when we met.

I told the Parliamentary Delegation that heralded the Cabinet Mission and the Cabinet Mission itself that they had to choose between the two parties or even three. They were doomed to fail, if they tried to please all, holding them all to be in the right. I had hoped that you were bravely and honestly trying to extricate yourself from the impossible position. But my eyes were opened when, if I understand you correctly, you said that Quaid-i-Azam Jinnah and the League members were equally in the right with the Congress members and that possibly Quaid-i-Azam Jinnah was more so. I suggested that this is not humanly possible. One must be wholly right in the comparative sense. You have to make your choice at this very critical stage in the history of this country. If you think that Quaid-i-Azam Jinnah is, on the whole, more correct and more reasonable than the Congress, you should choose the League as your advisers and in all matters be frankly and openly guided by them.

You threw out a hint that Quaid-i-Azam might not be able even to let you quit even by 15th August especially if the Congress members did not adopt a helpful attitude.

This was for me a startling statement. I pointed the initial mistake of the British being party to splitting India into two. It is not possible to undo the mistake. But I hold that it is quite possible and necessary not to put a premium upon the mistake. This does not in any way impinge upon the very admirable doctrine of fair-play. Fair-play demands that I do not help the mistaken party to fancy that the mistake was no mistake but a belated and only a partial discharge of an obligation.

You startled me again by telling me that, if the partition had not been made during British occupation, the Hindus being the major party would have never allowed partition and held the Muslims by force under subjection. I told you that this was a grave mistake. The question of numbers was wholly untenable in this connection. I cited the classic example of less than one hundred thousand British soldiers holding India under utter subjection. You saw no analogy between the two instances. I suggested the difference was only one of degree.

I place the following for your consideration:

(a) The Congress has solemnly declared that it would not hold by force any Province within the Union.

(b) It is physically impossible for millions of caste-ridden Hindus to hold well-knit though fewer millions of Muslims under subjection by force.

(c) It must not be forgotten that Muslim dynasties have progressively subjected India by exactly the same means as the English conquerors later did.

(d) Already there has been a movement to win over to the Muslim side the so-called scheduled classes and the so-called aboriginal races.

(e) The caste Hindus who are the bugbear are, it can be shown conclusively, a hopeless minority. Of these the armed Rajputs are not yet nationalists as a class. The Brahmins and the Banias are still untrained in the use of arms. Their supremacy where it exists is purely moral. The Sudras count, I am sorry, more as scheduled class than anything else. That such Hindu society by reason of its mere superiority in numbers can crush millions of Muslims is an astounding myth.

This should show you why, even if I am alone, I swear by non-violence and truth, together standing for the highest order of courage before which the atom bomb pales into insignificance, what to say of a fleet of dread-naughts.

I have not shown this to any of my friends.

If I have misunderstood you in any single particular you have only to correct me and I shall gladly accept the correction. If I am obscure anywhere, I shall try to remove the obscurity either by letter or by meeting according to your wish.

My anxiety to save you from mistakes as I see them is the sole excuse for this letter.

Yours sincerely,

H.E. the Viceroy,   M. K. GANDHI
New Delhi.

The Viceroy's House
New Delhi

Dear Mr Gandhi,   *28th June 1947*

Thank you for your letter of this morning, which I have read with much interest.

I am glad you wrote because after reading your letter I feel that almost from first to last I must have failed to make clear to you my meaning. I am glad that you have not shown your letter to others, since I should be very sorry that views should be attributed to me which I did not, in fact, express.

I hope you will agree to discuss these matters again at our next meeting.

Yours sincerely,

Mr Gandhi.   MOUNTBATTEN OF BURMA

Government House
New Delhi

My dear Gandhiji,   *26th August 1947*

In the Punjab we have 55 thousand soldiers and large scale rioting on our hands. In Bengal our forces consist of one man, and there is no rioting.

As a serving officer, as well as an administrator, may I be allowed to pay my tribute to the One Man Boundary Force, not forgetting his Second in Command, Mr Suhrawardy.

You should have heard the enthusiastic applause which greeted the mention of your name in the Constituent Assembly on the 15th of August when all of us were thinking so much of you.

Edwina has gone off to-day on a courageous mission to the Punjab with Rajkumari Amrit Kaur, to see what they can do to help relieve the suffering and distress among the refugees.

Yours very sincerely,

Mr Gandhi.   MOUNTBATTEN OF BURMA

Calcutta

Dear Friend,   30th August 1947

Many thanks for your letter which His Excellency the Governor sent me yesterday afternoon. I do not know if Shaheed Saheb and I can legitimately appropriate the compliment you pay us. Probably suitable conditions were ready for us to take the credit for what appears to have been a magical performance.

Am I right in gathering from your letter that you would like me to try the same thing for the Punjab? I am in correspondence with the Pandit and the Sardar.

I hope your new office is not unduly more arduous than as Viceroy.

It filled me with joy when I read in the papers that Lady Mountbatten had flown to the Punjab. I hope she is none the worse for the trying visit.

Yours sincerely,

M. K. GANDHI

H.E. the Lord Mountbatten of Burma,
Government House,
New Delhi.

PART IX

Aphorisms and Extracts

My writings should be cremated with my body. What I have done will endure, not what I have said and written. I have often said recently that even if all our scriptures were to perish, one *mantra* of *Ishopanishad* was enough to declare the essence of Hinduism, but even that one verse will be of no avail if there is no one to live it. Even so what I have said and written is useful only to the extent that it has helped you to assimilate the great principles of truth and *ahimsa*. If you have not assimilated them, my writings will be of no use to you.

(*Harijan*, 1st May 1937)

Let Gandhism be destroyed if it stands for error. Truth and *ahimsa* will never be destroyed, but if Gandhism is another name for sectarianism, it deserves to be destroyed. If I were to know, after my death, that what I stood for had degenerated into sectarianism, I should be deeply pained. We have to work away silently. Let no one say that he is a follower of Gandhi. It is enough that I should be my own follower. I know what an inadequate follower I am of myself, for I cannot live up to the convictions I stand for.

(*Harijan*, 2nd March 1940)

If we are armed with that attitude of mind, we may hope to propagate *ahimsa* principles. Without that, books and newspaper propaganda is of no avail. You do not know with what indifference I used to run *Young India*. I did not shed a single tear when *Young India* had to be stopped.

(*Harijan*, 13th May 1939)

My own experience has led me to the knowledge that the fullest life is impossible without an immovable belief in a Living Law in obedience to which the whole universe moves. A man without that faith is like a drop thrown out of the ocean bound to perish.   (*Harijan*, 25th April 1936)

I have made the world's faith in God my own, and as my faith is ineffaceable, I regard that faith as amounting to experience. However, as it may be said that to describe faith as experience is to temper with Truth, it may perhaps be more correct to say that I have no word for characterizing my belief in God.   (*Auto.*)

God is that indefinable something which we all feel but which we do not know. To me God is Truth and Love, God is ethics and morality. God is fearlessness, God is the source of light and life and yet He is above and beyond all these. God is conscience. He is even the atheism of the atheist. He transcends speech and reason. He is personal God to those who need His touch. He is the purest essence. He simply Is to those who have faith. He is long suffering. He is patient but He is also terrible. He is the greatest democrat the world knows. He is the greatest tyrant ever known. We are *not*, He alone *Is*.

                    (*Young India*, 5th March 1925)

I do not regard God as a person. Truth for me is God, and God's Law and God are not different things or facts, in the sense that an earthly king and his law are different. Because God is an Idea, Law Himself. Therefore, it is impossible to conceive God as breaking the Law. He, therefore, does not rule our actions and withdraw Himself. When we say He rules our actions, we are simply using human language and we try to limit Him. Otherwise, He and His Law abide everywhere and govern everything. Therefore, I do not think that He answers in every detail every request of ours, but there is no doubt that He rules our action and I literally believe that not a blade of grass grows or moves without His will.   (*Harijan*, 23rd March 1940)

You cannot realize the wider consciousness, unless you subordinate completely reason and intellect, and the body too.   (*Harijan*)

But I know that I have still before me a difficult path to traverse. I must reduce myself to zero. So long as one does not of his own free will put himself last among his fellow creatures, there is no salvation for him. *Ahimsa* is the farthest limit of humility.   (*Auto.*)

But He is no God who merely satisfies the intellect, if He ever does. God to be God must rule the heart and transform it. He must express Himself in every smallest act of His votary. This can only be done through a definite realization more real than the five senses can ever produce. Sense perceptions can be, often are, false and deceptive, however real they may appear to us. Where there is realization outside the senses it is infallible. It is proved not by extraneous evidence but in the transformed conduct and character of those who have felt the real presence of God within. Such testimony is to be found in the experiences of an unbroken line of prophets and sages in all countries and climes. To reject this evidence is to deny oneself.

(*Young India*, 11th October 1928)

No one can attain perfection while he is in the body for the simple reason that the ideal state is impossible so long as one has not completely overcome his ego, and ego cannot be wholly got rid of so long as one is tied down by the shackles of the flesh.   (*Young India*, 20th September 1928)

We are living in the midst of death. What is the value of 'working for our own schemes' when they might be reduced to naught in the twinkling of an eye, or when we may equally swiftly and unawares be taken away from them? But we may feel strong as a rock, if we could truthfully say 'we work for God and His schemes'. Then nothing perishes. All perishing is then only what seems. Death and destruction have *then, but only then* no reality about them. For death and destruction is then but a change.

(*Young India*, 23rd September 1926)

Prayer is the very soul and essence of religion, and therefore, prayer must be the very core of the life of man, for no man can live without religion.

(*Young India*, 23rd January 1930)

Prayer is not asking. It is a longing of the soul. It is daily admission of one's weakness. . . . It is better in prayer to have a heart without words than words without a heart.

(*Young India*, 23rd January 1930)

Means and end are convertible terms in my philosophy of life. (*Young India*, 26th December 1924)

I have nothing new to teach the world. Truth and Non-violence are as old as the hills. All I have done is to try experiments in both on as vast a scale as I could. In doing so I have sometimes erred and learnt by my errors. Life and its problems have thus become to me so many experiments in the practice of truth and non-violence.
(*Harijan*, 28th March 1936)

Good travels at a snail's pace. Those who want to do good are not selfish, they are not in a hurry, they know that to impregnate people with good requires a long time. (*I.H.R.*)

Love and exclusive possession can never go together. Theoretically, when there is perfect love, there must be perfect non-possession. The body is our last possession. So a man can only exercise perfect love and be completely dispossessed, if he is prepared to embrace death and renounces his body for the sake of human service.

But that is true in theory only. In actual life, we can hardly exercise perfect love, for the body as a possession will always remain with us. Man will ever remain imperfect, and it will always be his part to try to be perfect. So that perfection in love or non-possession will remain an unattainable ideal as long as we are alive, but towards which we must ceaselessly strive. (*M.R.*, 1935)

I saw that nations like individuals could only be made through the agony of the Cross and in no other way. Joy comes not out of infliction of pain on others, but out of pain voluntarily borne by oneself.
(*Young India*, 31st December 1931)

Sex urge is a fine and noble thing. There is nothing to be ashamed of in it. But it is meant only for the act of creation. Any other use of it is a sin against God and humanity. (*Harijan*, 28th March 1936)

Abstract truth has no value unless it incarnates in human beings who represent it by proving their readiness to die for it. (*Young India*, 22nd December 1921)

I do dimly perceive that whilst everything around me is ever changing, ever dying, there is underlying all that change a living power that is changeless, that holds all together, that creates, dissolves and recreates. That informing power or spirit is God. And since nothing else I see merely through the senses can or will persist, He alone is.

And is this power benevolent or malevolent? I see it as purely benevolent, for I can see that in the midst of death life persists, in the midst of untruth truth persists, in the midst of darkness light persists. Hence I gather that God is Life, Truth, Light. He is Love. He is the supreme Good.

(*Young India*, 11th October 1928)

Human society is a ceaseless growth, an unfoldment in terms of spirituality. (*Young India*, 16th September 1926)

I claim that human mind or human society is not divided into watertight compartments called social, political and religious. All act and react upon one another.

(*Young India*, 2nd March 1922)

I do not believe that the spiritual law works on a field of its own. On the contrary, it expresses itself only through the ordinary activities of life. It thus affects the economic, the social and the political fields.

(*Young India*, 3rd September 1925)

I believe in absolute oneness of God and therefore also of humanity. What though we have many bodies? We have but one soul. The rays of the sun are many through refraction. But they have the same source.

(*Young India*, 25th September 1924)

The individual is the one supreme consideration.

(*Young India*, 13th November 1924)

Rationalists are admirable beings, rationalism is a hideous monster when it claims for itself omnipotence. Attribution of omnipotence to reason is as bad a piece of idolatry as is worship of stock and stone believing it to be God. I plead not for the suppression of reason, but for a due recognition of that in us which sanctifies reason.

(*Young India*, 14th October 1926)

It is my firm conviction that nothing enduring can be built upon violence.   (*Young India*, 15th November 1928)

They say 'means are after all means'. I would say 'means are after all everything'. As the means so the end. There is no wall of separation between means and end. Indeed the Creator has given us control (and that too very limited) over means, none over the end. Realization of the goal is in exact proportion to that of the means. This is a proposition that admits of no exception.

(*Young India*, 17th July 1924)

The means may be likened to a seed, the end to a tree; and there is just the same inviolable connection between the means and the end as there is between the seed and the tree.

(*I.H.R.*)

Though you have emphasized the necessity of a clear statement of the goal, but having once determined it, I have never attached importance to its repetition. The clearest possible definition of the goal and its appreciation would fail to take us there, if we do not know and utilize the means of achieving it. I have, therefore, concerned myself principally with the conservation of the means and their progressive use; I know if we can take care of them attainment of the goal is assured. I feel, too, that our progress towards the goal will be in exact proportion to the purity of our means.

This method may appear to be long, perhaps too long, but I am convinced that it is the shortest.

(*A.B.P.*, 17th September 1933)

The true source of rights is duty. If we all discharge our duties, rights will not be far to seek. If leaving duties unperformed we run after rights, they will escape us like a will-o'-the-wisp. The more we pursue them, the farther will they fly. The same teaching has been embodied by Krishna in the immortal words: 'Action alone is thine. Leave though the fruit severely alone.' Action is duty; fruit is the right.

(*Young India*, 8th January 1925)

But some comforts may be necessary even for man's spiritual advancement. One could not advance himself by identifying himself with the discomfort and squalor of the villager.

A certain degree of physical harmony and comfort is necessary but above that level, it becomes a hindrance instead of help. Therefore the ideal of creating an unlimited number of wants and satisfying them seems to be delusion and a snare. The satisfaction of one's physical needs, of one's narrow self must meet at a point a dead stop, before it degenerates into physical and intellectual voluptuousness. A man must arrange his physical and cultural circumstances so that they may not hinder him in his service of humanity, on which all his energies should be concentrated.

(Harijan, 29th August 1936)

As long as you derive inner help and comfort from anything you should keep it. If you were to give it up in a mood of self-sacrifice or out of a stern sense of duty, you would continue to want it back, and that unsatisfied want would make trouble for you. Only give up a thing when you want some other condition so much that the thing no longer has any attraction for you, or when it seems to interfere with that which is more greatly desired.

(Vishva-Bharati Quarterly, New Series II, Part II.)

Political power means capacity to regulate national life through national representatives. If national life becomes so perfect as to become self-regulated, no representation becomes necessary. There is then a state of enlightened anarchy. In such a state everyone is his own ruler. He rules himself in such a manner that he is never a hindrance to his neighbour. In the ideal state therefore, there is no political power because there is no state. But the ideal is never fully realized in life. Hence the classical statement of Thoreau that that government is best which governs the least. *(Young India*, 2nd July 1931)

I look upon an increase in the power of the state with the greatest fear because, although while apparently doing good by minimizing exploitation, it does the greatest harm to mankind by destroying individuality which lies at the root of all progress.

The state represents violence in a concentrated and organized form. The individual has a soul, but as the state is a soulless machine, it can never be weaned from violence to which it owes its very existence.

It is my firm conviction that if the state suppressed capitalism by violence, it will be caught in the coils of violence itself and fail to develop non-violence at any time.

What I would personally prefer, would be, not a centralization of power in the hands of the state but an extension of the sense of trusteeship; as in my opinion, the violence of private ownership is less injurious than the violence of the state.

I read Carlyle's *History of the French Revolution* while I was in prison, and Pandit Jawaharlal has told me something about the Russian Revolution. But it is my conviction that inasmuch as these struggles were fought with the weapon of violence, they failed to realize the democratic ideal.

We want freedom for our country, but not at the expense or exploitation of others, not so as to degrade other countries. I do not want the freedom of India if it means the extinction of England or the disappearance of Englishmen. I want the freedom of my country so that other countries may learn something from my free country, so that the resources of my country might be utilized for the benefit of mankind. Just as the cult of patriotism teaches us to-day that the individual has to die for the family, the family has to die for the village, the village for the district, the district for the province, and the province for the country; even so, a country has to be free in order that it may die, if necessary for the benefit of the world. My love therefore of nationalism, or my idea of nationalism, is that my country may become free, that if need be, the whole country may die, so that the human races may live. There is no room for race-hatred there. Let that be our nationalism.   (*I.V.*)

You will see that my influence, great as it may appear to outsiders, is strictly limited; I may have considerable influence to conduct a campaign for redress of popular grievance because people are ready and need a helper. But I have no influence to direct people's energy in a channel in which they have no interest.   (*Harijan*, 26th July 1942)

My *ahimsa* would not tolerate the idea of giving a free meal to a healthy person who has not worked for it in some honest way, and if I had the power, I would stop every *sadavrata* where free meals are given. It has degraded the nation and it has encouraged laziness, idleness, hypocrisy and even crime.   (*Young India*, 13th August 1925)

Do not say you will maintain the poor on charity. Only two classes of people are entitled to charity and no one else—the *Brahmana* who possesses nothing and whose business it is to spread holy learning, and the cripple and the blind. The iniquitous system of giving doles to the able-bodied idle is going on to our eternal shame and humiliation, and it is to wipe out that shame that I am going about with the message of the *charkha* up and down the whole country.   (*Young India*, 24th February 1927)

Monotony is the law of nature. Look at the monotonous manner in which the sun rises. And imagine the catastrophe that would befall the universe, if the sun became capricious and went in for a variety pastime. But there is a monotony that sustains and a monotony that kills. The monotony of necessary occupations is exhilarating and life-giving. An artist never tires of his art.

The present distress is undoubtedly insufferable. Pauperism must go. But industrialism is no remedy. The evil does not lie in the use of bullock-carts. It lies in our selfishness and want of consideration for our neighbours. If we have no love for our neighbours, no change, however revolutionary, can do us any good.   (*Young India*, 7th October 1926)

I would say that if the village perishes India will perish too. India will be no more India. Her own mission in the world will get lost. The revival of the village is possible only when it is no more exploited. Industrialization on a mass scale will necessarily lead to passive or active exploitation of the villagers as the problems of competition and marketing come in. Therefore we have to concentrate on the village being self-contained, manufacturing mainly for use. Provided this character of the village industry is maintained, there would be no objection to villagers using even the modern machines and tools that they can make and can afford to use. Only they should not be used as a means of exploitation of others.   (*Harijan*, 29th August 1936)

The conflict between monied classes and labourers is merely seeming. When labour is intelligent enough to organize itself and learns to act as one man, it will have the same weight as money if not much greater. The conflict is really between intelligence and unintelligence. Surely it will be folly to keep up such a conflict. Unintelligence must be removed.

Exploitation of the poor can be extinguished not by effecting the destruction of a few millionaires, but by removing the ignorance of the poor and teaching them to non-co-operate with their exploiters. That will convert the exploiters also. I have even suggested that ultimately it will lead to both being equal partners. Capital as such is not evil; it is its wrong use that is evil. Capital in some form or other will always be needed.   (*Harijan*, 28th July 1940)

By political independence I do not mean an imitation of the British House of Commons, or the Soviet rule of Russia or the Fascist rule of Italy or the Nazi rule of Germany. They have systems suited to their genius. We must have ours suited to ours. What that can be is more than I can tell; I have described it as *Ramaraj*, i.e. sovereignty of the people based on pure moral authority.

    (*Harijan*, 2nd January 1937)

It is my certain conviction that no man loses his freedom except through his own weakness.

Even the most despotic government cannot stand except for the consent of the governed which consent is often forcibly procured by the despot. Immediately the subject ceases to fear the despotic force, his power is gone.

    (*Young India*, 30th June 1920, *Tagore*)

I do not believe in armed risings. They are a remedy worse than the disease sought to be cured. They are a token of the spirit of revenge and impatience and anger. The method of violence cannot do good in the long run. Witness the effect of the armed rising of the allied powers against

Germany. Have they not become even like the Germans, as the latter have been depicted to us by them?

That nation is great which rests it head upon death as its pillow. Those who defy death are free from all fear.

FAREWELL[1]

. . . To see the universal and all-pervading Spirit of Truth face to face one must be able to love the meanest of creation as oneself. And a man who aspires after that cannot afford to keep out of any field of life. That is why my devotion to truth has drawn me into the field of politics; and I can say without the slightest hesitation, and yet in all humility, that those who say that religion has nothing to do with politics do not know what religion means.

Identification with everything that lives is impossible without self-purification; without self-purification the observance of the law of *ahimsa* must remain an empty dream; God can never be realized by one who is not pure of heart. Self-purification, therefore, must mean purification in all walks of life. And purification being highly infectious, purification of oneself necessarily leads to the purification of one's surroundings.

But the path of self-purification is hard and steep. To attain to perfect purity a man has to rise above the opposing currents of love and hatred, attachment and repulsion, and to become absolutely passion-free in thought, speech, and action. I know that I have not in me as yet that triple purity in spite of constant ceaseless striving for it. That is why the world's praise fails to move me; indeed, it very often stings me. To conquer the subtle passions seems to me to be harder far than the physical conquest of the world by the force of arms. Ever since my return to India I have had experiences of the dormant passions lying hidden within me. The knowledge of them has made me feel humiliated but not defeated. The experiences and experiments have sustained me and given me great joy. But I know that I have still before me a difficult path to traverse. I must reduce myself to zero. So long as a man does not of his own free will put himself last among his fellow

1. *Mahatma Gandhi's Ideas*, ed. C. F. Andrews, London, Allen and Unwin Ltd., 1930.

creatures, there is no salvation for him. *Ahimsa* is the farthest limit of humility.

In bidding farewell to the reader I ask him to join with me in prayer to the God of Truth, that He may grant me the boon of *ahimsa* in thought, word and deed.

BIBLIOGRAPHY

BOOKS BY MAHATMA GANDHI

Cent per Cent Swadeshi or *The Economics of Village Industries*, Ahmedabad, Navajivan Publishing House, 3rd Ed., 1948.

Christian Missions—Their Place in India, ed. P. Kumarappa, Navajivan, 2nd Ed., 1957.

Constructive Programme: Its Meaning and Place, Navajivan, 2nd Ed., 1945.

Delhi Diary, Navajivan, 1948.

From Yeravda Manir, Navajivan, 3rd Ed., 1945.

Gandhi: An Autobiography or *The Story of My Experiments with Truth*, trans. Mahadev Desai, London, Jonathan Cape, 1966.

Gandhiji's Correspondence with the Government, 1942-4, Navajivan, 2nd Ed., 1945.

Glances at Islam, trans. V. G. Desai, Navajivan, 1938.

Hind Swaraj or *Indian Home Rule*, Navajivan, 2nd Ed., 1939.

The India of My Dreams, Bombay, Hind Kitabs, 1947.

Key to Health, trans. Sushila Nayyar, Navajivan, 1948.

The Nation's Voice, eds. C. Rajagopalachar and J. Kumarappa, Navajivan, 2nd Ed., 1947.

Non-Violence in Peace and War, Vol. I, Navajivan, 3rd Ed., 1948.

Satyagraha in South Africa, trans. V. G. Desai, Navajivan, 2nd Ed., 1950.

Self-Restraint v. Self-Indulgence, Navajivan, 1947.

Songs from Prison, London, Allen & Unwin, 1934.

Speeches and Writings of Mahatma Gandhi, Madras, G. A. Notesan & Co., 4th Ed., 1933.

The Indian States' Problem, Navajivan, 1948.

Women and Social Injustice, Navajivan, 4th Ed., 1954.

Young India, Vols. I and II, Madras, Ganesan Ltd, 1922.

Young India, Vol. III, Ganesan Ltd, 1924.

BOOKS ABOUT MAHATMA GANDHI

N. K. Bose, *Selections from Gandhi*, Navajivan, 1948.

W. Crocker, *Nehru*, London, Allen & Unwin, 1966.

Mahadev Desai, *The Gita According to Gandhi*, Navajivan, 1946.

Mahadev Descri, *The Story of Bardoli*, Navajivan, 1929.

Manubehn Gandhi, *Bapu—My Mother*, Navajivan, 1949.

S. K. George, *Gandhi's Challenge to Christianity*, Navajivan, 1947.

R. B. Gregg, *A Discipline for Non-Violence*, Navajivan, 1941.

R. B. Gregg, *Economics of Khadar*, Navajivan, 1946.

A. Kaur, *To the Women*, Navajivan, 1945.

J. C. Kumarappa, *Christianity—Its Economy and Way of Life*, Navajivan, 1945.

J. C. Kumarappa, *Clue to Keynes*, Navajivan, 1947.

J. C. Kumarappa, *Practice and Precepts of Jesus*, Navajivan, 1945.

K. G. Mashruuala, *Practical Non-Violence*, Navajivan, 1941.

Pyarelal, *The Epic Fast*, Navajivan, 1932.

Rajendia Prasad, *Constructive Programme*, Navajivan, 1942.

BIBLIOGRAPHICAL NOTE FOR 1983 EDITION

The Collected Works of Mahatma Gandhi are being published by Publications Division, Government of India, New Delhi (1958-). Eighty-two out of a proposed ninety-one volumes have so far appeared.

The following titles have been published since the first edition of this book:

Geoffrey Ashe, *Gandhi, a Study in Revolution*, London, Heinemann, 1968.

Joan V. Bondurant, *Conquest of Violence: the Gandhian Philosophy of Conflict*, Princeton University Press, revised edition, 1965.

N.K. Bose, *My Days with Gandhi*, Calcutta, Indian Associated Publishing Co., 1953.

———— *Gandhi in Indian Politics*, Bombay, Lalvani Publishing House, 1967.

Judith M. Brown, *Gandhi's Rise to Power*, Cambridge University Press, 1972.

D.M. Datta, *The Philosophy of Mahatma Gandhi*, University of Wisconsin Press, 1961.

Louis Fischer, *The Life of Mahatma Gandhi*, London, Jonathan Cape, 1951.

Chandra Kumar & Mohinder Puri, *Mahatma Gandhi: His Life and Influence*, London, Heinemann, 1982.

Ved Mehta, *Mahatma Gandhi and His Apostles*, London, André Deutsch, 1977; Penguin 1978.

Robert Payne, *The Life and Death of Mahatma Gandhi*, London, Allen & Unwin, 1958.

INDEX